Geo S Balcom

GAIL HAMILTON'S WRITINGS.

SKIRMISHES AND SKETCHES.

One Volume.

A NEW ATMOSPHERE.

One Volume.

STUMBLING-BLOCKS.

One Volume.

GALA-DAYS.

One Volume.

COUNTRY LIVING AND COUNTRY THINKING.

One Volume.

The above are published in uniform style, by

TICKNOR AND FIELDS.

SKIRMISHES

AND

SKETCHES.

BY GAIL HAMILTON.

BOSTON:
TICKNOR AND FIELDS.
1865.

UNIVERSITY PRESS:
WELCH, BIGELOW, AND COMPANY,
CAMBRIDGE.

CONTENTS.

Skirmishes and Sketches.

I.

CHILD-POWER.

CORNY was a disappointed man. When he came over from Ireland, he thought he was coming to El Dorado. Not that he had ever heard of such a place as El Dorado, but he had heard wonderful stories rehearsed by his kinsfolk and neighbors, and he imagined that our rivers were milk, and our lakes honey; that gold was to be had for the asking, and silver was nothing accounted of in "Ameriky." So Corny kissed his father and mother, took his brown-haired, bright-eyed young wife, his pipe, and his flute, and sailed over to the Land of Promise. He found that it promised more than it performed; or rather Irish lips had reported and Irish ears heard more than was ever spoken. The soil of Columbia, like the soil of green Erin, is coy to cold suitors. Fortune here, as fortune there, will be wooed, and not unsought be won; and the long and the short of it was, that Corny, instead of measuring out gold dollars by the sieveful, had to take his hod and hoe and go to work like the rest of us. Is it any wonder that he was disappointed? Who would not be disappointed to make a sea-journey and a land-journey of three thousand miles, leaving father and mother and mother-land behind, and at the end of it find — a shovel? It was as if, tired of the toil and turmoil of this work-a-day world, you should take up your pilgrim-staff some fine evening, and travel on to the turreted castle that rises royally in yonder sunset sky, — a castle whose walls are amethyst and its portals pearl, — which seemed to beckon you on to eternal ambrosia and nectar, to promise nothing less than that you should be served by Hebes, and companioned by gods; and after weeks of weary wandering, footsore and forlorn, you reach your sunset castle, and find that you will not be invited to so much as a supper of Johnny-cake and milk till you shall have baked the Johnny-cake and milked the cow.

But Corny put the best face on the matter, and the best hand too, which in fact amounts to pretty much the same thing, and went to work. Indeed, there was nothing else for him to do. He had spent all his money in coming over, and in America, as everywhere else, must either work or die. He was a sturdy lad of fields and pastures, so he went into the country and mowed great swaths through the waving valleys, and hoed straight rows through the brown corn-lands, and smote the threshing-floors with regular, strong beats, and pressed the sweet, rich, foaming cider into the scented vats. In winter he helped to gather in abundant crops of solid, steely ice to cool the sherbet of sultanas, or he drove his large-limbed, steaming oxen over the frozen roads into the silent woods, and made the country-side ring with the stroke of his sturdy axe. So, many a board was crowned and many a hearth-stone warmed by the willing hand of this swart, hale, hearty Irish exile.

All this while bright-eyed Kathleen kept everything snug and nice in the two rooms of their little cottage, her own self the snuggest and nicest thing in it, and that Corny knew right well. To this little cottage there presently came a great joy and a great sorrow, — a great joy of hope and anticipation, a great sorrow of disappointment for a little girl "that was dead before she was born"; and then another joy of hope and anticipation, and another sorrow of deep disappointment for a little boy that was but a few seconds a baby before he was an angel; and yet a third time hope budded and bloomed, — yes, thank God! bloomed into a big, burly, scowling, healthy baby, hideous to the unprejudiced eye, but handsome as babies go; and he clenched his fist and vowed in baby fashion to live as long as Methuselah. And they called his name Corny. Then in all the land was nobody so happy as Corny and Kathleen. Corny the Great worked all day long, and then came home and fluted to Corny the Less, and Kathleen washed and scrubbed and scolded, and said the baby was cross, and such a trouble she could n't do any work, laughing in her heart the while for pure delight, and would have torn your tongue out if you had asserted or even assented that the baby was the least bit cross or troublesome.

But strange to say, Corny, who had borne his disappointment bravely before, now that he was drinking down great draughts of fatherly joy began to grow discontented. There came over him a mighty yearning for the Old Country. I think he wanted to show his foreign-born baby to his Cork county friends, and perhaps this new paternal love in his heart revived and strengthened the old filial love. Just now, too, letters came from the Irish homestead. His old mother declared that she believed she should live twenty years longer if she could see his face once more. His old father made generous Irish proffers of unlimited peat, perpetual house rent, and probable inheritance; and Corny hung up his scythe and threw down his hoe, and said he would go. Then he and Kathleen talked it over; and Kathleen did not care for the peat nor the house rent, and not over much, I am afraid, for the father and mother whom she scarcely knew. She only saw a long, tiresome, and dangerous voyage for the prince in the cradle, and she rocked him with an emphatic foot, and made no scruple of letting it be known that she had a very contemptuous opinion of migration, and still Corny said he would go. Then there came stories of destitution, distress, and impending famine in sorrow-stricken Ireland, and Kathleen saw a horrid vision, — a pair of quivering jelly cheeks growing thin, and sharp, and still; dimples flattening out of little hands, creases straightening out of little legs; and what 'll the boy do for milk on shipboard? asks Kathleen Avourneen, a slight savor of acid in her honest, ringing voice.

"Sure, an' he 'll drink tay now like an ould woman," answers Corny; and the more lions ramp and roar in his path, the more he determines to go, and gives notice accordingly to his landlord.

"The whole world cannot stop me from going," says Corny O'Curran.

But away off in the northwestern corner of this country, terrible things were happening, — children torn from their mother's arms and beaten to death against rocks, husbands shot down in their wheat-fields, wives at their cottage-doors, and blood and rapine and the wild war-whoop scattering horror and dismay. Men left their mown grass in the fields, their oxen standing by the nebs, the cake smoking on the hearth, and fled for life, for love, by day, by night, through the woods, for the nearest forts and towns of refuge. One father and mother deserted their log-house just built, their rich lands just tilled, all their past toil and hope of future harvests, sorrowing only for one little mound in the corner of the garden, but unspeakably glad for one little head that rested still on their bosoms, and turned their steps to the remembered farm-house in New England, and to gray-haired parents that went in and out under the broad elm-shadows. But the journey, easy for the strong man and woman, was too hard and long for the baby feet. They faltered, they turned aside, they went up the shining steeps and walked with God.

Corny sauntered past the old farm-house under the elms, one afternoon, the very day he had given notice to his landlord, and there was a funeral. Some one standing outside told him the sad story of that little life. He went in. He saw a tiny coffin, white flowers, a dead baby face, and came out shuddering. When he went home that night, he went straight to the cradle. Baby Corny kicked and crowed and flung up his warm, mottled arms, and Man Corny took kicking legs, and crowing lips, and mottled arms, and pressed them all in a huddle close against his heart.

"Corny," calls Kathleen, from the oven in which her head is thrust; "Jem has been here, and says he 'll give you a dollar for the table."

"Let him keep his dollar, and I 'll keep me table," says Corny, tossing baby up to the ceiling.

"It 's all ye 'll be likely to git," says shrewd Kathleen.

"An' more," answers Corny, shamefaced. "Katie, I don't believe we 'll go this fall"; — and he mumbles something about work and wages; but Kathleen will not rest till she has the whole story, and glad enough is she. Now the winter is upon us, and Corny is harvesting great granaries of ice, with never a thought of fatherland, because he dreads the journey for his boy.

So I find that one little baby in long frocks wields a stronger power than "all the world" besides!

II.

"GLORY, HALLELUJAH!"

EVIDENTLY this lyric has a mission. It would not be surprising if the National Hymn — which the thirteen wise men of Gotham went a-fishing for last May, baiting their hooks with golden eagles, and getting many nibbles, but no fish — should be found at last in this rousing song. It is a wonderful combination of incongruities, and can scarcely have been marked out for an ordinary career. There is high, religious fervor; a sense of poetic justice and righteous retribution; a scorn of grammar and rhetoric and rhyme and reason; an incoherence, a brutality, a diabolism, a patriotism, and a heroism, which must make it go down the popular throat sweetly as the grapes of Beulah. It has something for everybody. It appeals to all the emotions. It sounds the gamut of humanity. It is like the great image which Nebuchadnezzar saw in his dream. Its head is of fine gold, its breast and its arms of silver, its belly and thighs of brass, its legs of iron, and its feet of clay. All this eminently fits it for a national song, since a national song is not a song of the poets, but the song of a people; and a people is heroic, and unreasonable, and incoherent, and brutal, and noble. Head of gold and feet of clay.

The origin of this song, like that of England's National Hymn, is somewhat foggy, — or will be, if it is let alone a little longer. "God save the Queen" is said to have been a lay of the plotting Jacobites, who, in the early days of the Hanoverian dynasty, were continually scheming its downfall, and the restoration of the Stuarts; and the king who was sung to and prayed for was the exiled Stuart, not the "great George" actually on the throne. But the song somehow worked itself into the public taste, and by a high-handed process was furbished and handed over to the loyal Georgians "as good as new." Was not this "Glory, Hallelujah!" sung by Colonel Ellsworth's Zouaves on their march from New York to Washington, and was it ever sung before? It seems about three hundred years since then; and, after such a lapse of time, one cannot, of course, certainly locate all events in the exact order of their occurrence, nor have I any documents at hand to verify my conjecture, but the "March till the battered gates of Sumter shall appear," savors of the honest and patriotic, but ignorant, "on to Richmond" enthusiasm of those early days. That line surely cannot have been written since Bull Run, and the "pet lambs" point directly to the Caliban Zouaves, who, if I recollect right, christened themselves thus. Does any one know the author of the song, or the time of its first appearance?

Let us look at its head of gold.

> "John Brown's body lies a-mouldering in the grave,
> John Brown's body lies a-mouldering in the grave,
> John Brown's body lies a-mouldering in the grave,
> His soul is marching on."

There is a slight suggestion of John Brown and the little Indian of the fossiliferous ages that preceded Fort Sumter, but it fades away before the real grandeur of the idea. The rude genius which struck out this lyric has hit upon a sublime principle. It is Bryant's royal thought clad in peasant garb.

> "Truth, crushed to earth, shall rise again;
> The eternal years of God are hers."

In homely phrase it recognizes, seizes, and promulgates the immortality of right, the indestructibility of truth; and the people recognize and receive it with a unanimity and an enthusiasm which reconcile one for a moment to that most capricious of apothegms, the voice of the people is the voice of God. On that summer day set in the brow of winter, that June morning lost amid December snows, when John Brown cast his eyes over the pleasant land which he had come to redeem, as he passed to the gallows which was to be his triumphal car down the centuries, — when he stood guarded by twenty-five thousand soldiers, and surrounded by an innumerable throng, — when throughout the South there was terror and hatred and exultation, and throughout the North admiration and sore regret, — who foresaw — to-day? Who looked forward through these two memorable years, and beheld the bristling hosts of Freedom pressing down upon Virginian soil, and ringing out the "Glory, Hallelujah!" on the spot made forever sacred by that martyrdom? Is there in history a retribution more swift, a justice more complete? Whatever may be the issue of the war, Virginia, mother of Presidents, mother of abominations, the cruel and cowardly State that was frantic with terror before a handful of brave men, and frantic with lust for their blood when other hands than hers had given them into her power, — the traitorous and braggart State, fit offspring of fathers scummed from English cities and mothers bought for a hundred pounds of tobacco, — has felt by her own firesides the bitterness of death and the sharper bitterness of desolation. John Brown violated law in his eagerness to dispense justice. Virginia violated law in her eagerness to dispense injustice, and "the curse shall be on her for ever and ever." Virginia slew John Brown in the interests of slavery, and in her despite of Freedom.

A hundred thousand men, imbued with John Brown's spirit, and armed by the law which he broke, march past his gallows-tree, and Freedom is avenged. He wrought ill for a noble cause. He confounded wrong with right. He would punish wrong by wrong. But the good that he did lives after him, and the evil is interred with his bones. The people recognized his single eye, and his pure heart, and when he went, they felt that virtue was gone out from them. They forget now the illegality of his measures, and remember only the purity of his motives. His death atoned for his errors. His hatred of slavery, his energy and courage and fortitude in attacking it, were the day-star of this dawn ; and so, because he wrought ill, his body lies a-mouldering in the grave, and because he purposed well, his soul is marching on. The idea for which he laid down his life, like the stone which was cut out without hands, is becoming a great mountain, and filling the whole land. It shall yet smite the image before which John Brown was sacrificed, and break it to pieces, and grind it to powder. His solitary footstep in the wilds of Virginia heralded that grand army whose tramp is the death-warrant of slavery. Virginia has herself severed the cords that held back the knife from her throat, and now vengeance, and justice, and mercy, join hands to drive it in! No longer covertly, stealthily, with veiled designs, by crooked ways, but in open day, of set purpose, with erect form and defiant mien, Freedom goes down to give light to them that sit in darkness and the shadow of death.

Glory, Hallelujah! that we live to see this day!

"O, sad for him whose light went out
Before this glory came,
Who could not live to feel his kin
To every noble name;
And sadder still to miss the joy
That twenty millions know,
In Human Nature's Holiday,
From all that makes life low."

There is space for only a glance at the less comely parts of the song. Here are its breast and arms of silver:—

"He 's gone to be a soldier in the army of the Lord," &c.

The popular recognition not only of the soul's immortality, but of its immortal activity. The life that battled so bravely, endured so constantly, and yielded so heroically, was not wasted, but is working still in another sphere, and working for the Lord.

"We mourn for the fallen one, we weep for the brave,
Who to this holy cause his noble life he gave;
Sadly yet proudly we shout forth thy name,
As we go marching on!"

Pathetic, and a little pleonastic, but the people is not nice as to its ear, nor fastidious as to its taste, and the sorrow is sincere.

His belly and thighs of brass: —

"Gird on the warrior's armor, the battle ne'er give o'er;
March till the battered gates of Sumter shall appear;
Rest not by the way, till you plant the Stars and Stripes
Where the traitor's flag now waves."

A glorious impulse, but praiseworthy and practicable only as it is consolidated into principle. It savors of indignation rather than determination; and determination only, guided by prudence, and strengthened by obstacles, wins the day.

Legs of iron and feet of clay: —

"John Brown's knapsack is strapped upon his back," &c.
"His pet lambs will meet him on the way," &c., &c., &c.

A sudden and somewhat unaccountable return to the original subject. Evidently the author is more thoroughly at home with John Brown than with abstractions, and goes back to him with a spring. But the meaning is involved in doubt. There seems to be a blending of the literal and the figurative. His knapsack on his back, may be but a vivid way of saying that he is still in good working order; but "his pet lambs" are in the flesh. How can the actual lambs meet the abstract John Brown? or does it mean that they will fight to the death, and so meet him martyrs in the same good cause?

The next —

"They will hang Jeff Davis to a tree," &c., &c. —

brings out the small boys, the hard men, and the

rough people generally, in full force. It is a perfect brutality meter. When an assembly sings it, you shall see the civilized people look a little startled, — as if they were getting rather more than they bargained for; but it is too late to do anything about it, so they lean upon each other for support, smile compromisingly, and conclude to keep on. But all the wild beasts are mad with delight; they find their blood-thirst suddenly legalized; their tumultuousness is orthodox, and they make hay while the sun shines.

The last —

> "Now three rousing cheers for the Union!" —

is a universal solvent. Man and beast, rough and smooth, are melted down into a mere mass of swaying, sonorous patriotism, whose enormous pressure would certainly result in an explosion, were it not for the safety valve of the final, deafening "Hip! hip! hip! Hurrah!"

If, now, a song whose marvellous adaptation to the people is shown by the universality of its reception and the utter abandonment of its execution; if a song as coarse as England's and a good deal finer; a song whose music is — at least to an uncultivated voice and ear — at once simple and magnificent; a song born, as it were, by accident, and left to itself, but working its way by its own inward energy into the public heart, so that it is sung by regiments marching through crowded New York, and through deserted Charlestown, and by all the girls they left behind them, and boys too,—if this is not to be the National Hymn, I should like to know the reason why!

III.

A FOLLY IN ISRAEL.

[Motto: At it again!]

THERE is a class of subjects, not innumerous, which nearly concern the interests of the Church, but of which only one side can be easily presented. You may fill columns of the religious newspapers with the good that is done by Sunday schools, but it is not lawful to recount the evil which they do. You may point out from the narrative of the thief on the cross any moral which the Church has educed and taught, but you may not deviate into lessons of your own learning. You may exhort men to come to Christ, you may even describe his excellences for their imitation, if you will depict only such as the Church has agreed to attribute to him; but if, suspecting that the traditions of men have somewhat overlaid the original manuscript, you should attempt to erase the one and restore the other, you may count on small furtherance in your work. New England Puritanism is very far from Popery, but it is also very far from a practical acknowledgment, in its true significance, of the right of private judgment.

In one respect the children of light are wise in their generation. The "religious newspapers" are probably well acquainted with the tastes and distastes of the "religious public." They know what it will bear, and against what it will rebel; and they doubtless have learned more thoroughly than any others the lesson enunciated by Niebuhr, — "How much is there which we may not say aloud for fear of being stoned by the stupid good people!"

But the question is, whether it is not better to be stoned by the stupid good people than to buy them off by pandering to their prejudices. If they are restless under a presentation of opinions differing from their own, shall those opinions be withheld, or shall they be gently instructed in the true nature and uses of opposition? Are leaders given to the blind for the purpose of guiding them, with some difficulty perhaps, along safe paths, or, for the sake of unity and peace, shall they all settle down comfortably together in the ditch?

It is not a question which can be evaded with impunity. If reformatory opposition be not permitted, destructive opposition will come without permission. If the Church will not tolerate free discussion among its members, there will be riotous attacks from without, and a decay of all its forces within. A "be it resolved" cannot change the face of nature. A community may refuse to tolerate any exposition of the faults in its pet plans or of weakness in its pet beliefs, and then congratulate itself that they are faultless. But facts do not disappear because men refuse to contemplate them. If the Sunday school is working mischief upon our children, its work is mischief, however strenuously we persist in calling it benefit. If it is the glory and beneficence of the age, nothing that even an angel from heaven can say against it will have any other permanent effect than to fasten it still more firmly in the affection and respect of the people. For the Sunday school is not an experiment, struggling up timidly into existence, to be tenderly entreated till a fair trial shall have shown whereunto the thing shall grow. It is an institution, of years and full strength, extending with every month, and enjoying the almost unclouded sunshine of popular favor. It ought to be in a condition to court the freest discussion. If it is what it ought to be, every attack will only bring discomfiture to its foes and advantage to itself. If it is not what it ought to be, it should welcome every suggestion, and carefully consider before deciding upon adoption or rejection. But the fact that an opinion adverse to the common features of the Sunday school and to the current topic of thought regarding it, especially an opinion emanating not from a hostile and inexperienced Gentile, who may be assumed to be ignorant of its workings, but from an Hebrew of the Hebrews, who is, as touching the law, a Pharisee, and concerning zeal, absolutely persecuting the Church, — that such an opinion should be considered too detrimental to be allowed expression, is an argument against Sunday schools which comprises the essence of every hostile charge. If that which professes to be a plan for good working may not be freely and publicly discussed by the lovers of good works, it must lie under the suspicion of harboring some fatal flaw.

If the religious public does not see this by its own unaided vision, for what are religious periodicals established but to lend themselves to the work of enlightenment? Or is it so that while the customs of the world may be rigidly scrutinized and unsparingly condemned, the customs of the Church shall not be so much as looked into to see whether they deserve condemnation? Then, after the woe and warfare of centuries, we are reverting again to an infallible Church, with the singular and signal disadvantage of having for our Divinity no recognized oracle. What came well-defined, if imperative, from the lips of King Pope, now clamors, discordant and unintelligible, from the hundred mouths of King Mob.

This paper was originally written for an able, catholic, and courteous religious newspaper. The watchman of Zion, a mighty man of war, slumbered at his post, I suspect, and the vanguard rushed in and gained a foothold; but before the second detachment could knock at the gates, the sentinels were on duty, the drawbridge was up, and the portcullis down!

This, as well as all the other papers, is written from the point of sight of Orthodox Congregationalism, to which, let my conservative but sweet-tempered brethren of that denomination be assured I adhere with the devotion of Mr. Micawber, and to whom I might not inaptly address the words of the bricht ladie of Elfinland Wud, who clung so desperately to the scared and shuddering Erl William: —

> "Gang ye eist, or fare ye wast,
> Or tak ye the road that ye like best,
> Far owir mure, and far owir fell,
> Thorow dingle, and thorow dell,
> Thorow fire, and thorow flude,
> Thorow slauchtir, thorow blude,
> Eerilie sal nicht wyndis moan,
> Ghaist with ghaist maun wandir on."

But the Sunday school is not the peculiar institution of any sect. It is a matter of deep and broad concern to Presbyterians, Episcopalians, Unitarians, and all such outside barbarians, who are cordially invited to reap for themselves every possible benefit from the following remarks, as freely as if they belonged to the true Church. For the Transcendentalists, Swedenborgians, and other sesquipedalian riff-raff, who are so deeply sunk in original sin that a little more or less of it will make no appreciable difference in their condition, they may as well, perhaps, pass by on the other side. And now, having made peace with all the world, I will, like Pius Æneas, begin.

The Sunday school, as at present conducted, is not an unmitigated blessing.

The old-time fashion of assembling young people together on Sunday in order to indoctrinate them into the truths of Christianity, and guiding them through a regularly prescribed three years' course, must have been very profitable. In the younger, but still old times, Martin Luther's plan of gathering into Sunday schools the children who could not attend day schools, and teaching them to read that so they might have direct access to the Bible, was also most commendable. In still later times, Robert Raikes, the rich and liberally educated Gloucester philanthropist, smitten to the heart by the vice and ignorance around him, hired rooms, gathered in the forlorn, neglected children, and paid poor women a shilling a day to teach them to read. At the same time, Katy Ferguson, who was neither rich nor liberally educated, who was, on the contrary, so abjectly poor that she had rights which white people were bound to respect, but who showed a sagacity which all must admire, and a benevolence which we cannot choose but love, herself organized and taught a Sunday school in New York for the benefit of the poor children of her own people. These schools did a truly Christian work. They took up Christ's little ones, the neglected children of society, miserable waifs tossed on the turbulent tide of life, unhappy wretches straggling up into vice and crime, and set them where they could be warmed by the Sun of Righteousness. Reading, writing, arithmetic, the common things which more favored children learned on week-days, were taught to them on Sunday, mingled with as much religious instruction as they were able to comprehend. But, except in our mission schools, the original idea of the Sunday school seems to be entirely lost. Our ordinary Sunday schools are composed of children who have every opportunity for instruction at home during the six days of the week, and who are regular attendants at church on Sunday. Where lies the need or the propriety of Sunday schools for them? A school is for study, for training; but mental discipline is not necessary for children who are already undergoing strict mental discipline in grammar and high schools. And surely it cannot be necessary to establish a school for the moral and religious training of children who have moral and religious parents at home and a minister for Sundays.

Moreover, what is the kind of instruction which children receive in Sunday schools? The answer may be found, partially, by looking at the instructors. Our Sunday-school teachers are selected from the general community by the superintendent, and often secured with much difficulty. Many to whom he appeals utterly decline to serve, others serve reluctantly, and only from an unwillingness to seem disobliging or from a sense of duty, not from any spontaneous desire or bent. They plead earnestly, sincerely, and often no doubt justly, their unfitness for the work; but he pleads with equal earnestness the difficulty of obtaining teachers at all, and they yield. They are the ordinary fathers and mothers of society, with no especial training for, or adaptation to, the work. They are no more capable of wisely and worthily instructing the young people committed to their charge than are the parents who are not teachers. By what right, then, on what principle, do parents go home or stay at home to read or rest or enjoy themselves in quiet, and send their children away to church or chapel to be looked after by people to whom they do not belong, and who would like to stay at home and have the Sunday-school hour in quiet as well as these parents? Why should parents throw the burden of their children upon other parents when they are just as able to bear the burden themselves, and when it belongs to them by Divine allotment?

Or, again, Sunday-school teachers are young men and young women who have never assumed the responsibilities or learned the duties of the family. They not only have no especial fitness, but they have an especial unfitness for the work. I know of Sunday-school teachers who are merely gay young people, without religious principle or even religious habits, who, out of school, make a mock of their Sunday instruction. Not very numerous, it is to be hoped, is this class of teachers; but very many there are, who, however well disposed they may be, are yet, from their youth and inexperience, unfit to be intrusted with the care of souls. Fatherhood, motherhood, by some mysterious and beautiful Divine arrangement, brings its own wisdom with it; a very ordinary man or woman may be an excellent — the very best — teacher for his own child; but Sunday schools take children away from the ordinary people who have this extraordinary fitness and put them into the hands of people equally ordinary, but without the fitness. These teachers do not have that intimate acquaintance with the children which their parents possess, and which is indispensable to a right and sufficient guidance of their young lives, nor is it possible that they should have that deep, abiding interest which the parents feel. How is it, then, that parents dare commit their children to such unskilful hands? How dare they intrust interests so important to an agency so inadequate?

Probably not one parent in a hundred makes a point of knowing the character of the instruction which his child receives. What the child voluntarily discloses, they know; but they do not systematically, by careful questioning, by indirect application, by pleasant but pertinent conversation, ascertain whether their children are learning Arminianism, Socinianism, Calvinism, or any other *ism*. It is hardly to be doubted that a person might go into the most orthodox Sunday school, and — possibly by the use of a little adroitness and possibly without it — might teach almost any form of heresy without the smallest danger of discovery by the parents. Probably there are few who teach heresy, but a great amount of disjointed reasoning and loose theology is current in Sunday schools. Assertion takes the place of argument. Opinions are inculcated rather than conclusions reached. One woman once asked her boys what the teacher said to them. "O, well," was the reply, with something like a yawn, "he heard us say the lesson, and then he asked us if father had got his haying all done, and said he 'd been to *mash* three days last week, and had got to go again Tuesday." This may be an exceptional case, but so far as I have seen, earnest, systematic investigation — which is implied in the idea of school — is a thing most rare. It is not probably the fault of the teachers. Their education was very likely conducted in the same inconsequent and incoherent manner. They were never taught to think consecutively, or they have not the capacity to teach others so to think. They are at their wits' end to keep their classes going through the prescribed hour, and not unfrequently they cannot do even that. No one can be more keenly alive to their incompetency than themselves, and it would be cruel to cast the shadow of a reproach upon them.

The positive harm that is done in this direction is small, because so little of anything is done. What mischief is wrought lies in mistaking this desultory hour's talk, interspersed with a thousand irrelevant matters, for theological and religious education.

Somewhat of the character of Sunday schools may and indeed must be learned from the aspect of the schools themselves, both while they are in session and after they are dismissed. The adults in school are generally interested in their study; a very few of the young girls, and perhaps of the elder lads, are somewhat interested, — perhaps it would be more correct to say, discover a possibility of interest; while many are far more observant of the dress and demeanor of their companions than of the lesson. The small boys and girls are restless and troublesome, not vicious, but simply child-like, with all their natural propensities for mirth and mischief brought into play emphatically by each other's presence, and only partially restrained by the presence of authority which is but partial. It is a matter of so great difficulty to fasten the children's thoughts on the subject presented to them, that teachers seem forced to expend the greater part of their energy in keeping them quiet, rather than in instructing them. There is no compulsion to insure either decorous behavior or perfect lessons. The children titter, giggle, whisper, stare, compare hats and bonnets, and in ways many and various evince their entire indifference to the matter in hand. They are irreverent during the prayer, distracted and consequently impolite during the recitation; and when school is over they go home talking of dress, play-day, school, and other themes entirely irrelevant and unbecoming holy time. Before they have passed the porch-door you may hear such remarks and questions as "I think your ribbon is ever so much prettier than mine," "Is your veil just like Susey's?" "Why don't you ever wear your blue dress to meeting?" "D' you know Joe got fourteen perch yesterday, 'n' I'm going Wednesday." The children are more elaborately dressed and far more disorderly and intractable than on week-days, and there is little else to show that they are attending a religious and not a secular school.

But Sunday schools, like everything else, must be judged by their fruits. This is a somewhat difficult matter. We must decide not only from what they do, but from what they leave undone and from what they cause others to leave undone. Sunday schools are organized, it is admitted, for the study of the Bible, with or without the aid of Question Books. How much knowledge of the

Bible our fathers and mothers had in their youth, we do not, of course, certainly know; but it is certain that a very great number of young people are growing up as ignorant of the Bible as it seems possible for children in Christian communities to be. They know in a general way that Jesus Christ died for sinners, and that Abraham and David are Bible characters, but of the history, chronology, actual teachings, and in fact, of almost all the priceless lore of the Bible, they are in a state of profound and lamentable ignorance. The light of the Bible reflected from the objects among which they live shines upon them; but so far as light direct from the Bible is concerned, they are walking in a darkness that may be felt. They cannot prove doctrines from the Bible; they do not even know with any definiteness or certainty what is the creed of their own church, much less can they trace its origin in the Bible. With the simple and most charming or most striking narratives of both the Old and the New Testament, they are often entirely unacquainted. They cannot explain Bible allusions from Judæan scenery or manners. Out of a group of a dozen or twenty lads and lasses from thirteen to seventeen years of age, all intelligent and all members of Sunday schools, you may often find not one who can tell whether Achan is the name of a man or a mountain, what is the connection between Jonah and Nineveh, or what is the direction in which one should push his researches if he would learn the story of Mephibosheth or Onesimus or Ahithophel. Such ignorance is the rule and not the exception in some of the most intelligent religious communities in New England villages and cities, where Sunday schools have been in what is called successful operation time out of mind. What I mean is, more definitely, this: gather parties of intelligent young people, between twelve and eighteen years old, who belong to certain flourishing Orthodox congregations in city and country,—children of church-members, and pupils of Sunday schools, —and those who will be able to give correct information on the points I have mentioned, and on others of similar importance, will be rare exceptions. As these congregations are not below others in point of general intelligence, it is not probable that they are below it in Scriptural knowledge.

This I understand to be the main thing. It is of no use to report large numbers, sweet singing, prompt and constant attendance, bright and happy faces. These are but mint, anise and cummin. These indeed ought to be secured if possible; but if with all these, the facts and principles of the Bible are not learned, the Sunday school fails of its end. Its avowed aim is not to give an hour's enjoyment or a centre of attraction to children, but to root and ground them in the faith once delivered to the saints; and if they fail here there is no success. The Sunday school is sometimes said to be the nursery of the Church; but I am "sore sick at heart" for the world, if the Church is to be stocked with such spindlings as the Sunday school produces.

Granting, however, that the Sunday schools accomplish very little, if it can be proved, or if it is altogether probable, that still less would be done without them, — that, dense as is the ignorance with them, it would be still more dense without them, — then we have only to thank God and take courage. But can the proof or the probability be produced? Fifty years ago there were few if any Sunday schools in New England. Are the men and the women who have grown up in Sunday schools any more thorough masters of Bible truth than the men and the women of fifty years ago who were brought up without Sunday schools? Are the lads and lasses of 1864 better acquainted with the facts which pertain to salvation than were the lads and lasses of 1814? Are the common people, the young mechanics, farmers, tradesmen, able to give a reason for the hope that is in them any more clearly and forcibly than the common people were fifty years ago? Are the boys and girls now any more truthful, obedient, respectful, unselfish, than the boys and girls of the last century?

It may further be said that, although Sunday schools may not diffuse or deepen Biblical knowledge so much as is to be desired, the salvation of souls is the ultimate object of Sunday schools, to which all Biblical knowledge tends, and very many trace back the commencement of a new life to the influence exerted upon them in Sunday schools. In view of such facts, how can there be any questions of benefit? If one sinner were converted from the error of his ways by Sunday-school teaching, we should be amply rewarded for all our labors; how then when great numbers look back upon it as the spot "where their weakness first fell bleeding when their first prayer rose to God"?

Waiving now the question of the value that is to be attached to a "salvation" which is not founded upon the rock, and fed by the waters of Bible truth, let us inquire if there must not be somewhere a fatal defect, when the children of Christian families receive their first impulse towards the divine life in Sunday school? If it has come to a general fact that more children accept divine truth from Sunday-school influence than from home influence, must it not be an equally general fact that homes are very much at fault? It is fathers, not Sunday-school teachers, who are commanded to bring up their children in the nurture and admonition of the Lord; and however Christian parents may rejoice in the conversion of their children from the error of their ways, come when and how it will, it is hardly a question whether such conversion, caused by instruction or warning received in Sunday school, does not imply a rebuke for parental unfaithfulness. The promises of the Bible are emphatically "unto you and to your children." The promises of God are in Christ yea, and in him amen; and those promises are most explicit. "Train up a child in the way he should go, and when he is old, he will not depart from it." There is no modification, no condition, no exception. "As arrows are in the hand of a mighty man, so are children of the youth." What are arrows in the hands of a mighty man? Wavering, wandering, uncertain things, which will, perhaps, hit the mark, and perhaps go wide of it; which may do his work, but which also may not, — may even recoil against himself, to wound and torture and kill? Is it not plain that just as the mighty man, the warrior, the sharpshooter, wings his unerring shaft whithersoever he will, and finds in it a sure defence, a strength and support, so the father may bring up his children to be what he wills, the staff of his age, the joy of his soul, the hope of the world? If the Bible does not mean this, what does it mean? And if it does mean this, ought parents to be content that their children should trace back their change from the ways of death into the ways of life to the influence of one stranger who was with them one hour a week, rather than to the influence of two persons who were with them nearly all the other hours, and who had all the advantages of consanguinity, intimacy, interest, and a common love, care, duty, and delight? Surely parents must have cause to look lightly on their duties, and value lightly their privileges, before they can with complacency see their children attribute to outside agency the good that should have been wrought in the sacred privacy, and by the constant healthful influences of home.

But it may be claimed this is putting too fine a point upon it; if the work is done, if the children grow up into men and women who fear God and keep his commandments, it may seem to be a matter of minor importance whether it be the work of parents or others.

But is even this work done? At a recent State Sunday-school convention, the proportion of those who became Christians in Sunday schools was said to be one in nine. At another convention it was said to be one in fifteen. If this is success, what would be counted failure?

Nor does the quality of our religious life, any more than its quantity, tend to inspire confidence in the means adopted to awaken and nourish it. Religious society is too largely frivolous in its tastes, absurd in its fears, and narrow in its views; religious experience is shallow, and religious principles are weak, and it can be for no other reason than that religious training is so imperfect. There is no subsoiling, — no under-drainage, no thorough working of the soil, — and, in consequence, our crops are scanty and stunted. The religious element of New England possesses not a tithe of the power it ought to wield, because it is so feebly managed. The Sunday school is partly, though unconsciously and innocently, to blame for this. It comes in, not with the intention, but in fact, to relieve parents from responsibility for the direct religious training of their children, and is itself wholly inadequate to its assumption. When parents used to hear their children recite the Catechism on Sunday evening, and the minister heard them publicly once a month, something was accomplished. The little people may not have understood what they were saying, but seed was planted in their minds which presently grew, and flourished, and brought forth fruit an hundred-fold. I do not think the Shorter Catechism, agreed upon by the Reverend Assembly of Divines at Westminster, is the best possible mode of presenting Bible truths to infant minds, but it is much better than the Sunday-school mode. It did no moral harm, and much intellectual good; the Sunday school does much moral harm, and no intellectual good that I could ever see. I should be glad to behold every church Sunday school in the land swept out of existence, if by such act the Westminster Catechism could be restored to the place it once occupied in the church homes. It was a tough old crust for young teeth to gnaw, but it was excellent for the teeth. Contrast with the diluted pap which is presented to children in the shape of leading questions with monosyllabic answers, which can be given nearly as correctly without study as with it, the sturdy, sententious, uncompromising answers of the Westminster Catechism: —

"What is God?"

"God is a spirit, infinite, eternal, and unchangeable, in his being, wisdom, power, holiness, justice, goodness, and truth."

"Did all mankind fall in Adam's first transgression?"

"They did," is all you would get from a Sunday school; but hear what the Westminster Catechism saith: —

"The covenant being made with Adam, not only for himself but for his posterity, all mankind, descending from him by ordinary generation, sinned in him, and fell with him in his first transgression.

"Wherein consists the sinfulness of that estate whereinto man fell?

"The sinfulness of that estate whereinto man fell consists in the guilt of Adam's first sin, the want of original righteousness, and the corruption of his whole nature, which is commonly called original sin, together with all actual transgressions which proceeded from it.

"Did God leave all mankind to perish in the estate of sin and misery?

"God having, out of his mere good pleasure, from all eternity, elected some to everlasting life, did enter into a covenant of grace, to deliver them out of the estate of sin and misery, and to bring them into an estate of salvation by a Redeemer."

It is not necessary to believe in the truth of these doctrines in order to see that the child who has mastered the one hundred and seven answers containing them, has gained a victory over sloth and weakness and the natural inclination to shilly-shallying, which will stand him in good stead all his life. When he grows up to a comprehension of the statements, he may accept or reject them, but he will know what he is about. The mental activity which they have caused will have given him a firmness of fibre that will preclude all weak yielding and swaying hither and thither. His reason will have something to work on.

Apart from the truth of the answer, its form is a model of condensation and completeness. No answer hangs upon its question, but each stands upon its own foundation. Each is a separate proposition, crystallizing its own truth, a part of a symmetrical whole, yet complete in itself. Intellectually, a thorough course of the Westminster Catechism may be considered about equal to three terms in college. Certainly I would not retain the Catechism when something better is offered; but as certainly, I would not give it up for something worse.

We had another blessing under the reign of this deposed monarch. It was a family-centralizing power. It was a focus of household light. It is remembered with father, mother, brothers, sisters, gathering about the well-swept hearth, and beautiful in the yellow fire-light. With it comes back the pride of youthful vigor, the joy of youthful innocence. Here, shy and smiling, on papa's feet sat the little sister whose shining curls toss only in your dreams. There, behind the light-stand, was the broad-browed brother who went up to heaven from the "battle in the clouds." One gathering golden harvests in California, and one tossing somewhere on the broad ocean, you can still see, side by side, on the settee in the corner. The old homestead is gone to ruin, the family name is passing away; but in your memory the unbroken circle gathers about the fireside on Sunday evening, type of the reunion that shall be. The simplest and sweetest pleasures of life, the tenderest affections of the heart, the most hallowed associations, the most sacred hopes, are entwined with the memories of that Sunday evening exercise.

What have we gained for this? Heterogeneous crowds jostling into a public room, and jostling out again. Dozens of children gathered into dozens of classes, with dozens of teachers such as could be had for the begging, keeping them under partial control through a prayer, or suffering them to shout out responses with the fury of a caucus hurrah, — coaxing, cajoling, or commanding them through lessons which are sometimes half learned and sometimes not learned at all. A gay, often boisterous walk, an hour without quiet, — parade and publicity, — only this and nothing more.

For the sanctity of home we have the secularity of the Sunday school.

The abandonment of Sunday schools would not necessarily improve home education, but it would have a tendency to do it. A divided responsibility is far less effective than an undivided one. It is a homely but a true saying, "what is everybody's business is nobody's business." If Christian parents knew that whatever religious education their children have must be given by themselves, they would be far more concerned to bestow it. If they would not, — if with the cessation of Sunday schools, religious education would cease altogether; if the hearts of Christian men and women are so little engaged in the truth which their minds profess to believe, that they would not take the trouble to teach them to their children; that, unless they can induce some stranger to do the work, it will not be done at all, — then I have only to say that our profession of Christianity is the most wretched deceit and mockery, is indeed the most dreary and hopeless form in which atheism can present itself. I assume without misgiving that the present defects in religious training have their origin in want of just observation. Parents fancy themselves to be doing the best thing for their children when they send them to the Sunday school. It is difficult to believe that it is conscious, deliberate laziness, for such a belief would strike at the root of Christian character. It is equally difficult to believe that parents who do not send their children to Sunday school, nor cultivate their religious nature at home, can find in my suggestions any justification of their course.

So I cannot think it too much to hope that our lost Sunday evening may yet be restored to us. At present, what with one thing and what with another, we seem to have forfeited it altogether. Our fathers kept both Saturday and Sunday evenings. We make the balance true by keeping neither. We have churches and gas-lights, singing and sermons, walking and talking, but we have no Sunday evening. There is a prayer and conference meeting, a Union lecture, a Sunday-school concert, one or another form of gadding about for change, christened with some pious sounding name, but no sweet, systematic home-keeping. We are all gone astray after gayety and dissipation. There is none that stand in the ways, and see and ask for the old paths, where is the good way, and walk therein and find rest on the rest-day for their souls. It was a small thing for some well-meaning persons to put in their officious hands and draw away the children for a short space on Sunday from the family fireside; but somehow the whole family is dragged after them and the hearth-stone is cold. An hour in a chapel need not change the whole Christian Sabbath, the whole family arrangement; but it created a new centre of attraction, and all the moons and stars seem to have left their orbits to circle around it,—and the poor old honest earth sits in darkness, weeping for her children and will not be comforted because they are not.

There is another evil found in connection with Sunday schools, but when or how it arose, whether from them or simply along with them or entirely apart from them, I do not know. I mean the avalanche of silly books which is continually sliding down upon the young mind, and which threatens to bury all vigor, all intelligence, all intellectual activity, under a mass of stilted, sentimental nonsense. We often hear and read ecclesiastical deprecation of novel reading; but do Christain parents know that their children are surfeiting themselves at the Sunday-school libraries with weak and worthless novels? If false views of life, if unnatural representations of character, if appeals to passion and vanity, if melodramatic scenes and sensational incidents, make novels pernicious reading for the young, then are our Sunday-school libraries dealing out pernicious reading. How long this evil has been in existence I do not know, but it seems to be at full tide now. I have looked over an old catalogue of a Sunday-school library collected about sixteen years ago, and compared it with catalogues of several late collections. Judging merely from the titles, the books of the old library are of a far higher class than those of the new. Among the former I find such books as "Anabaptists," "Arabia Petrea," "Allein's Alarm," "Bible Dictionary," "Babylonish Captivity," "Bible Chronology," "Baxter's Saint's Rest," "Bible not of Man," "Bible is True," "Bunyan's Holy War," "Child's Guide through the Bible." In the modern catalogues, I look in vain for books of similar substance. The greater number are pathetic stories of little girls who died and who ought never to have lived; scaring stories of little boys who went to a circus, and thence by short and easy stages to the state-prison; fascinating stories of beautiful misses in pure white frocks, who suffered the horrors of remorse for having once gone to the opera with the family where they were visiting, and whose penitent and patient sweetness won over wicked but dark-eyed and chivalrous young men to give up wickedness and painting and take holy orders, and the white-robed girl to wife; thrilling stories of pious lads who rush through ridicule, persuasion, and sundry forms of opposition, converting all before them. The story, as a form of entertainment or instruction, has its appointed place, and is open to no objection ; but such stories as run riot through our Sunday-school literature are neither sweet to the taste nor to be desired to make one wise. They do not appeal to the imagination, nor to the consciousness, scarcely at all to the conscience, nor to any faculty of the soul, save a languid curiosity or a morbid craving for sentiment. Their work is doubly harmful. The mind cannot long preserve its balance, if forced to subsist on any one kind of food ; how much less if that food be largely adulterated. If we must have a diet composed chiefly of sugar-plums, let us at least have them from established factories, where we may be sure of a good article of its kind, and not content ourselves with a sickly concoction of sugar, flour, and water, simmered together in a thousand kitchen kettles. The lords and ladies of Waverley, the men and women of Thackeray, Trollope, Mrs. Stowe, Miss Muloch, or George Elliot, would be a great improvement on the interminable procession of Hatties and Katies and Nellies and Georgies and Willies and Harries that now mince their missish ways over the library shelves.

But must we have only sugar-plums? Is it necessary that we confine ourselves to stories? Must we leave all our interesting and momentous Church history and Bible history in the background, and give ourselves over to fifth-rate romances? Why are not girls and boys of fourteen, fifteen, twenty years of age occupied with studying the story of their own Church, interwoven as it is with some of the most important political crises of the world? Why do they not study the scenery and history of the Bible, the customs and manners of Judæa, which throw so much light on Bible narratives? Why do they not trace back the paths of the early churches, which would make the Epistles clear, curious, and practical? Why are they not versed in the sinuosities of Hebrew and Greek life, that they may follow the Scriptural sinuosities through all their Divine adaptations, and so discern their Divine origin, instead of viewing the Bible as one dead and dismal level of practice and precept?

It is said that they will read such books as they have, and others they will not read. Of course it is of no use to cumber our shelves with books that will never be touched. Little children must have little stories, and larger children must have larger stories, and the supply only answers to the demand. But if the argument holds good with regard to Sunday-school books, it holds still better with regard to novels. I shall, however, be slow to believe that the children of Christian parents cannot be educated into higher tastes. If this unsubstantial but highly seasoned food were withheld from them, I cannot but think they would presently come to a healthy appetite. If they turn away from wholesome bread and butter and cry for tarts and jelly, let them cry till they are hungry, and then the bread and butter will have a fair chance of being appreciated. Turn off entirely the "weak, washy, everlasting flood" of sanctimonious sentimentalism, and see whether there will not presently be a return to the living springs of the Bible. Provide only such books as have in them material for thought. If they be stories of character and development, let them be true to human life, and not painted caricatures. The baptized weaklings who tread our aisles so softly are no more capable of healing the hurts of the infant soul with their theological abracadabra than were the sturdy old pagans of Haroun al Raschid, Sinbad the Sailor, and Mother Goose. If we have history let it be history, not the diluted residuum of history. The pulling down of a noble work to bring it within a child's reach is little less than sacrilege. If the rugged, simple, and homely English of the Bedfordshire tinker is not to be comprehended by the youthful reader, let the youthful reader comprehend as much of it as he can, and strive assiduously to grow up to the rest; but let us have no "Child's Pilgrim's Progress," culling for him the flowers which he is abundantly able to cull for himself, and permanently spoiling for him the garden, which his own hands would never do. For the youngest children stories need to be just as true to nature, and inculcations just as firmly founded on reason, as for their elders. There are also the inexhaustible narratives of the Bible told in language as fit and simple as any modern writer could frame. If paraphrase be necessary, let it come from parental lips, suggested by the conditions of the moment; but it is a most venturesome service for a man to sit down in cold blood and presume to clothe Bible stories in better guise for another man's children than that which the firesides of two nations and two centuries have sanctified.

Looking at this whole matter, we are led to conclude that, until children have attained sufficient intellectual maturity to be able to investigate a question, to approach it and attend to it from no external pressure, but from inward enthusiasm, the Sunday school must be an injury to them, and an injury in vital points. It mars a delicacy which cannot be too devoutly defended. The more intimate the sensitiveness, the more fatal its violation. A shop plundered is but robbery; a church rifled is sacrilege. I cannot conceive of an institution which should promise any benefit that could counterbalance the harm of a separation on Sunday between parents and young children, and especially the harm of putting the religious life of children at the mercy of strangers. On other days the conduct of affairs requires separation, and seems to require, for the sake of economy, a partial transfer of duty; but the Lord blessed the Sabbath day and hallowed it, — hallowed it for home, for rest, for privacy; hallowed it for sanctification of the past and redemption of the future; for the divine work of the week to blossom in the blessed, beautiful worship of the holy Christian family. For many parents it is the only day which they can spend with their little ones, and no work but of necessity or mercy should be allowed to interfere with it.

Mission schools stand, it will readily be seen, on different ground. As the state of war, which is a retrogression for the North, is an advance towards civilization for the South, so the state of being in Sunday school, which is a desecration of the Christian Sabbath, is a consecration of the pagan no-Sabbath. To gather poor little vagrants from their gutters and alleys into decent rooms, and teach them mental, moral, and Christian truth, is a very different thing from luring children away from the privacy of Christian homes into the glare and distraction of mixed assemblies.

To adults, — to all who are old enough to pursue a subject systematically, — a Sunday service conducted on the theory of the Sunday school can hardly fail to be of great value. If, instead of our present superficial desultory reading, which is our main reliance, outside the pulpit, for theological thought, and which greatly detracts even from the benefit of pulpit ministrations, the rank and file of the churches, all the grown men and women, were engaged, under the leadership of some persons of superior knowledge and culture, and of tact, candor, and reverence, in the careful, critical, and devout study of the Bible; a study which should at once enlist and cultivate energy, attention, and all the powers of research at the command of ordinary minds; a study which should enable men to discern between Bible teachings and human traditions, between what the Lord Jesus Christ said and what commentators declare him to mean, between the inspiration of the Holy Spirit and the inspiration of unholy pride of opinion, or partisan violence, or innocent prejudice; a study which should be study, and not a travesty of it; investigation, not gossip; man's work, not child's play, — we might hope that religious thought would be reawakened, religious feeling deepened and made effective, religious principle strengthened and wisely directed. (This would be a very different thing from that movement which is now so warmly advocated and so stoutly opposed, — the substitution of the Sunday school in its present form for the afternoon sermon and service. It is easy to conceive the scorn with which a divine "of the old school" should look upon this proposed encroachment of the new.) Children accompanying their parents through such an exercise would be no more wearied than by any ordinary Sunday service, and would naturally and gradually, as their minds unfolded, be drawn into sympathy with it, and derive from it an advantage proportioned to their capacity. Not turned loose among themselves, they would have small temptation to deviate from that propriety of demeanor which the day and the occasion demand, and which, in spite of Mr. Turveydrop, is no unimportant element of good morals as well as good breeding. The lore learned by parents from the oracles of God would be taught with fatherly and motherly love to the little ones at home. The meat of the Gospel, in the alembic of the parental heart, would be transmuted into the pure and sincere milk of the word, by which young souls should increase in wisdom and stature, and in favor with God and man. Children whose parents are members of the congregation and not of the church would be gathering religious instruction along with their parents; and the parents themselves, no longer able to lean upon some teacher, who, though consciously incompetent to cure the child's soul, is consciously competent to salve the parent's conscience, would be far more likely to think upon their ways, and turn both their own and their children's feet unto the testimonies of God. Instead of laboring to bring children into the Sunday school, we should be laboring to bring families; and the solitary children who might be drawn in would be distributed among families, and be watched over as children by parents, instead of being herded together as pupils under the care of a perplexed amateur teacher. We should at least know that sacred things would be cherished in sacred places; and besides whatever positive good were accomplished, we should be spared the pain of seeing religious sentiment defloured before it is developed.

IV.

A LANDMARK REMOVED.

WHEN the wires flashed across the country the brief tidings, "Owen Lovejoy died last night at half past eleven," many hearts must have sadly felt that he died too soon. It was not only that he was in the prime of life, in the full maturity of his powers, with many a hard fight still in his strong right arm, but that the battle-flag fell from his dying grasp while yet the strife was hot. The victory toward which he had all his life been pressing hovered before his eyes, but could not perch upon his banner, and he passed away with the war-cry still ringing in his ears. But our regrets are as needless as vain. "It is not the victory, but the struggle, that makes the happiness of noble hearts." He was called away in his prime, but his work was done. There was a time when he was needed. He is needed no longer. There was a time when Liberty passed through the land with a staff; now she is become two bands that stretch across a continent. From shore to shore the echoes of her voice resound, and deep calleth unto deep.

Through the hillside hamlets of New England and the prairies of the West, here and there, years ago, was found a man with an impracticable twist in his character; all together they were not enough to do anything, but they were quite enough to hinder other people from doing anything, — sturdy, indomitable men; sometimes speaking aloud with eloquent lips to the utter thwarting and discomfiture of those whose great principle it was to float with the current, and sometimes bearing testimony only by a silent, stubborn refusal to pour libations at the shrine of others' idolatry. But they were mighty men of valor in their generations. They buckled on armor and girded sword for the war. There was no place nor power nor pelf to lure easy-goers or the devotees of pride and ambition. All who embarked with them must sail in the teeth of wind and tide. They met somewhat sharper than swords, nothing warmer than contemptuous compassion. Their neighbors, who were kindly disposed and fain to defend them, said they were good men, but mulish. Their hearts were in the right place, but their heads were clean given over to one idea. That idea has become a great mountain, and filled the whole earth.

Rufus Choate, in one of his impassioned addresses, represented the two parties of Whigs and

Democrats as sweeping the ocean with their ships of the line wherein were marshalled the forces of a mighty nation, "except a few Free-Soilers whose bark was never built to brave the stormy sea, but only to traverse the solitudes of the serene upper air." But the Whig Ocean Queen has gone down, and not so much as a floating spar reveals where she sank. The Democratic three-decker has parted her keel, and many a splintered fragment goes careering madly over the waves to tell of the wild work that has been; while the part that is afloat keeps close alongside the little Free-Soil craft, now a mighty man-of-war, flying the flag of a nation at its mast-head, bearing in its bosom the hope of the world.

On such a seemingly frail craft, with such a seemingly insufficient crew, Owen Lovejoy embarked and did soldierly service. He plunged into the "thunder-storm of battle" for moral right, not personal revenge. He fought for love of man, not hatred. Doubtless, the death of his brother at the hands of Slavery intensified, but it did not create, his horror of the accursed thing. When the sword pierced his own soul, it did not awake him from a dream; it only made him grasp more firmly the blade he had chosen so wisely, and wielded so well. All his life he walked along the heights of eternal justice, and, whether with fierce denunciation, or with a gentle persuasion, he bade his fellows, Come up hither. As a pastor he preached the Gospel of the true Messiah, whose glad tidings were to loose the bands of wickedness, to undo the heavy burdens, to let the oppressed go free, to break every yoke, to deal bread to the hungry, to bring in the poor that are cast out, and to cover the naked. But the pulpit was too far from the wrong, and his attack seemed to him feeble from distance. He longed to lay at the very heart of the man of sin; and putting from him, with no irreverent hand, the robes of his priesthood, he gave himself thenceforth to the one cause of freeing his country and the slave from the curse that bound them both. The two stood as one in his conscience and in his heart. He could not walk to his country's greatness over "the friendless bodies of unburied men," even though they were black. He sought both to raise a prostrate and free an enslaved race, and to raise and free the race that humbled itself to the dust in compassing such prostration and enslavement. Laboring as a patriot and a statesman for large ends, he did not overlook smaller ones. He did not forget the individual in the race. Not only has the black man cause to bless his name and memory, but black men and women and little children recall him as a benefactor. It was meet that a negro, a freedman, should aid in bearing his body to its final resting-place, for he maintained the cause of the negro at all times as the matter required.

He has gone over to the majority, but not too

soon. His eye was not dim, nor his natural force abated. The years had taken no firmness from his step, no clearness from his judgment, no hope from his heart. He had travelled through the wilderness his forty years, and he might not enter the Land of Promise, but the Lord had led him up from the plains of Moab unto the mountain of Nebo, to the top of Pisgah, and showed him fair Canaan, and he saw that rest was good, and the land that it was pleasant.

His fame, too, is assured, — such honorable fame as befits honorable work, such fame as good men love. In the days that are to come, when even Ethiopia, in the land of her captivity and her redemption, shall stretch out her hands unto God, not last nor faintly outlined among the names which she will delight to honor shall stand this name which we sadly pronounce to-day. Nor has he died too soon for his fame among his own people. He has gone over to the majority as the ancients held it, but in our later phrase the majority has gone over to him. The people have climbed up to where their leaders stood. Not his courage, — that was never questioned, — but his wisdom is vindicated. There is no need to say what will be. Men see now that what they thought fanaticism was the true sagacity. Optical illusion was clear vision. The solemn claims of justice, and love, and human brotherhood were at one with the claims of honor, and purse, and the naked needs of existence, nay, even of existence itself. He asserted and defended those claims manfully, Christianly; and the generation that scorned and scoffed is forward to-day to wreathe a glory round his brow.

The world will do justice to his bravery, his single-mindedness, his statesmanship; but the softer lights that played around his soul it had scarcely space to see. There is small shining for dewdrops when lightnings flash. The occasion was so earnest, that he was fain to cry aloud and spare not. It is as a reformer, as a champion, as a knight without fear and without reproach, that he is known and lamented.

> "Fleet foot on the correi,
> Sage counsel in cumber,
> Red hand in the foray,
> How sound is thy slumber!"

But the firelight from household hearths that fell upon him revealed a gentle grace, a happy humor, wit lambent, unfailing, but harmless; a heart which, far away, clung to all the little tendernesses of home. Brave old war-horse that he was, snuffing the battle from afar, a little child could lead him, and be no tenderer than he! Brawny and huge, no footfall was softer than his, no voice more low and quiet. Roused sometimes, even in the pleasure of social talk, to indignation and loud-voiced eloquence over the wickedness which it was his life-trust to combat, he was always tolerant of the hand that pulled the valve-string of his balloon, and he ever came earthward again with a half-ashamed smile, with a deprecatory look, or a mock ferocious threat. He was such a good-natured, sleepy-eyed lion, roaring you so gently, for all his shaggy strength, so meek and submissive and long-suffering, when his antagonisms were lulled asleep, and he could, with good conscience, take his ease among his friends, that he was an irresistible target for teasing. The harder the storm of banter and browbeating that pelted him, the more he enjoyed it, nor ever a ripple broke the surface of his large-hearted placidity. No sharper weapon than a Latin epigram, or a verse from Virgil, or some quiet little home-bent blade did he ever draw upon his assailants, but so apt and ready was he with these small arms that he generally came off victorious. But conquered or conqueror, his good nature was invincible. The low, deliberate voice, the quaintnesses of word and manner, the smile, so mingled of amusement, assumed toleration, real enjoyment, and all manner of good wit and good will, were never wanting, nor will their memory fail. As the necessity for hostilities grew less, as truth marched on to triumph, as righteousness and peace approached to kiss each other, and the sorrowful land returned again to the allegiance to which the fathers bound her, and from which traitorous sons had dragged her, his genial qualities would have had opportunity to blossom· out into the light, and to soften what seemed rugged in his character. The rock would have been no less firm, but it would have been draped with all graces of bloom and spray. His inner and outer, his private and public life, would have blended into harmony, and he would have been known for the man he was.

Now the harmony is complete; but, alas! eye and ear fail us to perceive it.

On the hillsides of New England, on the prairies of the West, beyond the sea, among the palaces of forgotten kings, there are hearts that will fondly linger over the memory of pleasant evenings which return no more.

With many a prayer for those to whom morning and evening rest alike in shadow, a friendly hand lays this wreath of forget-me-nots upon his new-made grave.

V.

DOUBTFUL ARGUMENTS.

IT is but natural, it is indeed every way imperative, that men who are called upon to preach a doctrine of import so fearful as that of the eternal punishment of the impenitent, should make constant efforts to explain its necessity and enforce its reasonableness. God's character seems to be concerned, and those who reverence his great and fearful name, and strive to bring it to the regard of the world, cannot fail to vindicate it against every possible stain of injustice, by trying to show that even in this most awful of all the doctrines of the Church, justice, no less than judgment, is the habitation of his throne. The attempt to do so is always praiseworthy, though not always wisely directed. Some of the arguments are of such a nature that they can hardly convince, and must, therefore, strengthen the opposition which they are designed to destroy.

To the assertion that so small a thing as the sin

which a man may commit in the few years of life cannot righteously be punished by unalleviated misery through unending years, a very common reply is, that sin may be a much more terrible thing than we know. It may cause derangement and disaster through worlds and ages, of which we have no conception. We see but in part; the All-Seeing considers not simply our act of transgression, but all its far-reaching consequences, and punishes according to his sight, not ours.

Is this explanation quite satisfactory, even as far as it goes? Is it according to analogy? You may say that it seems to the strong man a very small thing to sit a few moments in a draught of air; nevertheless in those few moments are sown the seeds of a disease which presently brings him to the grave. A little child does not know why he is bidden to play within the garden paling; but thoughtlessly straying beyond, he plunges down a precipice into the engulfing waters. Law is inexorable; its penalties must be enforced.

So far as pertains to physical matters, the analogy seems to hold. If a man commits a trespass against material laws, it matters not whether he did it wilfully or ignorantly, he incurs the penalty. There is no exemption. But in moral, and even in civil law, another rule obtains. An infant is suffering from ear-ache. Too young for self-control or intelligent consciousness, in a frenzy of pain and passion, its little hands strike wildly out at the loving mother, who shares the anguish which she cannot relieve. What an act is this, if intelligently done! What a monster of iniquity and ingratitude is the child to turn against the heart which aches with pity, against the hands which never weary with striving to mitigate his suffering, to expend all his little rages on the bosom that yearns to soothe him into peace! The natural law of love and the Scriptural command to honor are alike violated. Does he suffer the penalty which attaches to such double violation? Does any one consider him unnaturally bad, and deserving the severest reprobation, as would infallibly be the case if he knew what he was doing? On the contrary, his ignorance is his adequate excuse. He has no suspicion that he is breaking the fifth commandment and verging upon the crime of matricide; and because he knows nothing of all this, we — do not justify laws which mete out to him the punishment due to such sin and crime, but we rather count it, therefore, a trivial thing, to be overlooked rather than forgiven, to stand not at all in the way of every possible well-doing towards the suffering child. We should say the mother was of a very harsh temper who should suffer her indignation to be roused, and very weak who should permit her feelings to be wounded, by such an exhibition on the part of her unwitting little one.

This, of course, is not, and is not intended to be, a strictly parallel case. We can have no parallel case, for the Lord our God is one Lord, and there is none like him; but it may help us to the truth. We shall get still nearer the truth if we take an instance of conscious ill-doing. A man is your enemy, and designs to inflict harm upon you. He means to increase his own wealth at the expense of yours. But he opens his eyes one day to find that his dislike to you was unfounded, that you were his benefactor when he thought you his tyrant, sympathizing when he thought you unfeeling; and to find, also, that your hurt is far greater than he intended, that in depriving you of your property he reduced your family to beggary, took away your staff of life, and brought you to the gates of death. His guilt is great; it is difficult to measure; but do you think it is just as great as it would be if, instead of unwittingly firing this mischievous train, he had with malice aforethought set the match to the powder? If you can say in your heart, Bitter as was my foe, he never would have done this had he known what such doing meant; he never would have done this had he known my real character and my relations to himself,—do you not attach less blame to him than if you see his hand deliberately lifted to every successive injurious act, his eyes open to all their results and to the full integrity and innocency of the person against whom every fresh expression of his malignity is directed? Is it not true, that, instead of visiting moral reprobation and punishment strictly in proportion to the dimensions of the act, we diminish it in proportion to the man's ignorance of those dimensions?

In the manifestation of the world's worst wickedness, when Evil laid its hand upon the only Good, and requited beneficence with crucifixion, what lesson fell from holy lips, what prayer went up to the Heaven of heavens? "Father, forgive them, for they know not what they do."

Paul, who was not one whit behind the very chiefest apostles, who though brought up at the feet of Gamaliel according to the perfect manner of the law of the fathers, was yet so overpowered with the excellency of the glory which met him on the way to Damascus, that he gave up all reliance on excellency of speech or of wisdom, and determined to know nothing among his congregation but Jesus Christ and him crucified, — even he believed that the hidden wisdom which God ordained before the world unto our glory could not have been known to the princes of this world, "For," he insists, out of his great, loving heart, with infinite pity and yearning, "For had they known it, they would not have crucified the Lord of glory." And if Paul, transfigured forevermore in the light that shined round about him from heaven, could find a good word, a regretful word, an excusing word, to say for those who had done the foulest deed that ever stained, or ever can stain, the records of our earth, — nay, if the Sinless One, knowing to the utmost the indignity put upon the Most High, could crave forgiveness for the criminals on the very ground that they knew it not, — shall we believe an angel from heaven if he preach any other gospel? Shall we not rather give good heed to the lesson which teaches that God is not strict to mark our iniquities to the farthest bounds of their consequences, and that man, defiled, degraded, outcast, instead of being punished for the baleful work which he wrought unawares, shall be the more likely to obtain mercy, because he did it ignorantly, in unbelief?

I know that this truth has its corresponding falsehood, which may be mistaken for it by the unwary. Ignorance itself may be a sin. But it is no more likely to be a sin now than it was in the days of Christ; and if Jesus and his great apostle to the Gentiles ventured to make the statement, running the risk of men's wresting it to their own destruction, it cannot be unsafe for us to follow their example. Moreover, there is always less danger to be apprehended from the abuse of truth than from the use of falsehood.

Another argument frequently brought forward in proof of the doctrine of eternal punishment, and lately published widely in the newspapers, with the indorsement of some distinguished archbishop, is, that in the original Greek of the Bible the same word is used to express the duration of the happiness of the righteous and of the misery of the wicked; so that the interpretation which revokes the doom of the latter sweeps away the bliss of the former. If we will abrogate the threat of unending woe, we must also abrogate the promise of unending happiness.

This argument must be understood as addressed to the Church, not to the world; to those who are confident, not to those who are careless, of eternal life. For the man who does not purpose to attain heaven has but a small interest in its existence. If he has only wretchedness in store, or if he has no definite future hopes, the reality of a place of happiness is the last thing about which he will concern himself, is a matter which furnishes him with no motive, and influences neither his belief nor his life. It is the Church, the people who believe in and who are supposed to be pressing towards heaven, who are addressed in such appeals.

And I for one accept the issue, — if I understand it aright. If by giving up the certainty of future bliss for ourselves we could also be relieved of the certainty of future woe for another, we should not only relinquish it with gladness and singleness of heart, praising God, but we should esteem ourselves of all men most miserable, most vilely selfish, if we could for a moment hesitate to do it. Look at what is set before us. On the one side there are spared to us of the Bible its precepts, its examples, its ideals. We have the story of the spotless life, the sacrificial death. We know what is the character of God, what is the type of human character in which he delights, and what the path he has traced for human feet. We know, in short, what is right and well-pleasing in his eyes. What does a man need more than this? Can he not trust his Maker without guaranty? Must God give bonds for the final disposal of the soul which strives to be like him; for the destination reserved to those who walk his appointed paths? Cannot faith trust implicitly in goodness? With abundant promises of help, can we not dispense with promises of happiness? It seems to me that we might take away from the Bible every direct prediction of future unending bliss, of that which is commonly understood as heaven, and then leave enough to stand on and defy a thousand hells. To do his will is to enter into his rest. He who receives Christ into his heart is in heaven already. The true disciple is dead; no harm can happen to him: his life is hid with Christ in God; and that which is so hid must be forever beyond reach of the powers of evil. Who is he of man or devils, principalities of earth or air, that can harm you, if ye be followers of that which is good? A truce to our shadowy Mohammedan heaven! The kingdom of God is within you. He that has the testimony within himself that he pleases God, may laugh to scorn the hope that hangs on a promise.

Do you say, then, why were the promises given?

Tell me first, why did the father go out to meet the prodigal son when he was yet a great way off? Why are a thousand seeds scattered for every tree that grows? Why is the love of our heavenly Father not doled out after our scant mortal measure, but lavished with the profusion of boundless benignity?

On the other side what? Eternal impurity, eternal rebellion. Eternal looking backward upon unrepented sin; eternal looking forward to accumulated guilt. On every side judgment and fiery indignation. Infinite regret, but no penitence; infinite rage, and no power; infinite rebellion, and no reconciliation; infinite remorse, no forgiveness; infinite agony, without hope, for millions upon millions of sensitive souls, born with no volition of their own into circumstances not subject to their control; moulded by evil for evil before they were capable of resisting, or even of recognizing evil; all the horror and hate of time duplicating and reduplicating themselves forever and forever through the countless ages of eternity. What price would be too great to pay for the possibility of escape from the infinite despair of such a prospect? We see the work of evil begun in this world; we seem to see in its beginning the elements of perpetual reproduction. The Divine revelation of the Word and the demoniac revelation of wickedness seem to point in the same direction: but if in the path of ultimate restoration there stood no greater obstacle than indefiniteness regarding the duration of the Christian heaven, if the oracles of God could be softened down to meet a surrender of that which is only sweet but not essential, what radiance of unspeakable hope would arise! By some way which we know not, through the introduction of some power whose workings we had never beheld, by some brighter vision of the love of the atoning Saviour than the earth had ever yet witnessed, we should be sure that the wandering sheep would finally be brought back into the fold. It was more than any promise, which Moses relinquished: "Yet now, if thou wilt forgive their sin —; and if not, blot me, I pray thee, out of thy book which thou hast written." Commentators have found trouble in explaining this passage, but it needs not to be explained to those who go to the Bible for truths, not texts, and carry thither the hearts which God gave them. It is but the instinctive cry of the clinging, loving human soul, — the "Would God I had died for thee!" Paul felt it in the great heaviness and continual sorrow in his heart: "For I could wish myself accursed from Christ for my brethren, my kinsmen according to the flesh." All understand it who have ever felt the throbbing of human brotherhood. In this world we can bear the pain and peril of those we love, the groan and travail of creation. We soothe our sympathy with active effort, and hope, unreasonable perhaps, but spontaneous and irresistible, underlies every evil. How in any future world we are to endure peace, not to say happiness, knowing that in any remotest corner of the universe a solitary, sentient being is shut up to irremediable, unmitigated torture, is to me, I must admit, a hitherto insoluble problem. Organized as we are, I could almost say that life would be more tolerable in hell, preaching to the spirits in prison, sharing the sorrow which we could not alleviate, than in heaven, conscious of the existence of that sorrow-full world. Better, it would seem, to labor without reward for the upspringing of a little light in the outer darkness, than to sit down in the full blaze of light, knowing all the while that there were souls shrouded in the impenetrable gloom. There is said to be a skeleton in every house; but more dreadful, more awe-inspiring than any earthly terror, would be that skeleton in the heavenly mansions. Only a ceaseless endeavor for the restoration of these lost could atone for the grief of living.

But God is good. Through every creed, in spite of every contradiction, past all bewilderment, his tender mercies are over all his works. It is ours to judge only of what we see and from what we see. We behold mortal pain, finite suffering, and find that they are not irreconcilable with Divine love. If the time ever comes when we behold immortal pain, infinite suffering, there will be some further revelation which will save to us our God unchangeable in goodness. Meanwhile, let us not reason from the untrue to the unknown; from selfishness to severity; but seeing what is revealed of the terror of the Lord, *persuade* men to holiness.

VI.

CHRIST AS A PREACHER.

THE general opinions of the Orthodox Church regarding the relations between man and the Gospel are well represented by the following extracts from two criticisms. The first says: "You sometimes fall into fallacious reasoning: as, for instance, when you argue that men want the Gospel and appreciate it as they do law and physic. They need it, but they do not want it. The ministers of Christ contend, as did their Master, with a natural opposition to divine truth. Man has a capacity but not a passion for spiritual realities. And with all the charm of novelty on his side, with all his beneficent and miraculous gifts of healing, with all the marvel of a faultless presence, and of wise and apt words such as man never spake, directed by a knowledge of what was in the hearts of men, knowing just how to read and meet men, yet according to your Yankee standard of success, Christ's life as a minister was one signal failure."

4

The second says: "Permit me to say that I think you have hardly done justice to the inherent depravity of human nature. It seems to me that your positions in favor of more brightness, vigor, thought, &c., in the pulpit and prayer-meeting, having an immediate and necessary effect in winning a hearing are more sunny and golden than facts will confirm. I endorse your general position, but I also think that there is another side which you do not bring out quite sharply enough; that is, that the Gospel *does meet* under *all* conditions a stubborn resistance from the heart."

These opinions seem to me to be the traditions of men and not the word of God. From the four Gospels which are our authority regarding Christ's history, it is easy to prove that men want the Gospel and appreciate it as they do law and physic; that Christ's life as a minister was, even according to the Yankee standard of success, a signal success; and that the Gospel so far from meeting under all circumstances a stubborn resistance from the heart, did, when proclaimed from the lips of the Saviour, meet with acceptance, gratitude, and enthusiasm. The people who are reported as having despised and rejected his Gospel are a comparatively small, though very influential minority. It was chiefly composed of the learned, the wealthy, the scribes and Pharisees, and elders of the people, the professed teachers of righteousness; while by the common people, the masses, the Gospel was welcomed with gladness and singleness of heart. They felt that here was the truth for which they had languished, and their thirsty souls drank it in as the water of the river of life.

The immediate object in view, let it be remembered, is to ascertain whether Christ obtained a hearing, or preached to "empty pews"; whether he secured attention, confidence, and respect, or whether he met violence and opposition.

Our first report of Christ's preaching is from Matthew, who tells us that Jesus began to preach, and to say, "Repent: and he went about all Galilee, preaching the Gospel of the kingdom, and his fame went about all Syria, and there followed him great multitudes of people from Galilee, and from Decapolis, and from Jerusalem, and from Judæa, and from beyond Jordan." And seeing these multitudes, he went up into a mountain and preached a sermon to them, and they were astonished at his doctrine. Why? He taught them as one having authority, and not as the — scribes. Nay, so impressed were they with his loving, comforting, instructing words that they could not leave him when the sermon was over. They hung upon his footsteps. Even when he was come down from the mountain, great multitudes followed him. They crowded about the houses where they knew he was. When he came out and walked down to the seaside to be fanned by the cool breezes, so great multitudes were gathered together unto him that he put off in a boat, and spoke to them as they stood on the shore. Again and again we are told, with simple unimpassioned reiteration, of the great multitudes that followed him and glorified the God of Israel, when they saw the mighty works that he did, and heard the words that proceeded from his mouth. When he went up to Jerusalem, the people in an outburst of love and enthusiasm made him spontaneously a triumphal procession. "A very great multitude spread their garments in the way; others cut down branches from the trees, and strewed them in the way. And the multitudes that went before, and that followed, cried, saying, Hosanna to the Son of David! Blessed is he that cometh in the name of the Lord! Hosanna in the highest!" It was like the coming of a king, so that "all the city was moved, saying, Who is this? And the multitude said, This is Jesus, the prophet of Nazareth of Galilee." But "when the chief priests and scribes saw the wonderful things that he did, and the children crying in the temple, and saying, Hosanna to the Son of David! they were sore displeased." Mark tells us that the people were astonished both at his doctrine and his works. They were all amazed, insomuch that they questioned among themselves, saying, "What thing is this? What new doctrine is this?" And all the city was gathered together at the door. As soon as it was noised that he was in a house in Capernaum, so many gathered together that there was no room to receive them, no, not so much as about the door. In his absence, great multitudes flocked about his disciples; but as soon as he came in sight, they all left the disciples and ran to him and saluted him. When Jesus heard of the slaughter of his herald, his kinsman, his baptizer, he naturally wished to be alone, and withdrew to a desert apart: but when the people heard of it, they followed him on foot out of the cities. When, after spending the whole night in words and works of love, he departed at dawn into a desert place for rest and solitude, again the eager, longing, but somewhat inconsiderate people could not bear to be separated from him, but sought him, and stayed him, that he should not depart from them, and could only be pacified by the gentle assurance that he must preach the kingdom of God to other cities also. Yet they were not always inconsiderate. They tried to silence Bartimeus, fearing evidently that his cries would disturb the Master. Again and again their love and faith interposed between him and violence. It is instructive to mark the different effects which were produced on the people and on their leaders. When Jesus healed the palsied man, "certain of the scribes said within themselves, This man blasphemeth." "But when the multitudes saw it, they marvelled, and glorified God." When the devil was cast out, and the dumb spake, the multitudes marvelled, saying, "It was never so seen in Israel." But the Pharisees said, "He casteth out devils through the prince of devils." When he healed the man who had the withered hand, the Pharisees went out and held a council against him, how they might destroy him. But when Jesus knowing it, withdrew himself, the great multitude followed him just the same. When the chief priests and Pharisees heard his parables, and perceived that he spake of them, they sought to lay hands on him, but they feared the multitude, because they took him for a prophet. When he destroyed the traffic which defiled the temple, the scribes and chief priests sought how they might destroy him: for they feared him, because all the people were astonished at his doctrine. When he spoke to them the parable of the vineyard, they sought to lay hold on him, but they feared the people, and were forced to leave him, and go their way. While the scoffing scribes, the Sadducees, the Pharisees, and the Herodians tried to catch him in his words, the common people heard him gladly. The woman who was loosed from her infirmity glorified God, but the ruler of the synagogue answered with indignation. When Christ had discomfited the hypocritical fault-finder, all his adversaries were ashamed, but all the people rejoiced for all the glorious things that were done by him. When he was at the descent of the Mount of Olives, the whole multitude of the disciples began to rejoice, and praise God with a loud voice, for all the mighty works that they had seen; but some of the Pharisees among them bade him rebuke his disciples for their acclamation. When he taught daily in the temple, the chief priests, and the scribes, and the chief of the people, sought to destroy him, and could not find what they might do, for all the people were very attentive to hear him. When Jesus had raised Lazarus from the grave, many of the Jews believed on him, but the chief priests and the Pharisees, from that day forth, took counsel together to put him to death. While the people were going out to meet him with palm-branches and songs of welcome, the Pharisees in an agony of despair were saying among themselves, "Perceive ye how ye prevail nothing? behold, the world is gone after him."

Did not these poor people seem to want as well as to need the Gospel? Did they not give evidence of as true appreciation of it as ever was given of law or physic? Were not these circumstances in which the Gospel did not meet a stubborn resistance from the heart? From a clique, from a hierarchy, from a class eaten up with spiritual pride, the Gospel did meet with a stubborn resistance; for the spread of the Gospel was sure to be the downfall of their prerogatives. But by the masses of the people — by those who were to be elevated in this world as well as fitted for the next by this Gospel — it was warmly welcomed. It seemed almost from the beginning to be instinctively recognized as the good tidings of great joy to *all people.*

But though the people did flock after Jesus, does not the manner in which they finally turned against him and clamored for his crucifixion show that, although the novelty of his mission amused them for a while, they no sooner saw its real aim, — the purity of heart and life which he required, — than they revoked their former decisions, and cried, "Crucify him, crucify him"?

Who crucified the Lord?

Matthew says, "Then assembled together the chief priests, and the scribes, and the elders of the people, unto the palace of the high-priest, ... and consulted that they might take Jesus by subtlety, and kill him. But they said, Not on the feast day, lest there be an uproar among the people." Mark says they "sought how they might take him by craft." Luke still more definitely says, "The chief priests and scribes sought how they might kill him; *for they feared the people.*" Judas "communed with the chief priests and captains, how he might betray him unto them. . . . . And he promised, and sought opportunity to betray him unto them *in the absence of the multitude.*" So, then, it seems the people were so far from intending any harm to Christ that the chief priests and scribes were forced to lay their plans with the utmost secrecy, lest the people, hearing of them, should interpose to prevent their success. The people had not grown hostile or cold to Jesus, but were seen by the chief priests and scribes to be his enthusiastic defenders, who must by all means be eluded.

When Judas came to apprehend Jesus, he was indeed accompanied by a great multitude, but it was "from the chief priests and elders of the people" still. Luke tells us that Jesus spoke unto "the chief priests, and captains of the temple, and the elders, which were come to him." John explicitly says, "Judas then, having received a band of men and officers from the chief priests and Pharisees, cometh thither," &c. So that the people were entirely guiltless of Christ's apprehension, were indeed probably quite ignorant of the fact, as his enemies had designed they should be. At his trial it was still the chief priests, and elders, and all the council, who sought false witness against Jesus, to put him to death. It was the chief priests and elders of the people that bound Jesus and led him away and delivered him to Pontius Pilate, and accused him. Luke says, "The whole multitude *of them* arose and led him to Pilate." "Them" he has before designated as the elders of the people, and the chief priests, and the scribes. When the people were assembled on their feast-day, many of whom probably did not know Jesus except by hearsay, the chief priests and elders *persuaded* them that they should ask for the release of Barabbas rather than Jesus. Mark says that Pilate knew that the chief priests had delivered Jesus unto him for envy. And the chief priests moved the people, that he should rather release Barabbas unto them. As he hung upon the cross, some that passed by reviled him, but it was the chief priests and elders that took the most prominent part in mocking and reviling him; we are even told that, as Jesus was bearing his cross to Calvary, "there followed him a great company of people, and of women, which also *bewailed and lamented him.*"

It appears, then, that if any one fact is clearly attested in the Bible, it is that Christ was received by the people with a clinging, longing, mournful passion of appreciation. They felt through their dull lives, through their aching hearts, the beams of a spiritual sun; and, after their homely fashion, opened their souls to its shining. But the chief priests and scribes, perceiving that their craft was in danger, never wearied till, by indefatigable and unscrupulous machinations, — by hiring and cajoling the assistance of lewd fellows of the baser sort, and by playing upon the political ambition and personal fears of their military governor, — they had crucified the Lord of glory.

Let us not wrongfully accuse any; yet, if there is a class at the present day which in its functions and relations corresponds more closely than any other with that formed by the chief priests and scribes of Judæa, it is the clergy, the dignitaries of the Church. And for the clergy — the representatives of Christ's accusers and foes — to maintain that the people — the representatives of Christ's defenders and friends — are the natural enemies of Christ, — to prove the theoretical enmity of the people by pointing to the practical enmity of the priests, to foist the malignity of a clique upon the shoulders of humanity, and that too in the face of facts which repeatedly assert and imply the benevolence of humanity, — is a proceeding which to the uninstructed mind must be characterized as bordering on the extraordinary.

VII.

NATHANIEL EMMONS OF FRANKLIN.

PROBABLY there is a large class who never read, and would never think of reading, a book by Professor Park, or a memoir of an old New England theologian. They rank Dr. Emmons, Dr. Hopkins, President Edwards, Professor Park, under the same head, — the only difference between them being that some are dead and some alive. They look upon them all as a kind of ecclesiastical columbiad of ten-inch caliber, the glory and the safety of New England; but columbiads, however valuable, are not entertaining, not sympathetic, not attractive in the social circle, not the kind of toy one would choose to sit down to of an October afternoon or a November evening. These eminent names are names, and scarcely anything else. So far as a personality attaches to them, it is a shadowy and distant one. They are supposed to dwell in a region remote from common life. Their talk is of the volitions and the affections, of nominal essences and spiritual substances, of moral ability and disinterested submission. But with bread and butter, market-prices, the fashions, and the thousand little interests that agitate ordinary humanity, they have nothing to do. If this class of readers can be induced to take up the life of Dr. Emmons, by Professor Park, their opinions will be likely to undergo a radical change before laying it down. They will be surprised to find, instead of an uninteresting narrative of an uninteresting life, one of the raciest books that the American press has ever produced. It carries us into the intensity of New-Englandism. It takes us back into the life of the last century. It gives us a key to the strength of the clergy of that day. It shows us on what meat our fathers fed that they grew so great. It is invaluable as a portrait of the past. It is full of suggestiveness for the present. To a young clergyman it will prove a guide, philosopher, and friend. To his people, and to all people, it will come fraught with wisdom and power.

For Dr. Emmons was — eminently and preeminently — a man, and he is painted as such. It is no sublimated saintliness, but a picture from life, with all the lights and shadows. Bright as he was, we see the spots. Great as he was, we dare sometimes to dissent from his views. But his wisdom and his folly are the wisdom and folly of a strong, upright nature, and his very follies humanize, without degrading him. If he always lived on the level of his logic, we might feel that he was too far above our plane for sympathy, but the equilibrium is somewhat restored when we hear him confess, "I do not believe in signs, but I would rather not see the new moon over my left shoulder." We are delighted to see his unreasonable obstinacy in refusing to use his hands and feet. He early determined to devote himself to the work of the ministry, and this is the way he did it: —

"Although he boarded within sight of his own house (which he was repairing), and frequently passed it while under repair, he never allowed himself to see its interior, until it was finished."

"Walking over his farm one day, he saw the bars of his fence down. His first impulse was to put them up, and thus save his fields from the depredation of cattle. But no; 'If I say A, I must say B; and it is safer not to begin the alphabet.' With this favorite maxim on his mind, he left the bars down, and went into his study."

"At a time when a large quantity of his hay lay exposed in the field, his men were suddenly alarmed at the prospect of rain. Though they knew that in ordinary circumstances it would be in vain to expect any aid from him, yet as there was now so much at stake, ... one of them went to the Doctor's study and told him that the hay must be wet unless he would give them aid.

'Then let it be wet,' said he. 'I am not going to leave my work to do yours.'"

Often, we are told, he spent fourteen or fifteen hours a day over his books. "No one could look about in his room without knowing where the veteran's feet usually rested. The marks which they left upon the wainscot attracted so much attention from visitors, that he was obliged to procure a new panelling for one place in his room, which would suggest fewer queries." He did make to physiology the concession of rising from his meals with as good an appetite as when he sat down, but we cannot help thinking what a pity it was that he did not eat good, hearty, reasonable dinners, and take brisk and vigorous bodily exercise. It must have made him higher-toned. But his wife helped him on. When asked how he could live on his small salary without working on his farm, he replied, "My wife supports me." She made his pastoral visits as well as his ink and blacking, and respected the hook on his door, which was the "shut sesame" to all intruders.

He was scrupulously neat and orderly, not dwelling so high in metaphysical clouds as to be careless of the small proprieties. Though he once rode home with another man's horse without discovering it, he *would* have a horse and chaise worthy of being called "the minister's." His barns and grounds were always in order. *Precisely so* must the wood be laid on the fire. At *such* a time the wood-box must be replenished. No visitor was admitted to his study till his book or manuscript was tucked under the green baize table-cover. At the appointed hour he was at church, and expected to *find his hearers in their seats*, not loitering about the door.

Punctilious himself, he desired his people to be the same. Never but once, during the fifty-four years of his active ministry, did he go to the treasurer to receive his salary. Then a new treasurer thought he would turn over a new leaf, and make the creditors of the parish wait on him. He stayed at home. So did Dr. Emmons. Ten days passed. On the eleventh the treasurer "saw the neat carriage driving up to his front door, and the three-cornered hat in the carriage. The Doctor alighted from the chaise, holding his reins and the whip. He knocked. The door was opened. 'Is Mr. A. at home?' 'He is.' 'I should be glad to see him.' Mr. A. came and stood before his minister. 'Good morning, sir,' was the minister's word. 'Good morning, sir,' was the treasurer's reply. 'I have been expecting,' added the minister, 'for eleven days to see you at my house. Good by, sir,' and he added no more, but his fleet horse took him back straight to the parsonage, and the treasurer followed him before noon, carrying the delayed salary, and resolving to try no more experiments." He was careful, however, to award the same courtesy to others that he claimed for himself. After he had resigned his pastorate, he stayed in his pew after the benediction, waiting for the young preacher to pass out, and could with difficulty be persuaded to walk by his side.

He was absolute monarch of his little kingdom. "There goes a rumor, that a gleeful company made him a generous donation before they engaged in a frolicsome ride, and they hoped that his well-known politeness would prevent his reprimand of his benefactors on the succeeding Sabbath. But he did not keep back the dreaded reprimand, being stimulated to an unwonted plainness of speech by the generosity of his young friends." "When a very respectable clergyman of another denomination had appointed a religious meeting within the bounds of Dr. Emmons's parish, the latter met him and quietly informed him, '*You are expected to keep on your side of the parish line.*' He kept there." Another clergyman of a different sect had been invited by a parishioner to preach in Franklin. He soon after met Dr. Emmons in Boston and informed him of the fact. The Doctor pleasantly replied, "You have a very important sphere of labor assigned you where you are. You need not take the trouble to come to Franklin. I can take care of my own flock." "But you will not object to my coming?" "I do object. And if you come to Franklin in our present circumstances, I 'll consider and treat you as a wolf in sheep's clothing." He never came. Finding one day that his hearers were inattentive, he shut up his note-case and said, "I shall not preach again in this house, until I can be assured of better attention from my people," and walked off. He could not have done these things, however, if he had not been Dr. Emmons. His moral worth gave him moral weight; but let no ass put on this lion's skin, for it will surely be his death. He educated his people. He made them think. He was their pride and their glory. They could well afford to be domineered over by a man who, in devoting himself to them, secured honorable and undying fame for both.

He not only educated his people, but he interested them. He sent them home from church longing for the next Sunday to come. Whether they agreed or disagreed with him, they could not choose but hear him. Every eye was fastened on him. The stillness of the grave pervaded the assembly. Young women accepted marriage-offers on condition that the husband elect should engage to attend the Quarterly Lecture. The grand secret was,—let it be written in letters of gold,—"He made the impression on his people, and kept it up to the last, that his public services were *worth something*, and that to be absent from one of them was to sustain a great loss."

His sterling honesty was conspicuous. He refused to let a rich man indorse a debtor's note. "He will not be profited by the transaction, and it is not right that he should take the risk." He lost the debt, and rejoiced that there was no bondsman. In his dread of appearing to hide the sharp points of his creed, he makes them appear a little sharper than they are. The more unpopular a truth, the more inexorable was he in presenting it. Assailed for a political sermon, he stoutly stood his ground, sagaciously declaring, "They have no real objection against political preaching, but against what is preached upon political subjects."

His liberality and his royal good sense are a shame to the narrow-mindedness of some of our contemporaries. Let those whose indolence wrests to their own destruction St. Paul's declaration, "For I determined to know nothing among you save Jesus Christ and him crucified," heed Dr. Emmons: "The more I attended to theology, the more I was convinced of the importance of acquainting myself with history, ethics, metaphysics, and civil polity." "I made it a rule to select the *best* and the *worst* [authors]; that is to say, those who had written most ingeniously *in favor* of the truth, and *against* it." "I thought it was an injury and reproach to clergymen, that they so much disregarded general knowledge, and paid their whole attention to divinity. . . . . There is no doubt, but that many errors and wild notions in religion have originated in the ignorance of those who have undertaken to preach the Gospel, without understanding the connection and harmony of its fundamental doctrines. Such preachers seldom attend to any sentiments but the peculiarities of their own sect; and vainly imagine that all are heretics who do not subscribe to their contracted creed. To avoid this mistake, I resolved to read and study divinity in a liberal manner, and not to adopt the sentiments of my own denomination, nor to reject the sentiments of other denominations, without examining them for myself. . . . . I have made it my practice, in the whole course of my ministry, to read extensively, and to examine as critically and impartially as I could all ancient and modern errors and innovations in religion."

It would be pleasant to dwell upon his judicious treatment of the dissensions in his church, — how he "appeased his alienated hearers by preaching the doctrines of the Bible, aiming to exalt religion by preaching the doctrines *well;*" upon his sensible way of stopping short in a dispute the moment he saw nothing was to be gained by it, even at the risk of being considered defeated; upon the depth and strength of his tenderness, standing out in bold relief against his Christian resignation,—a tenderness that could scarcely suffer him, at the age of ninety, to speak the name of the wife of his youth, torn away in her springtime, — that choked his utterance when he would place the seal of baptism on the brow of a child who was to bear the name of his dead son, though it had not prevented him from pointing the sad moral of that son's life by his early grave, — a tenderness that drew his little grandchildren to his study the moment they entered his house, and made even the insane of his parish insist on being taken to the parsonage, that they might be soothed by his gentle ministrations. It would be instructive to dwell upon his noble maintenance of the dignity of man, to the discomfiture of those who make orthodoxy consist in debasing him; upon his objections to Sunday schools, evening meetings, protracted meetings, tract societies, &c., objections which time proved to have been valid, though time may also, in some measure, have obviated them; upon the vast influence which he exerted on and through his pupils; upon the sensitiveness which shrank from revealing his inward life, which "disliked the practice of living out-of-doors, of having all things common, and of giving publicity to all religious action"; upon the bashfulness which forced him to soothe the agitation that, to the last Sabbath of his pulpit-life, he felt in view of addressing a multitude, by reflecting, "In one hour it will be all over"; upon the wit, which, always under control, was always ready, for attack or defence; upon that vivid faith, that actual belief, that intimate acquaintance with God, and that strong realization of a spiritual world which saw "angels encamping on the plains of Franklin, and hourly ascending or descending to or from the skies," that made not only the quiet village, but the whole world, "aglow and astir with the Great Spirit"; upon the strength of that soul, which in the depths of a secluded parish left its mark on his own age, and must stamp it on the ages that follow; — but want of space forbids. No thoughtful person can read the book without feeling a deep gratitude to him who has turned aside from severer studies to enrich his generation with the knowledge of one whose life is a priceless legacy to his country.

VIII.

BRAIN AND BRAWN.

IT seems a great pity that right things have a tendency to rush into extremes, and become wrong ones; for too much of a good thing is very nearly, if not quite, as bad as a bad thing. From which text behold a short sermon.

In the Old World, and in portions of the New, labor is degraded. It is connected with ideas of servitude and incapacity. We, in New England, are trying to remedy the evil. We wish to redeem labor, — to make worth, and not occupation, the standard of rank. This is a laudable end, only in our eagerness to accomplish it, we are in some danger of over-doing, to the injury of the very individual whom we seek to benefit. We forget that labor is not, *in itself*, noble. It was denounced upon Adam, and his descendants, as a curse; and though prayer, and love, and faith transmute it into a blessing, it does not lose its original nature. It remains, in some aspects, a curse still. It is to be accepted, not chosen. The ox and the ass were, from the beginning, given to man, to serve him; but not till the flaming sword was drawn to keep the way of Paradise, was man, the master, doomed to eat bread in the sweat of his face.

But though labor has, of itself, no moral character, it can be rendered subservient to noble uses. It is to us what we make it. To George Stephenson, iron and water and burning coals were nimble servitors to do his will; and, at his bidding, they brought the sea inland, and bore the land seaward, and laid commerce, and civilization, yes, and Christianity too, at his feet; but scores of men hammered by the side of George Stephenson, and never struck out the spark of an idea. They, camel-wise, bowed their shoulders to a life-long burden: he chained it to his triumphal car, and rode, a conqueror. In the one case, labor was creative, and therefore godlike; in the other, routine, of the earth, earthy,— not a thing to be despised, but also not to be extolled. Hugh Miller breaking up stones by the roadside, and Patrick McCarty carting them to mend the road with, would seem, to a casual passenger, to be working together, with the same object in view; but they were ages apart.

Yet one might sometimes suppose that labor was the undoubted badge of a higher nobility, and the laboring man the true aristocrat, by divine right. Lyceum lecturers, agricultural-fair orators, county newspapers, cajole their listeners and readers with sounding words about a "bold yeomanry, our country's pride," and the "sturdy mechanic, the bone and sinew of the land"; and the bold yeoman and sturdy mechanic chuckle over the flattery, go home to their daily monotonous drudgery, and settle on their lees in self-complacent ignorance. But the yeoman, or mechanic, who delves without thought, or invention, or reflection, from sunrise to sunset, and spends the evening over his pipe and his mug of cider, is — a very great deal lower than the angels; is, I had almost said, a cumberer of the ground from which he draws his fancied nobility.

This is not to say aught against the honorableness of agricultural or mechanical occupations. It is only that, like all other occupations, they derive, but do not confer, honor or shame. Ignorance and stupidity are disgraceful in farmer or doctor. Intelligence and refinement are respectable in shoemaker or lawyer. The inheritance of an estate does not convert a clown into a gentleman, nor does its loss convert a gentleman into a clown. He that sweeps a floor as for God's laws, makes that and the action fine; and he that sweeps a floor, year in and year out, with no higher end in view, is fine and refined neither in himself nor in his action.

Yet you will often hear such encomiums passed

as, "He is the hardest-working man in town." "He is a fine man, — always at it, — up early and late." "He is a most industrious man. You always know where to find him. Go to his bench."

Such remarks are intended to indicate virtues, and perhaps they do, but not necessarily. If a man is forced, by untoward circumstances, either to labor unceasingly or to see his family suffer, then, if he perform cheerfully his unceasing labor, it is a great virtue. Or, if his mind has been sparingly endowed by his Creator, and he has to use the whole of it, and his body and time too, in the support of his family, and does it, it is still a virtue, but a little one. If he labors unceasingly because it is a habit, or to hoard up money, or because he has no taste for anything else, it is no virtue at all. It is a fault; not to say a crime. God did not create us to be "always at it." There are times and seasons when we ought to be away from "it." There are duties which lie otherwhere than in the shop or on the farm. Therefore, when you call upon us to admire one of your hard-working men, be so good as to inform us first, to which class he belongs; whether his lauded virtue is not his sin to be rebuked, or, at least, his weakness to be compassionated. Is not the very reason why he has to toil and moil over his corn and potatoes, that he has not intelligence enough to apply the best methods of culture to his farm, — methods which would give him greater crops and more leisure? Tell us how much he accomplishes by his work, not simply how much he works. It is no credit to a man to go round by Robin Hood's barn, when he can just as well take a short cut "across lots." If one man works twelve hours to earn the bread and butter for himself and his nine children, while his next-door neighbor does the same thing in five, what does it indicate? That the first necessarily has more virtue than the second, or that he has less mother-wit?

The flattery with which our assembled working-classes are apt to be served, undoubtedly contributes to keep many of them content to make no higher attainments. If they are not received with open arms by the educated and refined, they attribute it to their occupation, not to themselves; to the unreasonable pride and prejudice of others, not to their own deficiency. But water is not the only thing that will find its own level. Genius, wit, learning, ignorance, coarseness, are each attracted to its like. Two painters were overheard talking in the room where they were at work. "Lord!" said one, "I knowed him well when he was a boy. Used to live with his gran'ther, next door to us. Poor as Job's turkey. But I ain't seen him since, till I hearn him in —— Hall, t' other night. Don't suppose he 'd come anigh me now with a ten-foot pole. Them kind of folks has short memories, ha! ha! Can't tell who a poor working-man is, nohow."

No, no, good friend, you are in the wrong. There is, indeed, a great gulf between you and your early friend, but it is not poverty. To say that it is, is only a way you have of flattering your self-love. For, if you watch those who frequent your friend's house, you will find many a one who lives in lodgings, with the commonest three-ply carpets, cane-seat chairs, and one warm room; while you have a comfortable house of your own, with, very likely, tapestry and velvet in your parlor, and registers all about. No, sir, it is not because you are poor, nor because you work; for he is as hard a worker as you, though, perhaps, not so long about it; but because — begging your pardon — you are vulgar, and ignorant; because you sit down in your sitting-room at home, with your coat off, and your hat on, and smoke your pipe, — because you plunge your own knife into the butter, and your own fork into the toast, having used both in your eating with equal freedom, — because your voice is loud, your tone swaggering, and your grammar hideous, — because, in short, your two paths from the old school-house diverged; his led upward, yours did not; and the fault is *not his.* You both chose. He chose to cultivate his powers. You chose not to do so. Call things by their right names!

Be a gentleman; be a man of sense, intelligence, and refinement, and you need no other credentials to the best, the really best, society;

nor will you fail, ultimately, to receive the esteem and appreciation which your worth demands.

The Bible is a revelation of the Divine will and purpose, and by following its directions we may obtain eternal life. But the Scriptures are as profitable for the life that now is as for that which is to come. The lessons which the Bible teaches indirectly are surpassed in importance only by those which it teaches directly. Its worldly maxims are as admirable in their way as its religious maxims, and both are illustrated and enforced by noble and numerous examples. Never has the world seen specimens of better farmers, merchants, tradesmen, masters, servants, high-bred ladies, courtly knights, brave soldiers, skilful generals, accomplished statesmen, devoted clergymen, unselfish patriots, than those who pass in stately procession before the Bible reader. What a fine old Hebrew gentleman is Boaz! How courteously he steps upon the scene! A mighty man of wealth, of good family, a large landed proprietor, an influential citizen, belonging to the "best society," he comes down from his house in the city, to see for himself how matters are going. With a fine patriarchal courtesy he greets the reapers as he passes among them. "The Lord be with you," and with equal courtesy, honorable alike to him and to themselves, they answer, "The Lord bless thee." Is not here a lesson for master and servant, employer and employed? Does any one suppose that they served him any the less faithfully for his respectful kindness, or that there was any sycophancy in their cordial response? Was there anything in the interchange of pleasant feeling that trenched upon the dignity either of Boaz or his reapers? Is not the truest, the only Christian relation between master and servant, that which recognizes the underlying brotherhood of man, while it is equally cognizant of the surface discrepancies? Does not the servant best respect and most scrupulously serve the master who respects the servant? A consideration of others' rights is the surest way to compass the consideration of our own. To be polite to others is the best way to make others polite to us. Here as elsewhere, what measure ye mete shall be measured to you again.

But Boaz, with that keen observation which may perhaps have had something to do with his great wealth and high standing, notices a new face among the merry field-maidens, a graver, quieter face probably, and turning to his overseer he makes inquiry, and learns that it belongs to the young woman who has been talked about so much in the city, — the Moabitish damsel who left her own family and land for love of her dead husband's mother and his God. So, glad, doubtless, of the opportunity, he cheers her fluttering, frightened heart with gracious words. How soothingly and gratefully must have fallen on her ear:

"Hearest thou not, my daughter?" (never fear, Boaz; for all she has been gleaning so industriously, nor once raised her eyes to you, she has heard every word you said.) "Go not to glean in another field, neither go from hence, but abide here fast by my maidens: let thine eyes be on the field that they do reap, and go thou after them: have I not charged the young men that they shall not touch thee?" To the stranger unwonted to the customs of the land to which she had so lately come, unacquainted with the people by whom she was surrounded, these assurances from the master must have been doubly welcome. But his large-hearted hospitality was not yet exhausted: "When thou art athirst, go unto the vessels and drink of that which the young men have drawn. At meal-time come thou hither, and eat of the bread, and dip thy morsel in the vinegar. And he reached her parched corn, and she did eat, and was sufficed, and left." And, still further, with thoughtful kindness, Boaz commanded his young men not only not to hinder her, but to *let fall also some of the handfuls on purpose for her*. No wonder Ruth fell in love with him, — so gentle, so generous, so tender to the forlorn little foreigner.

Ruth was a Moabitess, a heathen by birth, a resident in a heathen country, and probably her first impressions of a country in which the true God was worshipped were received in the harvest-fields of Boaz. Suppose a young woman from the Feejee Islands were to be transported to the hay-fields of some of our large farmers on a fine day in July; would her impressions be as favorable as those of Ruth? Would she see a liberality, and kindness, and courtesy, which should at once recommend a Christian country to her favor? Do we always see in our barns, our cider-presses, our corn-fields, our potato-patches, our wood-sheds, a Christianity as decorous and well-behaved? There are farmers who, instead of being polite, rather pride themselves on the roughness of their dress and manners. They seem to think that to be polite is unmanly, — that blue overalls and swarthy arms must have coarse natures to match, — that refinement belongs only to broadcloth, and a soft address to dancing-masters; but is there any reason why a New England farmer should not be polite as well as a Bethlehem farmer? Farming is a noble occupation when it is nobly followed; but if to be a farmer it is necessary to be a boor, then farming is of all occupations the most ignoble and undesirable. The truth is, politeness is the prerogative of no vocation. A boot-black may be less accomplished than a prince, but he need not be less polite. Haymaking browns the skin and hardens the hands, but it need not make the heart callous nor the soul coarse.

Politeness is a Christian duty. A man has no more right to be impolite than he has to steal.

Politeness is often synonymous with Christianity; that is, politeness will often lead a man to do the same things which Christianity will lead him to do. Politeness keeps a man from saying that which will needlessly wound another's feelings. So does Christianity. Politeness keeps a man from indulging in habits which annoy those around him. So does Christianity. Politeness is often Christianity applied to the manners. Yet Christian people will often make remarks which they know will, and intend shall, give pain to others, and for no other purpose than to amuse themselves or gratify a petty malice. Sometimes it is simply that they do not care whether they wound or not. They never seem to think that religion has any bearing on such things. They will speak disparagingly of a person whom they know you like, when there is no possible worthy object to be subserved by it. They will ride rough-shod over the sensitiveness of those with whom they are associated, and if any one remonstrates with them, why, forsooth, "they are plain people,—they say what they think,—there is no hypocrisy about *them*." Woe to the man who is among them, but not of them! The only way for him to do is to shut up within himself everything that is vulnerable, and to go abroad always with his armor on. Thus it happens that it is often far pleasanter to live and mingle in society with gay, fashionable, worldly, and polite people than with some kinds of Christians.

The former may do many things of which you disapprove. They acknowledge no higher code than politeness, it may be, but they live up to it. They round off their angles, level down their protuberances, never say cross, or harsh, or ill-natured things. They are cushiony, and amiable, and restful. You glide smoothly among them. There are no tangles and collisions; whereas the Christian who despises politeness is angular, full of sharp corners which he continually thrusts in your way to make you stumble over them; he takes no pains to make himself agreeable, never seems to think that it is better to be loved than not to be loved. If you shun him, he thinks it is because he is sincere or you are haughty, when it is only because he is intolerably selfish and repulsive. He forgets that, though the Devil does appear sometimes as an angel of light, light is none the less on that account a divine and glorious thing; and he forgets also that the Devil in such a disguise is just about as comfortable to have about as would be an angel with the diabolic appurtenances.

Politeness if not godliness, is next to it, therefore let us be polite. If we cannot be as polite as we would like to be, let us be as polite as we can. The man who will not try to be polite is fit neither for the church nor the world. . Let him dwell apart among the tombs. Do our best, and we shall all probably be in some respects disagreeable to our warmest friends. The least we can do is to make ourselves as tolerable as possible.

IX.

GLORYING IN THE GOAD.

"LET the wealthy and great
  Roll in splendor and state,
I envy them not, I declare it;
  I eat my own lamb,
  My own chickens and ham,
I shear my own fleece, and I wear it;
  I have lawns, I have bowers,
  I have fruits, I have flowers,
The lark is my morning alarmer;
  So, jolly boys, now,
  Here 's God speed the plough,
Long life and success to the farmer!"

SO sings a certain venerable pitcher its untiring song. A brave pitcher it was in its day. A well-ordered farm lies along its swelling sides. A purple man merrily drives his purple team afield. Gold and purple milkmaids are milking purple and golden cows. Young boys bind the ripened sheaves, or bear mugs of foaming cider to the busy haymakers, with artistic defiance of the seasons. There are ploughs and harrows, hoes and spades, beehives and poultry-houses, all in the best repair, and all resplendent in purple and gold. Alas! Troy was. The gold has become dim, the purple is dingy, the lucent whiteness has gone gray; a very large, brown, zigzag fissure has rent its volcanic path through the happy home, dividing the fair garden, cutting the plough in two, narrowly escaping the ploughman; and, indeed, the whole structure is saved from violent disruption only by the unrelaxing clasp of a string of blue yarn. Thus passes away the glory of the world and of pitchers!

Is it not too often typical of the glory of our rural dreams? To live in the country; to lie on green lawns, or under bowers of roses and honeysuckle; to watch the procession of the flowers, and bind upon our brows the sweetest and the fairest; to take largess of all the fruits in their season; to be entirely independent of the world, dead to its din, alive only to its beauty; to feed upon butter and honey, and feast upon strawberries and cream, all found within your own garden-wall; to be wakened by the lark, and lulled asleep by the cricket; to hear the tinkling of the cow-bell as you walk, and to smell the new-mown hay, — surely we have found Arcadia at last. Cast away day-book and ledger, green bag and yardstick; let us go straightway into the country and buy a farm.

But before the deeds are actually delivered, it will be worth while to ascertain whether the pitcher's word is as good as its bond. If its fallen fortunes are indicative of what yours shall be,—if Arcadia blooms only in its gorgeous bosom, and will turn into an Arabia Petræa at the first touch of your spade, — better for you a pitcher of roughest Delft on board of deal than all this pomp and circumstance of lies.

Reports of societies are not generally "as interesting as a novel." Nevertheless, if one will consult the Report of the Commission of Agriculture for 1862, he will find, among fascinating columns of figures, bold disquisitions on the midge, a mirage of grapes, pears, and peaches, and uncomfortable-looking "thorough-bred" cattle, an essay, by Dr. W. W. Hall of New York city, which may assist him in forming his plans. It is not necessarily destructive of the most charming theories, but it is very definite and damnatory as to facts. Among other unromantic and disagreeable things, it asserts — and proves its assertions by still more disagreeable, because incontrovertible statistics — that, for all the sylvan delights of lawn and bower, and the exquisite sensation of eating your own hams, the largest class of patients in insane asylums comes from the "jolly boys" and their wives and daughters; but better watch a grass-blade struggling up under the curbstone of the sidewalk than view the fairest landscape in the world from behind a grated window. We learn also, that, in spite of his ample larder, his freedom from envy and carking care, the farmer does not live so long as the pale clergyman whose white hands he looks upon with only not contempt; but how sweet so-ever may be the scent of clover and buttercup, he little heeds their fragrance who lies beneath them. We are told that a very large part of our farming population have no breadth of view; that they cannot enter into a conversation beyond a few comments on the weather, the crops, the markets, and the neighborhood-news. The freshness, the beauty, the music and motion, that breathe and stir around them, can gain no foothold in the unvarying routine of their lives; but in vain do the heavens spread out their glory, and in vain the earth unfolds her loveliness, if

> "A primrose by the river's brim
> A yellow primrose is to him,
> And it is nothing more."

To these skeletons is added, perhaps, the casual and certainly the most common skeleton of all: in this rustic paradise, his home of all the graces and comforts, the grim spectre Debt stalks to and fro, eating out the farmer's substance, and giving him in return anxiety, make-shifts, irascibility, and despair. Three homes out of four, according to this writer's estimate, suffer from the ravages of debt.

This is a general, perhaps a national view. We may come a little nearer home, and find that a closer examination only confirms the conclusions arrived at by the broader survey. Thoreau, who "travelled a great deal in Concord," and whose keen eyes took note there for forty years, says,—"When I consider my neighbors, the farmers of Concord, ... I find that for the most part they have been toiling twenty, thirty, or forty years that they may become the real owners of their farms, which commonly they have inherited with encumbrances, or else bought with hired money, ... but commonly they have not paid for them yet. It is true, the encumbrances sometimes outweigh the value of the farm, so that the farm itself becomes one great encumbrance, and still a man is found to inherit it, being well acquainted with it, as he says. On applying to the assessors, I am surprised to learn that they cannot at once name a dozen in the town who own their farms free and clear. If you would know the history of these homesteads, inquire at the bank where they are mortgaged. The man who has actually paid for his farm with labor on it is so rare that every neighbor can point to him. I doubt if there are three such men in Concord. What has been said of the merchants—that a very large majority, even ninety-seven in a hundred, are sure to fail—is equally true of the farmers. . . . . Yet the Middlesex Cattle-Show goes off here with *éclat* annually, as if all the joints of the agricultural machine were suent."

If you do not trust the testimony of books, but

will turn to living men, you will scarcely fare better. One man, whose recreations have been rural, but his business civic, conducts you through his groves and summer-houses, his stone barns and his latticed cottages, but tempers your enthusiasm with the remark, that this fancy farming is sowing ninepences to reap sixpences. Relinquishing fancy farms, you go to the practical man swinging his scythe in his hay-field, his shirt-sleeves rolled above his elbows, and his trousers tucked into his boots. He shows you the face-walls and the compost-heap, the drains and the resultant hay-cocks, with measurable pride, but tells you at the same time that every dollar he has earned on that farm has cost him nine shillings. This will never do. A third farmer has inherited his farm, not only without encumbrance, but with money at interest. Under his hands it waxes fat and flourishing, and sends to market every year its twelve or fifteeen hundred dollars' worth of produce. But you overhear its owner telling his neighbor that "it 's a Cain's business, this farming: make any man cross enough to kill his brother!" You find this farmer racked with rheumatism, though in the prime of life, — bent with the weight of years before his time. He has lost his health just as he has improved his farm, by working early and late through sun and rain. You turn to still another farm, whose owner brings the learning of a college as well as the muscles of a yeoman to the culture of the soil. His nurseries and orchards are thrifty, his cattle sleek and comfortable, his yards broad, cleanly, and sunny. His fields wave with plenty, his granary overflows. Here, surely, you have struck into the Happy Valley. Here at last Tityrus reposes under the shade of his broad-spreading beech-trees. On the contrary, you find Tityrus in the sitting-room, rolling his eyes in a fine frenzy over a very prose bucolic on the Condition and Prospects of Sheep-Husbandry, which he is writing for the "Country Gentleman," at five dollars a page. All the cool of the day he works on his farm, and all the hot of the day he devotes to his manuscript; and he avers, with a solemnity which carries conviction, that he and his wife have come to the conclusion that they are carrying on their farm for the benefit of the hired help! He is devoted to farming; he is interested in its processes; but the men and maids get all the profits, and he supports his family by his pen. Everywhere you find one song with variations. Farmers and farmers' wives are not in love with their calling. They are not enthusiastic over it. The "smartest" of the children do not remain at home to take charge of the farm, unless impelled by a sense of duty to their aged parents, or lured by some promise of extraordinary recompense. Everywhere the farmer finds farming to be "a slave's life," "a dog's life," "delve all your days, and nothin' to show for 't," "hard scrapin' to make both ends meet." It is so unwieldy a mode of applying means to ends, that, if you must believe him, every quart of milk costs him six cents, with the labor thrown in, while you pay the milkman but five cents at your own door; every dozen eggs which he gathers from his own barn he gathers at the rate of twenty-five cents a dozen, while you are paying only twenty-two. And even when both ends do meet, and not only meet, but lap over, you scarcely find a hearty cheerfulness and sunshine, a liberal praise and unfeigned ardor, a contagious delight in the soil. "Jolly boys" in purple blouses may drive ploughs around pitchers, but they are rarely met on the hillsides of New England. If we credit Dr. Hall, they are quite as rarely seen on the rich, rolling lands toward the sunset.

Is this state of things inevitable? Farmers have a very general belief that it is. They not only plod on in the old way themselves, but they have no faith in the possible opening-up of any other way. Their sole hope of bettering their condition lies in abandoning it altogether. If one son is superior to the others, if an only son concentrates upon himself all the parental affection, they do not plan for him a brilliant career in their own line; they do not look to him to obtain distinction by some great agricultural achievement, a discovery of new laws, or a new combination of old laws; all their love and hope find expression in the determination "not to bring him up to farming." They "don't mean he shall ever have to work." Hard work and small profits is the story of their lives and of the lives of their ancestors, and they do not believe any other story will ever be truly told of the genuine farmer. And when we say small profits, we wish the phrase to hold all the meaning of which it is capable. It is hard work and small profits to body and soul; small profits to heart and brain as well as purse. But every plan which looks to better things is "notional," "new-fangled," "easier to tell of than 't is to do"; and so the farmer goes on his daily beat, with pride in his independence, fostered by the flattery of his county-fair orators, yet vituperating his occupation, bemoaning its hardships and depreciating its emoluments, stubbornly set in the belief that he knows all there is to know about farming, and scornful of whatever attempts to go deeper than his own ploughshare or cut a broader swath than his own scythe.

To suggest the possibility that all this is the result of limited knowledge, and that the most favorable and beneficial change might be found in a more liberal education and a wider acquaintance with the facts discovered and the deductions made by science, would be considered by a bold yeomanry, our country's pride, as an outbreak of "book-farming" in its most virulent form. "You may bet your hat on one thing," says the bold yeoman,

— "a man may know sunthin', an' be a good minister, an' a tol'able deacon, but he 's spiled for farmin'."

Two words are beginning to be coupled in the newspapers and to float about in the air, whose juxtaposition is the cause of many a demure jest among the rural population, — "Agricultural College." Separately, the words command all respect; united, they are a living refutation of the well-known axiom that "the whole is equal to all its parts."

"Gov'ment is goin' to build an Agriculteral College. Farmin' an' learnin' marry an' set up house-keepin'. Guess Uncle Sam 'll have to give 'em a hist with a donation-party now 'n' then. Agriculteral College? Yes, sir. Well, sir, if you 'll show me a man, sir, that 's a gradooate from that College, that 'll ever be seen with a hoe in his hand, I 'll give him leave to knock my brains out with it! Yes, sir! An' it 'll be the best use he can put it to, sir! He 'll do less mischief that way 'n any other! Agriculteral College! Edicated farmers! Yes, sir, I 've seen 'em! Got a grist up in Topsell. Jint-stock farm. The best talent in Essex County 's been a-carryin' on that farm, an' nigh about carried it off, an' themselves along with it. Yes, sir, the best talent in Essex County, an' had the farm given 'em, an' they 've sunk a thousan' dollars, sir, a'ready! That 's what I call a Sinkin'-Fund, sir! That 's to begin with. Jones is an edicated farmer. He made his cider last fall on scinetific principles. Well, sir, I could put an apple in my mouth an' swim down Merrimac River, an' have better cider 'n that all the way! Edicated farmin' 's a very pooty thing, if a man can be at the expense on 't; but when it comes to gittin' a livin', farmin' 's farmin'. Agriculteral College! Yes, sir, farmin' 's a hard life, lookin' at the best side. Soil 's light an' runnin' to stones. But this here college stuff 's the poorest kind o' top-dressin' you can give it. Learnin' 's a good thing. I 've nothin' agin learnin', but 't a'n't the best use you can make on 't to plough it in. The only way to promote the agriculteral interests of Essex County, sir, is to keep the farmers jest as they are. Greek 'n' Latin a'n't state-prison offences, but they 're sure death to pork 'n' potaters. Minute you edicate the farmers they 'll be as uneasy as a toad under a harrow. What kind of a hand would Doctor Hall or Squire Smith make, to come an' take a farm alongside o' me?"

This is the way our bold yeoman puts it. Planting himself on the indisputable facts of his pork and potatoes, he regards one who stands upon anything else as a dreamer. He forgets that pork and potatoes are not the only facts in the world. The earth itself is a larger fact than anything that springs from it. It is the inalienable inheritance, the sole support of man.

Mother and nurse, from the cradle to the grave, there comes no hour when he can withdraw from her nourishing bosom. But, by our farmers' showing, it is but a harsh and niggardly step-mother, opening the fountains of life only under enforcement. Is this reasonable? Is it reasonable to suppose that the one calling which is essential to life, the one calling on which every other depends, should be the Canaan accursed, servant of servants to its brethren? Is it reasonable to suppose that God gave us this beautiful round world, source of all our wealth, almoner of every comfort, possessor and dispenser of all grace and loveliness, yet with such poison in her veins that they alone are safe who deal with her at a remove, — she withers the hand that touches her? The ancients believed better things than these. They reverenced the Mighty Mother, and fabled a giant's strength to him who craved a blessing by the laying on of hands. We know that a curse was pronounced upon the earth, but why farmers should be so forward to monopolize the curse it is difficult to conceive. It is generally supposed that all the descendants of Adam are equally implicated. It is not for the farmer alone, but the minister and the mechanic as well, who is to eat bread in the sweat of his face. Wheat and barley and corn are no more under a ban than gold and iron and timber, which all come from the same bountiful earth; but while artificers in gold and iron magnify their office and wax fat, the farmer depreciates his, and according to his own showing is clothed upon with leanness.

Surely these things ought not so to be. Looking at this earth as the divinely-prepared dwelling-place of man, and looking at man as divinely appointed to dress and keep it, we should naturally suppose that there would be an obvious and a pre-eminent adaptation of the one to the other. We should naturally suppose that the primary, the fundamental occupation of the race would be one which should not only keep body and soul together, but should be exactly fitted to develop and strengthen all the powers called into exercise, and should also be most likely to call into exercise a great variety of powers to the fashioning of a beautiful symmetry. Looking still further at the secondary occupations, we find our views confirmed. The shoemaker must bend over his lapstone, and he becomes stooping and hollow-chested. The blacksmith twists the sinews of his arm to strength, but at the expense of his other members. The watchmaker trains his eyes to microscopic vision, but his muscles are small and his skin colorless. A very large majority of the secondary callings remove men from the open air, often from the sunshine, and generally train a few faculties at the expense of the others. The artisan carries skill to perfection, the genius towers into sublimity, but the man suffers. Not so the farmer.

His life is not only many-, but all-sided. His ever-changing employment gives him every variety of motion and posture. Not a muscle but is pressed into service. His work lies chiefly out-of-doors. The freedom of earth and sky is his. Every power of his mind may be brought into play. He is surrounded by mysteries which the longest life will not give him time enough to fathom, problems whose solution may furnish employment for the deepest thought and the most sustained attention, and whose solution is at the same time a direct and most important contribution to his own ease and riches. The constant presence of beautiful and ever-shifting scenery ministers to his taste and his imagination. Nature, in her grandeur, in her loveliness, in the surpassing beauty of her utilities, is always spread before him. All her wonderful processes go on beneath his eyes. The great laboratory is ever open. The furnace-fire is always burning. Patent to his curious or admiring gaze the transmutation takes place. The occult principle of life surrounds him, might almost bewilder him, with manifestations. Bee and bird, fruit and blossom, and the phantom humanity in beasts, offer all their secrets to him. Every process is his minister. His mental and material interests lie in one right line. The sun is his servant. The shower fulfils his behest. The dew drops silently down to do his work. The fragrance of the apple-orchard shall turn to gold in his grasp.

The beauty of bloom shall fill his home with plenty. The frost of winter is his treasure-keeper, and the snows wrap him about with beneficence. With nothing trivial, deceptive, inflated, has he to do. An unimpeachable sincerity pervades all things. All things are natural, and all things act after their kind. Is it a divine decree that all this shall tend to no good? Shall all this pomp of preparation rightly come to nothing? Do we gather the natural fruits of circumstance, when the mind travels on to madness, the body goes prematurely to disease and decay, and the heart shrivels away from love and is overcast with gloom? Is all the appearance of adaptation false, and do farmers gain the due emoluments of their position? Not so. It is their fault that they do not see the life which revels in exuberance around them. Earth with all her interests takes unrelaxing hold of their potato-patch, but they have eyes only for the potato-patch. Accustoming themselves to the contemplation of little things, considered separately and not as links in the universal chain, their angle of vision has grown preternaturally acute. Things they see, but not the relations of things. They dwell on desert islands. For all the integrity of Nature, they fail to learn integrity. The honest farmer is no more common than the honest merchant. He abhors the tricks of trade, he has his standing joke about the lawyer's conscience: but the load of hay which he sold to the merchant was heavier by his own weight on the scales than at the merchant's stable-yard; the lawyer who buys his wood, taught by broad rural experience, looks closely to the admeasurement; and a trout in the milk Thoreau counts as very strong circumstantial evidence. The farmer does not compass sublime swindles like the merchant, nor such sharp practice as the lawyer; but in small ways he is the peer of either. We do not say that farmers are any more addicted to their characteristic vices than the lawyers and merchants are to theirs; but that they have their peculiarities, like other classes, and that the term *honest* is as necessary a prefix to *farmer* as to any other noun of occupation. We admit all this, but we believe it is the fault of the farmer, and not of his circumstances.

"His fault!" says the farmer, and say many men of whom better things might be expected. "How can he get wisdom that holdeth the plough, and that glorieth in the goad, that driveth oxen, and is occupied in their labors, and whose talk is of bullocks?" How? By "seeking her as silver, and searching for her as for hid treasures." For remember, O farmer! the despairing question is from below, the inspiring answer from above. It is not the Bible, but the Apocrypha, that casts doubt upon agricultural education. There *is* wisdom to him that holdeth the plough. Honor and health and wealth and great-heartedness are to be found in the soil. Earth is not one huge encumbrance to weigh man down; it is the means by which he may rise to heavenly heights. Earth has been the mother of dignity ever since her Maker's eyes looked upon her, and the Maker's voice pronounced her very good. And "Very Good" is the true verdict. Ignorance, stupidity, and sin insist upon perpetuating the curse from which she has been once redeemed; but a blessing lies in her heart for him who has but the courage to grasp it.

What analogies have they to prop their conclusions withal, who maintain the necessary degradation of the soil? Fire, air, and water bow down and do obeisance to man. They are analyzed and recombined. They are studied with insatiable curiosity. They receive the absorbed attention of a lifetime. Daily their secrets are wrested from them. Their likings and their dislikings are forced into man's service; they are coupled in strange unions and harnessed to his chariot. Whithersoever he will, they bear him. They minister to his lowliest needs, they bend to his loftiest dreams. They have lifted him from the earth whereon he crept, and have given him the wings of the wind. Swifter than the eagle flies, swift as the lightnings flash, they run to and fro at his command. Nor has the limit of their capacities been reached, nor has man ceased to pry into the mysteries which lie hidden in their depths. He was once their abject slave. He is now their crowned king. He will one day be their absolute monarch.

But while the three ancient elements are thus wrought into glory and honor, the fourth sister, Earth, remains a clod. They give gifts to men, but she only sears him with the brand of servitude. Every bold seeker, adventuring into their arcana, bears back his treasure-trove; but the earth only mocks her wooer, and robs him of his strength who sleeps upon her knees!

It is easy to point to occurrences which apparently prove this, — to experiments which seemed fruitless, — to plans adopted only to be laid aside, — to new modes that were heralded with great flourish of trumpets, and shuffled ignominiously out through the pantry-door. But every science and every art has had its empirical age, and every age has its empiricists. Astrology spoke its great swelling words, made its cabalistic signs, and passed away to its burial; but astronomy remains eternal as the heavens. The stars cannot tell a man when he shall die, and they shine upon the shepherd as brightly as on the sage; but they have marvellous secrets to whisper to him who watches the long night through to behold their coming and mark the magic of their ways; and by so much knowledge unfolded Earth takes her place in the skies. There was no El Dorado beyond the western sea to bestow eternal youth upon the Spanish dreamer; but there was a land fairer than all his fancy painted, to whose light the Gentiles shall yet come, and kings to the brightness of its rising. The philosopher's stone has never been found which should transmute all metals to gold; but gold itself is worthless in the presence of such truths as philosophy reveals. All the way through, no science has been pushed to barren results. A thousand errors have branched off from the central truth, and have sometimes been mistaken for it; a thousand false steps have been made for one in the right direction; yet the truth is central and indivisible, and men have pressed on steadily to reach it. Counterfeits do not annihilate the pure coin. Pretenders do not destroy faith in the rightful prince. Failures lead the way to success. Honest, wise, persevering research has ever been rewarded in full measure, pressed down, shaken together, and running over. And it is not to be supposed that the one science of the earth, vaster and nobler than all others, the science that ministers most directly to man's life, shall be the one science to baffle his research and yield him meagre returns. We do not know what wealth the earth holds in store for us, and it is our shame and misery that we so little strive to know, so little care to seek. With an ignorance for which our rich experience leaves us no excuse, we doggedly assume that we have attained the ultimatum. The earth is to us but an immense pippin covered all over with the arrogant label, "Seek-no-further."

If farmers choose to accept this label as their motto, they should also accept the consequences without complaint. If they choose to live in a rut, they must not expect to breathe the air which they would find on a hill. Many readers will remember a passage at arms that occurred in the legislative assembly of one of our New England States. A clergyman, advocating a bill which was to help a certain class of young men in obtaining education, referred to several persons who had by assistance become men of note, but who without it would have remained "only farmers." Another member immediately took umbrage, avowed himself to be a farmer, and assured the assembly that he should not vote for a bill which was to educate young men to sneer at him! The bill failed,—whether from constitutional weakness or from this blow we are not informed, but are left to infer the latter. The repartee was very good as a repartee, and a respectable degree of Parliamentary skill was shown in seizing upon a plausible pretext for a foregone conclusion; but so far as the question was of principle, and not of repartee, the clergyman was right and the farmer was wrong. We may exalt democracy, and abase aristocracy, and cajole people with specious phrases. Ignorance and uncouthness may put on the garb of modest merit, and worthlessness seek to veil itself by an unattractive exterior; but under never so many layers the truth remains intact. "Only a farmer" expresses with all-sufficient accuracy the relative position of farmers, — not their necessary, but their actual position. The occupation which should be a liberal profession is a most illiberal labor. Farming is honorable, just as any other business is honorable, according to the amount of mind and heart brought to bear on it. Shoemaking will always be an inferior craft to statesmanship, because the amount of intellect required is less in the former than in the latter. The man who aims at the highest culture, both of his farm and himself, is aiming, whether consciously or not, at the highest rank, and he shall not stand among mean men; but he who simply delves in the dirt will find no laurels there. Fine-sounding phrases cannot give dignity to that which is in itself undignified. No amount of complaint can elevate prejudice, obstinacy, and routine into intelligence, generosity, magnanimity. Farmers themselves act upon this principle with entire unanimity, because it is a law of Nature, and not an effort of the will. The man upon whose experiments they look with utter distrust, ill-concealed contempt, and covert ridicule, whose science seems to them mere nonsense, extravagance, and recklessness, they at the same time regard with reverence and admiration. They look down upon him as a farmer, but they look up to him as a man. They are proud and pleased to have his family visit and receive theirs. They feel that he is of a different order from themselves. And if farmers persist in keeping education and science away from their farms, if they will bring only their hard hands to the work, and will leave their brains to shrivel in their skulls, this state of things must go on. The best of materials is of no use without will and skill to work it. Matter is a sorry substance until mind lays hold of it. The world was not made with tug and sweat, but He spake, and it was done, He commanded, and it stood fast. As the world was made, so must it be subdued, not by matter clawing at matter, but by the calm dominion of spirit over matter. Until intellect percolates the soil, the soil will not part with its hidden hoards. We shall have effort, struggle, wear, and weariness, but no victory. It is the strife of clod with clod.

So it is that the men who grieve to bring their minds into play will never make of their occupation a profession. The people who work mind and muscle, who turn knowledge into wisdom, shall stand before kings. Those who

> "Keep in uninquiring trust
> The old dull round of things"

shall be hewers of wood and drawers of water to the end of the days. If farming is doomed, farmers are doomed. For here is the earth ready-made, and however much we may dislike it, it is all we have and the best we shall get. If farming must be mere mechanical labor, — then there is a point where elevation and improvement must stop, for there must always exist a class of serfs, — serfs to the soil, slaves of their own farms; and none are more sure of this than those who have lived in a farming community, and seen how surely the adventurous spirits, the active, the energetic, the intellectual, the promising, turn away from the dismal monotony of the farm and launch out on currents of freer flow, or, if they remain at home, remain only in consequence of the continued and earnest expostulations and the fairest promises of parents, to rock the cradle of their declining years, and not unfrequently to rock it over.

But if the founders of our Agricultural College, or if any furtherers of rural education, propose to themselves to diffuse light by appealing to farmers, — if they think to correct the evils of ignorance by furnishing special opportunities to farmers, — if they flatter themselves that they can establish a college of aims and claims so moderate that farmers and farmers' boys will not be discouraged by the time, money, or mind required, — they are spending their strength for naught. No college and no school can be founded so wisely and fitly, that farmers as a class will send their sons to it. Why should they, believing, as they do, that the district-school already gives them as much "learnin'" as they need? Boys there can "read, write, and cipher." They gain knowledge enough to reckon with the hired man, to keep the tally of the marketing, to compute interest, and to do parish business. What more do they want? Your college-men will talk about selections and temperatures, silex and fluorine; but what has all that to do with planting the ten-acre lot? Timothy and red-top grew before Liebig was born. A rose by any other name is just as sweet to the agricultural nose. Farmers who have grown to manhood with full faith in the fixity of their condition, in the impossibility of its improvement, are not to be turned right-about-face by a programme. The best patent cultivator could not root out this main article of their creed. Agricultural colleges may spread all their blandishments; but farmers will not listen to the voice of the charmer, charm he never so wisely. The academic roof may be set low and the academic door flung wide open, and the academic Siren, with new and deeper meaning, may sweetly

"Sing a song of sixpence, a bag full of rye";

but before it reaches the rural ear, it will have transformed itself into a new rendering of the fatal entomological civility, —

"'Will you walk into my parlor?' said the spider to the fly."

Reasoning is of no avail. Farmers do not grasp the chances already offered them; how should they be expected to possess themselves of future ones? Able treatises on breeding, instructive, eloquent, and forcible, are written and printed; but these men continue to tie up nightly their ill-favored and lean-fleshed kine, and are weekly dragged to church by loose-jointed nags wabbling over the road, head between legs. There are yearly reports, rich in suggestion, well printed, cleverly illustrated, distributed without cost — to the receivers. They will not read them. They may glance at the foreign-looking sheep, with folds of wool on his throat; they will utter a strong idiomatic exclamation over the broad-sided shorthorn; but they will not go beyond the limits of their own township to replenish their stock. They have not time nor money nor heart for experiments. You prove to them beyond the possibility of gainsaying that their mode is cumbrous, and, in truth, extravagant; they will assent to your propositions, admit the force of your arguments, but inevitably leave your presence with the remark, that, "after all, they think, like Gran'ma'am Howdy, they 'd better go on in the good old diabolical way," — and there, accordingly, they go. Their logic is devious, but it is always ready. It may not be convincing, but it is conclusive. The major premise is often hidden, but it is as firm as Fate.

"Parson Edwards 's been round with the temperance-pledge," says one old farmer to another.

"Yes," answers the latter. "Came to me. Asked me, says he, 'Mr. Solomon,' says he, 'have you got any cider in your suller?' — 'Yes, sir,' says I, — 'sixteen barrels, good as ever was hossed up, I don't care *where* 't is.' — 'Well,' says he, 'Mr. Solomon, my advice to you is, to go an' tap them barrels, every one on 'em, an' let it run!'"

"Guess you told him you 'd wait a spell, did n't you?"

"Humph! Let it run! *I knew his gran'sir!* Meddlin' toad! Advisin' me to throw my cider away! I KNEW HIS GRAN'SIR!"

Whenever any amendment is suggested, some "gran'sir" or other will be sure to block the way. That he has been two generations dead, or that he has no apparent connection with the point at issue, may be indisputably proved, but it does not open the road.

Nor will the farmer's sons be any more ready to avail themselves of their college than the farmer's self. As a general thing, they have either ploughed their own furrow "in the good old diabolical way," and walk in it as their fathers walked, caring for no other, or they have acquired so unconquerable a repugnance to the uncongenial toil that they cannot conceive of any plan or process by which it can be made tolerable. To elevate farming by placing the lever under the farmers is to attack a fort where its defences are strongest. But we can apply socially as well as agriculturally the principle of a rotation of crops. Poets are not necessarily the sons of poets. We do not draw upon engineers' families for our supply of engineers. The greatest statesman of the age may come from the smallest estate in the country. So also is there no Medo-Persic law compelling the cultivation of our lands by farmers' sons. An infusion of fresh blood is sometimes the best remedy for long-standing disease and weakness, especially in social organizations. The end desired is not the education of any special existing class, but the establishment of a class fit to receive in trust special existing interests. We want our country's soil to be intelligently and beneficially cultivated. We desire that it shall be rescued from ignorance and from quackery, and placed in the hands of active intellect and sound sense. We want our farmers to be working-men, not day-laborers. We want them to be practical farmers, book-farmers, and gentleman-farmers in one. The proprietors of the soil stand at the base of society, and should constitute by themselves an order of nobility, — but eclectic, not hereditary. Whenever a boy displays a turn for agriculture, there is a fit subject for agricultural education, a proper student for an agricultural college, whether his father were merchant, farmer, policeman, or president. You cannot make a college so mean that farmers' sons will flock into it, but you can make it so great that the best of all classes shall press in. Endosmose and exosmose are the soul of growth; either, alone, would bring death, —

death on one side from exhaustion, on the other from over-fulness. The city is currently said to draw its best blood from the country. Let the city pour it back again over field and meadow, turning our wilderness into gardens. Country and city will be invigorated by an exchange of commodities, — the one giving of its nature, the other of its culture. We want no exclusiveness, aristocratic or democratic. We want intelligent men to develop the capacity of the soil. The problem is, to vindicate the ways of God to man, — to demonstrate that He spake truth, when He looked upon the earth which He had made, and pronounced it very good. It is the duty of this generation to show to the future that agriculture opens a career, and not a grave, to thought, energy, and genius. It needs strong arms and stout hearts, but there are bays to be won and worn. We want farmers who do not look upon their land as a malicious menial, but who love it and woo it, and delight in enriching and adorning it. We want men who are enthusiastic, — who will not be put down by failures, nor disheartened by delay, — men who believe that the Earth holds in her lap richer stores than gold or silver, — who are not deceived by all the niggardliness that has been laid to her charge, but know in their inmost souls that she is full of beneficence and power, and that it needs only to pronounce the "Open Sesame!" to gain admittance to her treasure-house and possession of her richest gifts. We want men who are willing to spend and be spent, not for paltry gains or sordid existence, but for gains that are not paltry and existence that is not sordid, — for love of truth, — men who attribute the failure of their experiments, not to the poverty of Nature, but to their own short-sighted, rough-handed endeavor, and who will simply take heart and try again, — men who are fully persuaded in their own minds that there must be, and are fully determined in their own hearts that there shall be, profit to him that glorieth in the goad.

It is left for our country to show that manual and mental skill, strength, exercise, and labor are not incompatible, — that hard hands may comport with gracious manners, — that one may be a gentleman digging in a ditch, as well as dancing in a drawing-room. The Old World groans under her peasant system, — even free England has her Hodge; but we will have no peasantry here, no Hodges in hobnailed shoes, no stolid perpetual serfdom to nurse our vanity and pride. The very genius of our nation makes every man's manhood his most valuable possession. America professes to believe that no one can with impunity evade the decree, "In the sweat of thy face shalt thou eat bread." She professes to hold labor in honor; but she should show her faith by her work. She should display her children of labor, fairer and fatter than the children of kings and princes. If they are seen to be decrepit in mind and body before their time, — if they have less happiness than the Austrian peasant, and less content than the English clown, and no breadth of vision or liberality of thought or clear foresight to atone for such deficiency, we shall have to compass sea and land before we make many intelligent men or nations proselytes to our faith.

The time especially has need of men. This hour, and every hour of the last three years, ought to prove to us beyond cavil that no class can safely be left in ignorance, least of all the class that holds in its hands a people's staff of life. Our country needs all the brain, all the conscience, all the nerve, and patience, and moral strength, that can be commanded. Her salvation lies in a yeomanry capable of comprehending the momentous issues at stake. "More light!" is the dying gasp of a dying people. Our republican institutions are but half completed. To give every man the right to vote, without giving him at the same time the power to vote intelligently, is but questionable service. If such an arrangement were perpetual, it would be unquestionable disservice. Only as fast and as far as we keep enlightenment abreast of power are we seeing that the Republic receives no detriment. Ignorance is the never-failing foe of freedom, the never-failing ally of despotism. We have organized and successfully fought a crusade against tyranny; we are now in the midst of our crusade against slavery; let us have one more, organized and efficient, against ignorance, that the fruit of our former victories be not lost to us for lack of wisdom to use them aright.

That the people who suffer most from want of knowledge should disdain it is but natural. To see the need of teaching, men must be taught. It is this very ignorance which is the strong buttress against education. Ignorance propagates itself. It can be subdued only by force or tact, not by argument. But for men who have attained by the help of their education whatever reputation they possess to affect to question its importance is to spurn the ladder by which they have mounted to eminence. We are sometimes almost tempted to suspect the existence of a petty jealousy in members of the learned professions. It would seem as if a small fear were indulged lest a wider diffusion of knowledge and a more thorough culture among the farming classes should detract from the supremacy of others. There is certainly, among some writers, a leaning towards a continuance of present abuses for which it is difficult to account. The shrewdness of the plain farmer is pitted against the science of the scholar, to the entire discomfiture of the latter. But would the plain farmer's shrewdness be at all diminished by educating the plain farmer? Would his sharp sense be blunted by being expressed with some partial subjection to grammatical forms? Would his observation be any less close for being trained? Would his reasoning be any less profitable by being wisely directed than by running at hap-hazard? Would it not be more economical to strengthen and polish his powerful weapons, and give them honest work to do, than to leave them rough and rusty from disuse? If education is not the foe of legal, mechanical, polemic, nor forensic acuteness, why should it be hostile to any?

No lover of his country who brings to this view the same clearness and sense which he takes to political or personal plans, but must hail as an omen of good the efforts now making throughout the North in behalf of agriculture and education. It is a cause for proud and grateful gratulation and congratulation, that our government is so wise and strong as to look through all the smoke and cloud of warfare, and set firm in the tumultuous present the foundations of future greatness,—that, calm and confident, it lays in the midst of the thunder-storm of battle the corner-stone of the temple of Peace. It is equally encouraging to see the States from east to west responding to this movement, consulting with each other, enlisting in the enterprise their best men, and sending them up and down in the land, and in other lands, to observe, and collate, and infer, that the beneficent designs of Congress may be carried out and carried on in the best possible manner for the highest good of all. So a free people governs itself. So a free people discerns its weakness and unfolds its strength. So a true aristocracy will yet develop a worthy democracy. From such living, far-seeing patriotism we augur the best results. Mistakes will doubtless be made; wisdom will not die with this generation; but a beginning is the sure presage of the end. Hesitation and precipitancy, unseemly delay, and ill-advised action, may retard, but will not prevent, a glorious consummation. In these colleges we look to see agricultural centres from which shall radiate new light across our hills and valleys. They will not at once turn every ploughboy into a philosopher, nor send us Liebigs to milk the cows; but to every ploughboy and dairyman in the country they will give a new and wider horizon. They will bring fresh and manly incentives into the domain of toil. They will establish in society a new order of men, — an order whose mere existence will give heart and hope to the farmer-lad disgusted with his narrow life, yet unable to relinquish it. They will send out to us men who have learned and who will teach that the plough, the hoe, the rake, are implements of profit and honor, as well as of industry. They will show that the hand and the head may work together, and that only so can their full capacity be tested. Science will be corrected by practice, and practice will be guided by science. These men will go over the land and quietly set up their household gods among our old-time farmers. They will gradually acquire influence, not by loud-voiced rhetoric, but by the silent eloquence of rich cornfields, heavy-laden orchards, full-uddered kine, and merry-hearted boys and girls, — by the gentle, but irresistibe force of kindly words, pleasant ways, ready sympathy, a helping hand in trouble, "sage counsel in cumber," —by the thousand little devices of taste and culture and good-fellowship, — by the cheap elegances, the fine endearments, all the small, sweet courtesies of life. They will approve the beneficence and the power of the Great Mother; they will demonstrate to farmers the possibility of large and generous living; they will teach them to distinguish between the mountebanks of pretended science and the apostles of that science which alone is truth; they will give to thought a new direction, to energy a new impulse, to earth a new creation, to man a new life.

X.

PICTURES AND A PICTURE.

TWO kinds of talk are extant concerning pictures. One is that which has seized a few of the floating technicalities, and discourses flippantly of light, and shade, and breadth, and tone, mouths the "old masters," rants of Italy, sneers at American art, and goes into raptures, in a public way, over a bit of old canvas, but is not so absorbed but that it has leisure to observe and brand the indifference of those who do not share its ecstasies.

The other prides itself on being "no artist." "It knows nothing of the rules of art. But it knows what it likes, and is going to like it, right or wrong. Artists may sneer, but it is not going to be driven from a picture, because the picture was not made with plumb and line." On the whole, this is rather more disagreeable than the first, since that only pretends to follow in the wake of excellence, while this sets up a claim to originality, strikes out boldly for itself, and is sure to find hosts of admirers among our rampant democracy. Ignorance on any subject is a thing to be repented of and forsaken if voluntary, to be silently borne if involuntary, but on no account to be exulted over. We, who boast our ignorance, forget, that though the artist, like the poet, is "born, not made," he is not born an artist. The germ is there, but many a spring's sunshine, and many a summer's shower, ay, and many a winter's frost, must ripen it into the mellow fruit. The possibility is there, but only by careful study, constant trial, severe culture, can it be wrought into a fact. Is it, then, reasonable to suppose that the untutored eye can fully appreciate the work of the tutored hand?

It is, indeed, a merciful dispensation of Providence, that the humblest day-laborer, going home from his work at six o'clock, with his coat swinging over his arm, and his tin pail in his hand, may feel the soothing, elevating influence of the calm sunset sky, the still fields, and the shining flood, yet he but enters the vestibule of the temple. Only to her importunate child, — only

> "To him who, *in the love of Nature,* holds
> Communion with her visible forms," —

does she disclose the arcana, — the mystic glory that shines in her holy of holies.

Thus a picture is not only the measure of the soul that conceived, and the hand that wrought, but of the eye that views it. If you see therein neither form nor comeliness, it may be either because form and comeliness are not there, or because your gross vision cannot discern their spiritual presence; and this incapacity may be the result either of native deficiency or lack of training.

Every true picture, everything worthy the name, has a body and soul. Canvas, color, contour, are the one. The idea that shines through them all, and invests them with life, and glow, and reality, is the other. Where the soul is wanting, all else may be perfect, the body complete, but the picture says nothing to you. It is mere dead matter. There may be pretensions to life, a convulsive and contorted struggling, as it were, to compass life, but you have no love wherewithal to endow the fair Undine with an immortal soul.

But this soul of the picture does not sit enthroned on the surface, to be profaned by vulgar gaze. Eye may meet eye, but heart alone can speak to heart. Of ten men who pass before a painting, nine may pass on unheeding. It is to them blank and meaningless, like the marks of certain chalk on window-glass; but when you draw near, you, the tenth, and breathe upon it the breath of your life, by an unerring instinct it recognizes your soul. Quickly life leaps into the picture, — flashes into the statue the Promethean fire, quivering in every limb, glowing in every lineament, till, as you gaze, it passes into your being, to become a part of yourself forevermore.

This life, this pathos and power, depend less on the subject than on the manner of handling it. We have all looked coolly on representations of dying saints, surrounded by a maze of infant cherubs and full-grown angels, wings and crowns and floating garments; and we have perhaps felt the cheek flush and the heart throb at the sunlight streaming in through a kitchen-window; for the one was vague, crude, and perchance ridiculous; while the other, simple and direct, carried us swiftly back to home, and childhood, and mother's love.

Yet mere fidelity is of little worth. You recognize the mechanical skill, but you say, "Why be at infinite labor to reproduce what is so much better at first hand?" An artist gives us a landscape wherein all the trees are of the requisite size and shape, — the rocks duly distributed and overgrown with moss, the brooks running the way of all brooks. We do not know why we are not moved, but we are not. We acknowledge a certain correctness. We cannot put a finger on this or that, and say, "It is not like." But we feel no coolness in the shadow of the rocks, — no longing to dint the soft moss with our weary feet. We do not hear the plashing of the water as we break with our hands its rippling flow, or the whisper of the south-wind in the tops of the pine-trees.

Another landscape laps us in the drowsy repose of summer. Herd-boys lie on the grass in all the luxury of outstretched ease, scarcely heeding the meek-eyed cows who chew the cud of their benevolent thoughts — cows always look benevolent, or at least complacent — in the shadow of the trees whose huge trunks and dense foliage make

"Rome's cathedral awe live in these woodland aisles."

The air of noonday, filtered of its heat, breathes, grateful and refreshing, through shadowy corridors defiant of the meridian sun. There is no merry, tricksy, "laughing water," or trim, turfed, well-bred pond, but a happy, languid, good-natured pool, on whose still surface the lazy lilies spread out their broad leaves and drink in the liquid coolness as they float. Gay flowers, that gather richness from unseen sources, flaunt in dank luxuriance on its margin, and homely weeds dip their feet unrebuked in its welcome waves. On every leaf, and twig, and blade of grass, is written, "Summer."

A third speaks also of repose, but repose under a different aspect. One is earthly; the other, spiritual. One is the dreamy, compulsory languor of the South; the other, the voluntary, serene revery of the North. One is an idyl piped by Arcadian shepherds in a vale of Tempe; the other is the pure soul of some silver-throated maiden, gushing out in low-voiced song at evening-tide. In one we

"Feel the warm Orient in the noonday air";

through the other we

"From cloud minarets hear the sunset call to prayer."

Land, water, and sky, combine to form that perfect beauty which "is a joy forever." A fairy lake, liquid gold where the light falls unobstructed, deepening into purple where the shadows linger, smiles back answering joy to the radiant heavens. From the purpling waters stretch away the purple hills, paling into violet, flushing into pink, glowing into gold, till, losing their earthliness, bathed and fused in the heavenly glory, they shine, translucent. Still and stately, the tall trees stand clearly outlined against the sky. Rose-tinted clouds float softly in the amber air. A white sail swells to the wooing breeze, but no sound breaks the charmed silence. The mists that spiritualized Helvellyn for her poet priest, wrap the scene in a delicious haze of softness and sweetness. Gazing, you are borne out beyond the world and the things of the world. Will that pleasant path, winding over the hills towards the sunset, lead you indeed to the sea of glass mingled with fire? On such a chariot as yonder lush cloud did the beloved of the Lord, in old time, pass from glory to glory? The dying day? Yea, verily, but the dying day folds her royal robes about her, and sweeps down to death with a grandeur and a grace that might well befit the majesty of her morning.

Looking at such a picture, fragments of verse, snatches of old songs, remembered tones of voices long silent, float murmurously through the chambers of your brain. Now, a ringing epithet from Tennyson, it may be; then, a diamond found among the toads and frogs that dropped from old Dekker's lips, or a self-singing line from the "poet of poets," or a sunbeam from some stray ballad that lives in the heart of a people, though the author's name and fame are buried with his unknown dust, — flitting so vaguely, yet chiming so perfectly, that we scarcely perceive their separate presence, yet are imperceptibly lulled by them into harmony and peace; just as the summer wind bears through the woods the mingled scent of violet, and pansy, and white-robed Innocence, and sweet-smelling arbutus, which yet we think not of resolving, but only stand in happy waiting, and snuff the odorous breeze. In smaller, in apparently trifling things, the same power is revealed. A child's shoe may be well painted, and yet be only a shoe. A hat is but plaited straw, and a top a bit of carved and painted wood. But, in the hands of a master, the worn shoe, the battered hat, and bruised top, will speak of a little form gone back to dust, — a silent chamber, wherein the patter of childish feet will never more be heard, — a hearth whose light and life and joy are quenched in sudden night. What a picture thus says to you, is the measure of its worth to you. You may see faults many and glaring, but everywhere we reverence a great purpose even if imperfectly fulfilled, a grand conception faithfully, honestly, even if unsuccessfully attempted, rather than petty ends achieved. Or the picture may be applauded by every one with unbounded enthusiasm, but if your own soul is not fired, it is no revealer to you. It may be from the old masters or the young pupils, from the world-renowned artist, or the obscure dentist's apprentice; but you alone must be the judge whether it speaks to you. If the wise, and learned, and good, are moved by what moves you, you may be glad thus to recognize kinship with them; but if otherwise, you may keep your own counsel, but you must be true.

Thus it is that, while painting holds out no invitation to arrogance and conceit, it offers no discouragement to ignorance. They who have never looked upon the masterpieces of the Old World may be lifted to a higher level by the masterpieces of the New.

It is not necessary to understand the technicalities of Art. If you do but love grassy plains and running water, if you ever admired a cloud, or thought of a mountain, you possess all the requisites for an interval of unalloyed happiness in looking at Bierstadt's picture of the Rocky Mountains. It is only to go up a staircase or two, through a passage or two, round a corner or two, into a darkness, into a light, and — you are no longer in the studio-building on Tremont Street, — you have crossed rivers, lakes, woods, and valleys. You have left behind you railroads, and batteries, and Boston, and civilization. You have stridden out to the border-lands of the Angles. You have struck the trail of the savage. You have mounted the crest of the great mysterious wave that swelled in the far Orient centuries and centuries ago, curving westward, sweeping over the steppes of Russia, over the meadows of Germany, over the vine-lands of France, surging up against the white-faced shores of England, pausing but for a moment, then, with gathered strength, thundering at the gates of our western world, curving westward, ever westward, over prairies and deserts, pursuing the pathway of the sun, till now it foams around the base of the inaccessible mountains. Here, beyond its farthest reach, you pause. Only the spray of the advancing tide flings its coolness at your feet. Here the Indian plants his tent-pole and takes his stand, — barbarism against civilization. But neither stand nor fight shall avail him. Already the wave, fretting within its rocky barriers, has found itself an outlet by the South, and while the "poor Indian" counts his wampum and smokes his pipe in fancied peace, lo! it storms up from the West, deep calling unto deep, till there shall be left for his wandering dove no olive-leaf, and pipe and wampum, wigwam and hunting-ground, are whelmed in the relentless flood.

Rest then, while we may, in this peaceful Indian village. A broad, level plain, fronting the mountains. Through the broad plain we may walk ankle-deep in the rich, dank verdure, but the mountains rise white and awful to the skies. Jagged and precipitous, unpressed by mortal foot but scarred with many a glacier, they lift their hoar heads, silent amid all the sound, wan amid all the color, still amid all the stir, shining amid all the shadow. Tender growths creep timidly up their furrowed sides, but quickly faint for want of cherishing, and pale into eternal snow upon their brows. Warmth, and greenness, and life, all are chilled in the pitiless cold that riots around those unscaled heights. Towering in the centre above his brethren, Mount Lander, king by virtue of pre-eminence, throws back his head and faces the sun with a royal disdain. Or, in softer mood, the afternoon light crowns him with such heavenly radiance that he stands bathed in glory, his face upturned in reverence to God. How late-born is society, how flitting is man, when we hold such communion! Yesterday a race was born; to-morrow it passes away; but the everlasting mountains are not scattered; the perpetual hills have never bowed. Monuments of God's might, they rise sublime above the littleness of life, confronting us with their desolation. No ingenuity, no avarice, no ambition, can clothe these rugged slopes with fertility, or mingle the song of bird or hum of bee with their pæan of the winds. Yet Grandeur and Beauty meet together there; Strength and Service have kissed each other. In the darkening day they frown, they lower, they menace, and we tremble under their overhanging steeps. But flooded with sunlight, a veil of silvery mist is flung about them, and the terrible outlines are lost in loveliness. Icy cold, they stand unceasing benefactors. Their wildest storm-song is a chant of peace on earth, good-will to men. Heaped and hidden in their perpetual snows, they keep the treasures of the valleys. Blessings of dale and upland, blessings of field and orchard, blessings of fruit and flower, trickle down to us from their bleak and stony breasts. The dew of our youth is in the womb of their morning.

Born of the glacier and the sunshine, little brooks leap down the dark defiles, rushing headlong into one wilful water, which rends for itself a chasm, and tears through the rocks, a reckless Undine, fantastic and uncontrolled. Now in the shadow, now in the sun, it tosses aloft its joyous spray, till you almost feel the grateful shower, almost hear the uproar of its wild wassail. But soon its uproar is hushed. Its headlong haste is lulled into a limpid calm. It floats out on the plain, a little lake, soft, clear, molten, holding in its deep heart the tender shadows of the mountains, sweet and pure and still. Ah! well may the frisky Undine pause in her morning song and steady her flying feet for the long journey that lies before her. This Laughing-water, this Minnehaha that darts out in a frolic from her mountain-home, shall broaden and deepen into grave Colorado. From her cradle in the rocks she shall go down her steep stairways into the Indian valleys, down among the waving wheat-fields and the golden corn-lands, through the depths of dreadful forests into the shining of hidden silver, through many a rift of tortured rock, with sweep and swirl, raging and raving, a thousand miles to the sea. Let her pause one breathing-space before she starts on her winding-way. But we will not follow her winding-way. Rather will we sit on the smooth green bank, under the shade of these cotton-wood trees, and dip our feet in the caressing waves. We will walk under these leafy arches, we will pierce this profound shade that is rest, not gloom, and stroll a half-mile up that lovely glen; surely we shall find there such a Happy Valley as Rasselas, Prince of Abyssinia, never saw or dreamed of. Faint and far the echoes of deadly warfare reach our ears, blending with the music of summer sounds that charm away their bitterness and bale. One moment die out, mad strife of might and right, and give for clashing, peace. Here are small interests, small acts, the homely life of a pristine race, — old, so old that no history, no tradition, reaches back to unfold the secret of its birth; yet forever young and crude and rude, impervious to civilization, but terribly open to deterioration and death. Tents of rough poles and rougher skins, blackened with smoke and hardened by wind and weather, form the straggling village. . They look not ill, harmonizing with the landscape, dotting the plain, or snuggling under the coverts of the trees, but they must be dingy and doleful within. You would say, however, that one need not go within. Domestic life seems to be carried on outdoors. Dusky figures reclining on the greensward, gay colors gorgeous in blanket and robe, grotesque shapes blazoned on tent-cloth and outlined on garments, — what wild life is this here in the heart of our nineteenth century? What paganism lurks in the outskirts of our Christianity? What religion stands side by side with the Bible, under the very shadow of the Cross, yet symbolizes itself with poles and embroidered cloth? For this it is that shall drive away the principalities and powers of the air and keep the village free from the wiles of imps. Occupations are intimated in the pile of slaughtered sheep and birds, and the great grizzly bear that lies outstretched and stiff, the centre of a gazing circle. The *cuisine* is simple and secure. Fishes, stuck lengthwise on a stick, hold grim conclave round a generous fire. The nursery discipline is direct and perfect. Witness the pappoose strapped to a board and set upright against a tent. O Civilization! which of your intricate systems furnishes any substitute for this summary and sensible process? It is a rural communism, a free, open, careless social life. Dogs, children, horses, all have a share in the common work and common weal. There is no fiery Bucephalus, no matchless Don Fulano, but weary nags that may have done their day's work handsomely, but stand now listless and limp, or crop lazily the rank herbage, or nestle head to head with dumb affection after the manner of horses. Mother and child, warrior and war-steed, all somewhat less regal than Cooper's genius limned them, stud the plain with their relaxed nomad life. One little fellow kneels breathless behind the burrow of a marmot, his tense bow set to twang death at the first pair of bright eyes that shall dare to peep out. Little Indian boy, the sheep and fatlings are enough. I truly hope you will miss your aim. I believe, indeed, that you are expending your patience in vain, for the very marmot you seek is perched here on a rock, and from the elevation of his hind legs, is laughing heartily at this safe distance to see what a fool he has made of you. And still above squaw and pappoose, above marmot and village and limpid lake, bends the blue sky, rise the solemn mountains, shines the summer sun, smiles the Eternal Father. It is difficult to remember as you gaze that it is but a picture. Once, twice, you may peer in from the outside, unacquainted, and not forget that you are in a great city, in her whirl of dust and din. But looking with fond persistence, suddenly the portals are swung open. You do not so much see,—you stand among the mountains. You feel the breath of their inspiration. The little clouds that sail so naïvely across the sun cast their umbrage at your feet. You watch the shadows chasing each other up the striated slopes, or stretching under the cliffs to melt and mingle with the shadowy waters, and cannot believe they are but "the consecration and the poet's dream." Your own head is bared to the balmy airs, and shines on you the fitful light that now dances along the steeps, toying with the sturdy verdure, now flickers over the fixedness, to crown with a glory this granite repose, now hovers above the shimmering mist of the cascade, or rests, a benediction, on the lake. The coolness of the valley, the silence of the mountains, the grand calm and peace fill your heart. A deep content, that has no speech nor language, settles into the inmost recesses of your life. An aspiration, divine, and yet most human, that soothes at once and stirs, shuts you in from the glare and glamour of earth-born strife, lifts you to the heights of heavenly fellowship, and while your feet press the clods of the valley, you stand face to face with the Immortals!

XI.

A SUGGESTION.

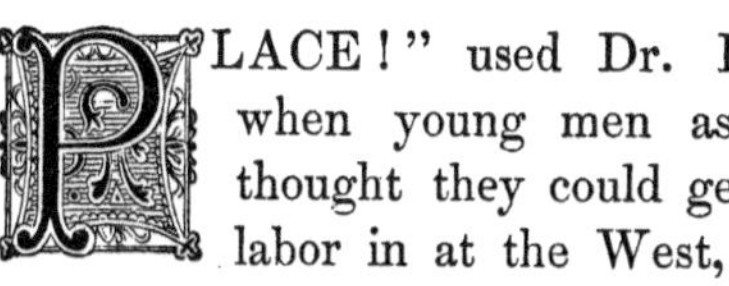

LACE!" used Dr. Beecher to say, when young men asked him if he thought they could get "a place" to labor in at the West, — "Place! the West is *all* 'place'; you can't go amiss of a 'place'; make one, anywhere!"

The West may be all place, but it is not the whole of place. Here in the East are many "places" unoccupied, and with no prospect of immediate occupation. At the same time there is a large floating population of ministers. Therefore one can but question whether our present mode of bringing demand and supply together is the best mode.

There is, for instance, a country parish in a country village, which for two or six or a dozen years, has been "running down." It has suffered from the presence of a feeble pastor, or from a heavy debt, or from the loss of its substantial members, or from the bitterness of some long-standing feud. From whatever cause, it is at ebb-tide, and suddenly finds itself without a pastor. It is not a particularly desirable field of labor, looked at abstractly; but there will be plenty of laborers to offer their services. Now there are many things to be considered. Perhaps in its palmiest days, the parish paid six hundred dollars a year to the clergyman. In its low estate it would hardly like to offer less; but if this sum is to be raised, it must be done either by having a man who will win over the disaffected pockets, or else by inducing the few who are conscientious and Christian to double and treble their own share, in order to make up for the deficiencies of the others. And these very men will probably be the ones who, from their superior intelligence and character, disburse the largest charities, and incur the largest expenses in other directions. The preaching of the Gospel, therefore, and the support of the minister, necessitate an indirect extortion. Those who do not guide their lives by strict religious principle, but by whim, prejudice, and likings, will not pay their share of the minister's salary, and those who do, have a heavy burden to carry, besides their own lawful part, which is no burden.

Now why should ministers adopt a course different from that which is adopted by doctors, lawyers, grocers, shoemakers? None of these ever go to the principal men in a village and bargain for a salary. They begin on their own responsibility. It is a run for luck. The lawyer and the doctor put up their "sign" and await briefs and patients. If they are skilful, practice comes, and sometimes if they are not. Without overpowering genius, they obtain a fair share of business, get a comfortable living, marry, are chosen selectmen and school committee, and to many other honorable offices, and live happily all their days. But nobody ever guarantees them anything. Why should not ministers follow their example? I know that there is a more settled routine for them, and therefore a fixed salary is more practicable. But though the routine is settled, the minister is not. Whether a young clergyman will be successful is just as problematical as whether a young doctor or a young lawyer will be. The only way they ascertain is by trying. Let the young minister adopt the same mode. He preaches awhile. He is liked by some, disliked by others, and causes but indifference in others. The former would like to "settle" him, but although they are in a majority, the minority is still large, and without the assistance of the latter his salary can hardly be wrenched out. Besides, if they should settle him, it is a question what the result will be. He may win over the hostile and the indifferent, or he may turn the latter into the former, and the former into active foes, and then in a few years there will be a quarrel, and a council, and heart-burnings, and mischief, and so the name of God is blasphemed among the Gentiles through them of the circumcision.

Now, when a young man, having been graduated from a theological seminary, hears of a "place," why could he not repair thither, and instead of terms, and bargains, and calls, and candidating, simply ascertain whether the situation is such that it is worth while for him to try to fill it? If he decides that it is, then why not apply to the authorities for permission to occupy the pulpit, and visit the people, and try his hand? Let no salary be so much as mentioned. The people do not yet know what he is, nor what he is worth, nor whether he is worth anything. By and by, if he is suited to the place, and the place is suited to him, the indifferent people will come to church, the indifferent hearts will be aroused, love will be awakened, justice will be revived, and the laborer having been found worthy of his hire, will be worthily paid. If some plan were devised by which every member of the parish should know every year exactly what his share of the parish expense ought to be, the minister would have a direct money criterion of his market value. So many as pay him, so many suffrages has he. So many as do not pay him, so many votes are cast against him. If, at the end of a year or two, he has not educated the people up to the point of paying him on the score of justice, or touched them to the depth of paying him on the score of love, he has so far failed. But, as it should be, the penalty of the failure rests on him, not on the few faithful and active members of his parish and church, who are in no wise guilty of his inefficiency. And if he is not able by his own powers and piety to lead the community, ought he to wish his weakness to be bolstered up by the kindness of friends. If he cannot stand alone, should he not go where he can, rather than remain leaning on this and that parochial staff?

The question may arise what is he to live on while he is passing through his probation, and receiving no pay? I reply, just what the doctor and the lawyer live on under the same circumstances. They obtain occasional fees for occasional services, and almost always there will be conscientious and just people in a parish, even when the minister enters it, who will, for the right's sake, be as prompt as client or patient. Meanwhile, let the young minister remember that he is the servant of Him who had not where to lay his head. Let him not shrink from faring, for love of Christ, no better than thousands fare for love of money. If worse comes to worst, let him try squatter sovereignty. A very little money and the labor of his own hands, will build him a shelter as good as the soldier's barracks, and this hut let him turn into a palace by the purity of his heart and the dignity of his life. Let him show the people indisputably, that he is in earnest, that he is not seeking salary, but souls; that his profession is not dilettanteism, but a life-work; that he counts fashion and style and luxury as nothing, if they stand in the way of his errand. Let them see that his mission is not of this world; that he is well content with locusts and wild honey, if so he can but feed them with the bread of life. Then the people will be divested of that feeling which many seem to have that the minister is despoiling them; that the money which goes to him is a gift, a gratuity. Of course, he must acquaint them in the beginning with his line of action, so that they, as well as he, may act intelligently. They must know that, however good or great he may be, his ultimate tarry with them depends upon his receiving an adequate support; but they must also know that his adequate support is only means to an end, and that he will show them that he is somewhat able to accomplish that end before they shall be expected to furnish means. The young man will perhaps have to endure hardships, but he is a soldier of the cross. Let him nourish the true missionary spirit, remembering that not pagans only bow down to wood and stone, but that Christendom, too, is but slightly Christianized. If he utterly fails to secure a generous support, let him console himself with the reflection that he is only bearing on his own shoulders the burden which would otherwise fall on the shoulders of a few men in his parish to whom it did not belong. And if repeated trials result in repeated failures, still the army and the navy, and the rich Western prairie lands lie open to him, and no man of ordinary sense, health, and prudence need starve in America.

XII.

A COURT CRIME.

IN superintending through stormy times the affairs of one's own country, one is sometimes obliged to let foreign misdemeanors pass unnoticed for a while; which explains the reason why I have suffered a crying sin in England's high places to go these four months all unrebuked.

An English correspondent of an American newspaper says: —

"I learn that there was quite a rebellion at Windsor Castle. The Princess vehemently opposed having a wet nurse, and the Prince took her side, and could not see why she should not be allowed to nurse the babe, as she strongly desired to do. But she was told that the court traditions could not be set aside; never was English prince or princess yet nursed by its own mother. So the healthy and virtuous Mrs. O'Somebody was sent for, and the Princess had a long cry. This is a true story, and somewhat more valuable than ordinary court gossip."

What a story is this to be true! True in a Christian country, and one that has been a Christian country for many a hundred years! If true, it is a blot on the British escutcheon, a shame to British civilization. Are there no women in England, that court traditions are allowed to lord it over instinct? Are there no men in England who have sentimentalized concerning maternity and infancy as the manner of men is, that they have not risen in a body to rescue from the hands of the Philistines this outraged young mother, — this poor little girl, who left father and mother, sisters and brothers, home and country, trusting herself to the promised love and tenderness of a strange and foreign nation? English women have been greatly shocked because slavery was permitted to exist under our flag of the free, and have counted and recounted, with ever-increasing horror, its dreadful deeds of darkness, — the slave-husband's inability to protect his wife, the slave-mother's agony for the baby torn from her arms. Their horror was just. It was honorable to their sensibility. It was the unerring testimony of Nature against a cruel wrong, — a crime against Humanity, — a sin against God. But if a child is to be torn wantonly and violently from its mother's bosom, does it make any difference whether it is done on the eastern or western side of an ocean? by the white, small hands of an English lady, or the sun-browned ones of an American slave-dealer? Is morality an affair of latitude or longitude, of pedigree or profession? If one must be bound, what matter whether the chain be of gold or iron? The difference between fetters and freedom is not a difference between one metal and another. If this story be true, the second lady in England is a slave. She is under the control of an arbitrary power, — a power which is not of God, and not of law, — and what is this but slavery? And this slavery concerns the most vital interests. This arbitrary, irresponsible power thrusts itself into the innermost sacred shrines of life, and is thus utterly offensive, utterly intolerable. This slavery England tolerates. Has a single protest been made against such usurpation? Has a single voice been lifted high enough to reach the ear of that court tyrant, Tradition, and to bring to his guilty heart one throb of misgiving? Yet if the English people really willed that their future Queen should not be deprived of the freedom which the meanest of her subjects enjoy, could they not accomplish it? Cannot the English voice penetrate the English court, and give to a father and mother control over their own child in matters where other control is contrary to the law of God?

That the Princess, in a strange land and a strange family, should have made so stubborn a fight as she did, is the best thing we have yet known of her, and all that we have known is good. I have heard that there are women who, of their own will and choice, not constrained by circumstances, decline to nurse their own babies; choose to give them over to hirelings! I do not know how that may be, but if such beings do exist, I should consider them as beings laboring under some moral deformity, — not to be blamed, perhaps, but very much to be pitied. Princess Alexandra is none of these. Evidently she holds "her uncrowned womanhood to be the royal thing." She is neither Queen nor Princess, but a happy wife and mother, counting nothing in court or kingdom so delightful as her own little pink, fat, shapeless, senseless darling; and having tasted the bitterness of death, which is spared to neither high nor low, she is denied the sweetness and solace which the humblest mother in the world may enjoy. It is an aggravated outrage! O poor little head waiting to be crowned! If the shadow of the bawble brings such sorrow, what will its pressure be?

Let us hope that the Prince of Wales, as he grows older, will grow stronger, — strong enough at least to rule in his own household when his rule is right, and in line with his wife's wishes. In the present case he seems amiable, but not commanding; less authoritative than might be reasonably looked for in a prince, and demanded in a husband and father. We are told that he is going to give a blow to tradition that will shake the whole island, by substituting the frock-coat for the dress-coat, — or the dress-coat for the frock, I cannot speak with certainty. But if the Prince of Wales is strong enough to make the solid earth tremble under his feet by causing a change of costume, surely he is strong enough to do it by causing a change of custom. If he can put down a fashion that overspreads his empire, he can certainly put down one that stalks only through Windsor Castle. If he can raise a great commotion for so small a matter as the shape of a garment, he can raise a small commotion for so great a matter as a soul's weal and a soul's happiness. We may hope too, that as the Princess grows older, and becomes more wonted to her position and mistress of the situation, she will take matters into her own hand, as she certainly gives promise of developing an ability to do, and cease to implore, where she has a right to command.

Meanwhile, where is Queen Victoria with her world-renowned home-virtues, that she should not have a queenly word to say in an affair so purely and vitally domestic as this? She whose pride and glory it has been to bring up her children herself, — could she not interpose in behalf of nature against an arbitrary, inexcusable, traditional whim?

One cannot help regretting that the pretty Princess did not cry longer. I suppose she did the best she could, and she showed admirable spirit, and a truly womanly and lovely character in doing what she did. Evidently she protested vehemently, entirely regardless of past and future, of fashion or etiquette, and indeed of everything but the one intense desire to nurse her own baby, like the good, honest girl she is. But there is never any use in crying for anything, unless you cry till you get it. To stop short of the object is worse than not to begin. And more than this, if you do stop, you are sure to stop at the very point where the opposition was beginning to give way. I have no doubt that, if Alexandra *could* have held out ten minutes longer, the healthy and virtuous Mrs. O'Somebody would have been directed to pack up her health and her virtue and go home, and the little lord would have been restored to his rightful lady; whereas by "behaving herself" prematurely, she is daily subjected to the unspeakable indignity of seeing her own baby at another woman's breast.

It is a great gratification to know that the little fellow cried vociferously through the whole ceremony of his christening. Virtuous wet-nurse, grandmother Queen, and court tradition were powerless to restrain or modify his shrieks. I have no doubt it was because his milk disagreed with him,—naturally enough since nature had not intended it for him, but made it to the order of another baby. I sincerely hope that he will continue to avenge his dear mamma, and disgrace the court by squalling at the top of his lungs on every public occasion, till he is twenty-one years old, and ceases in the eyes of the law to be an infant. Then, possibly, court tradition may no longer impiously set itself up against God's own beautiful ordinances, and unless it can dispense with the institution of babies altogether, may not deprive that institution of its most delightful features. Then it is to be hoped "the blessings happy peasants have" may belong also to crowned and uncrowned queens

XIII.

MOB PATRIOTISM.

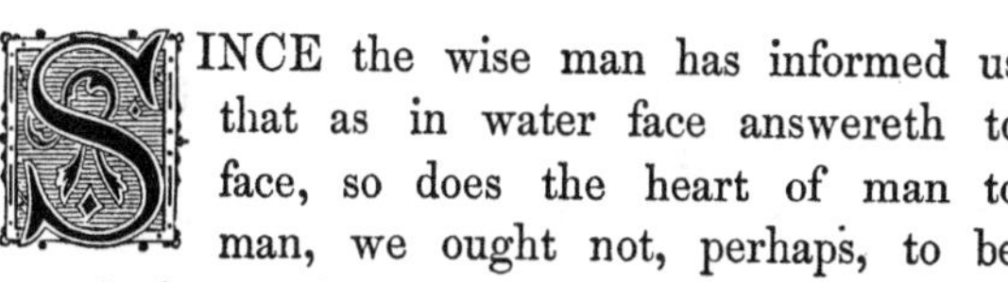

SINCE the wise man has informed us that as in water face answereth to face, so does the heart of man to man, we ought not, perhaps, to be surprised at seeing in our borders occasional outbursts of the same lawlessness as that which excites our reprobation in the South. Nevertheless we cannot look upon them without mortification. They tend to show that the anti-slavery sentiment of the North, and the pro-slavery sentiment of the South, are matters of soil, climate, and locality, not of intelligent, enlightened Christian principle. Mobs at the South attack a man for attachment to the Union. Mobs at the North attack him for indifference to the Union. The former, owing to their hotter blood, are, perhaps, more violent and demonstrative than the latter; but the two stand otherwise on the same footing. Both are equally brutal, cowardly, and indefensible. Nay, the Southern mob is more excusable than its Northern counterpart. They are in constant danger. They in many, perhaps in most cases, no doubt honestly believe that their victims have been tampering with destructive implements; that the loyalty of the slaves and the lives of the masters are at stake, and can be saved only by the severest treatment of those whom they believe guilty, — and it is sheer self-defence in them to ward off even the appearance of danger. If they go further than they need, if they sometimes see trouble where none exists, if they confound trivial with serious things, and by excessive caution and rigor accelerate and aggravate the evil which they dread, the greatness and imminence of the calamity is their excuse; but we do not believe that one man in ten at the North apprehends any personal, or municipal, or national danger from the man whose house or stall he surrounds, and whom he forces to raise a flag, or to disclaim or retract words which he had previously spoken. The obnoxious persons are in a hopeless minority, their reputation not brilliant, nor wide-spread, and their influence small. The proceedings against them are all that makes their names known beyond their own immediate circle. Moreover, if danger is apprehended, of what use are the means taken to prevent it? If a man is a traitor at heart, is he any less a traitor because a motley crowd forces him to raise the "Red, White, and Blue?". If he is concocting, aiding, or abetting rebellion, can he not go on just as blithely under the Stars and Stripes as under the Palmetto-tree? If a man does anything contrary to law, let the law be brought to bear upon him in full force. If he is not doing anything contrary to law, he should be left unmolested. If his sentiments are unworthy of a patriot while his words and deeds are not amenable to the law, you can refuse to buy his meat, or shoes, or broadcloth, or pills, or sermons, or grain. You can avoid social intercourse with him, and thus express your disapprobation, with sufficient force and distinctness for all practical purposes. But every time a mob collects and forces a man by threats to make a speech, or raise a flag, or do anything which of his own free will he would not do, the cause of Liberty and Republicanism is degraded. Every citizen who lends himself to such uses helps to lower his State to the level of the rebellious States, and sets Massachusetts side by side with South Carolina, or as much lower than South Carolina as the institutions of Massachusetts are higher. Cotton-mob men can hardly help being ignorant and brutal. Born in hovels, bred on whiskey, they naturally grow up into lewd fellows of the baser sort; but Massachusetts men have had opportunities enough to be intelligent and well-mannered, and if they are not, it is their own fault. Their moral education ought also to show them that there is an essential cowardice in assembling twenty, fifty, or a thousand men, against one. Their numbers give them immunity from danger, so that they run no risk, while making him run all risks. They are for the time voluntary slaveholders, and as tyrannical as it is possible for a slaveholder to be. They judge by hearsay, and in their riotous organization often do gross injustice, even on their own rude principle; insulting men who are just as patriotic as themselves. Patriotic! It is difficult to believe that the feeling which raises mobs is a whit more truly patriotic than the feeling which mobs are raised to suppress. Love of country which displays itself in violating the laws of country, is a very questionable sentiment. Freedom of speech and of opinion is the foundation-stone of the Republic. Anything which would destroy that, runs counter to the whole current of our institutions, and, in essence, is treason in the first degree

XIV.

ELLEN.

BEHIND yonder close-drawn curtain I know a still form lies.

For warmth, coldness, — for song, silence, — for mirth, mourning, — for life, death.

War has reaped his red harvests on many a battle-field. Sorrow has stalked through the land, scattering broadcast his seeds of woe. But no breadth of grief diminishes its depth. A desolated hearth is just as desolate as if desolated hearths were not shivering all around it.

There are tears for heroes fallen, for stately homes laid waste ; but none the less there shall be tears for a lowly life departed, a lamp gone out in a cottage chamber.

Irish Ellen. Good and faithful soul, with the warm, rich, island blood leaping in every pulse. Brown hair as deep, as glossy, and abundant as ever lay parted over royal brows, — brown eyes full of the soft light of love and laughter, — the sunshine nestles there no more. They have gone down to darkness and the grave.

I hear a little cooing voice that cannot yet even speak the mother's name, but only purrs out a blind, ignorant joy. I hear the wavering, unsteady tread of little feet that have but just learned their uses, and go stumbling and failing with keen delight in a new-found power. But I hear no more the old sound, — the mother's embracing voice that wrapped around the baby-gurgling with its caressing tones. Always I heard that sound responsive to the baby-voice, — never failing, never tired, never less full of fondness and freshness than at the first, — a dear duet, sweet as the song of the new creation when the morning stars sang together; joyful as that old acclaim when all the sons of God shouted for joy.

O, the unfathomable depth of the mother-heart that lies now all unheeding! The unutterable love that no pain could terrify, no care, no work, nor watching tire! War and poverty and taxation were nothing. Weariness, impatience, ambition found no entrance there. Love, —pure, clear, full, perfect content in a baby-life, made the evening and the morning the first and the eternal day. Even old Ireland beckoned in vain. All the music of the spheres was drowned in that little cooing voice. All the motion of the universe centred in those little stumbling feet.

And the baby will forget his mother. Now his

little heart feebly recalls her. Now and then a faint wail moans over his lips for the lips, the voice, the bosom that he vaguely misses. Now his blind hands fumble at the door, groping for the mother that lies within, — mother no more, — a statue, a stone, a death. Sad is the dim sorrow of that tiny life, but saddest of all the certainty that it will so quickly pass away. To-morrow and to-morrow it will be less. In a week there will be no trace. All that boundless love, that inexhaustible treasure-trove of tenderness, will be as if it had never been. Is it not a waste? He will grow up and never know it. No memory will recall, no inspiration will reveal to him that ocean of love in which his young life was lapped and lulled to dreamless ecstacy. Was it not a waste? O, Ellen, on whatever far-off world you walk in white, in whatever garments of praise your soul has robed herself, do you not miss and mourn this little cooing voice, these little stumbling feet? Even in the heaven of heavens can you find any joy that can quite atone for this? O, faithless heart! what words are these? Eye hath not seen, nor ear heard, neither have entered into the heart of man, the things which God hath prepared. He hath made man, male and female in his own image. Fatherhood, motherhood, meet in God. He will satisfy the wants which he has created.

It was but a homely life that Ellen led, and

homely virtues those with which she adorned it. A short and happy life seamed with sorrows, — a life spent in the kitchen, at the wash-tub and the ironing-table, — such a life has little to commend it to the world's regard. Yet many and many a man lives in the full blaze and bray of renown, and his passing away will be commemorated with the varied pomp of requiem, and slow-moving procession, and stately mausoleum, who will deserve less of his country than this young Irish exile. A humble work well done shall find a better, though not a surer, guerdon than the indulgence of an intellectual, æsthetic, or sensual selfishness, calling itself by whatever name it choose. Ellen stood at the wash-tub and the ironing-table, and neither crease nor stain marred the purity of the white folds that passed under her hands. She ordered the table, and every spoon knew its place. She went through the chambers, and no fairy's wand ever did completer work than mop and broom in those stout red arms of hers. Speck and fleck fled before her, giving up the battle half-fought from sheer faint-heartedness. And she wrought cheerily. Her work was a song. Nothing was too much for her. The day was never too long nor the task too hard. She never gave eye-service. She did everything, and then she polished it, — making a poem of drudgery. Dishonesty or falsehood never came near her. I think there were sharp possibilities in those soft brown eyes, but I never struck fire from them, nor ever saw the lightnings flash. Always beneficent herself, inexhaustible in kindnesses and all good deeds, she overflowed with gratitude. A little bunch of white Innocence, plucked for her dead-born baby about to be borne to his burial, commanded her perpetual vassalage. The smallest token of remembrance, slender services of the merest simple consideration, she repaid with such full measure of thanks, and such signal strength of thew and nerve, deeming no return sufficient, as put to shame our cold acknowledgments.

O sovereign mystery of death! What is this change that comes so swift, yet so slow, — so still, yet with such sudden shock? Yesterday, a warm, living, loving person; to-day a Thing, — a Terror. Yesterday, she; to-day, it. Yesterday, here, living among the old faces, the old places; to-day, no farthest star so remote.

And what *is* this that lies here pallid and unbeautiful? What is that which is gone and left it so? Whence came the life that flushed and filled this temple? Whither has it fled and left a tomb? Where in all the infinite universe, where among the ineffable glories of the visible or invisible heavens, where beyond all that eye hath seen or can see, dwells the flitted soul? Has the spark glowed into a flame? Is the little rush-light of earthly love lost?— no, that cannot be! God grant that can never be! but overflooded with the celestial radiance? What and whence and whither?

Vainly we question. There is no reply.

She has solved the problem. This Ellen, late so familiar to us; so humble, so deferent, so little wise, so ministrative to our comforts, so subordinate to our wants, — she has rent the veil. She has passed beyond our sight into the Unknown Land. She, who used to receive wonderingly our shreds of information, might now, if we could gather at her feet, tell us the strange story which no man knows. Statesmen, philosophers, sages, — all might hang on her lips, and learn the awful secret.

Ignorance, Doubt, Fear, hear what the Lord Jesus Christ saith: I am the resurrection and the life: he that believeth in me, though he were dead, yet shall he live.

XV.

A WORD TO THE INCONSIDERATE.

THERE is such a disease — especially in New England — as consumption. It is greatly dreaded because it is supposed to be incurable. It is not a positive thing that rushes at its victim and strikes him down in a day. It is a lurking, subtle foe, — flattering, deceiving, terrifying. The busy wife and mother has been weak and listless, and unable to "turn off work" for the last year or two; her step has grown manifestly feebler, and her cheek paler than it used to be; her husband has taken her to the seaside, and the Springs, and the mountains, and has consulted all the famous doctors, and even looks with interest at the column where patent medicines are advertised; notwithstanding, she occasionally loses her voice, and speaks in a whisper, perhaps for months together, — begins to lie in bed late in the morning, and to tremble before the raw northeast winds. It is very sad, and the hearts of those who love her are filled with foreboding. But do not therefore kill her with kindness. Oranges and grapes, cooling fruits and simple delicacies, to a limited extent, may be grateful to her; but a woman not in robust health is not a Wantley dragon, that can devour by the bushel cakes, jelly, pastry, highly-seasoned meats, and all manner of pickled and potted things. Reason would seem to teach that there cannot be much comfort in seeing one's self surrounded with dainties which one cannot touch. A bunch of flowers, or a single flower, or a curious moss, or a pretty engraving, or a pencil sketch, would be vastly better, — anything that takes the invalid out of herself, — that directs her attention to something else, which is one of the roads to recovery. But the sight of food that one cannot eat, forces attention to the fact that one cannot eat, and so the carefully prepared dish is not only useless, but discouraging, — to all except the Irish girl in the kitchen, who fares sumptuously as long as it lasts.

Nor is it well to question the invalid too often respecting her health. If she were suffering from an acute and violent disease, whose aspects have new significance every hour, and whose culmination is momently expected, inquiry would be excusable. But she is not. She is in precisely the same condition one day as another, so far as can be seen. If there is change, it is imperceptible. She and her friends are living, and waiting, and hoping, and trying. Did you ever think how much difficulty she finds in answering your inquiry? "Pretty well, thank you," is out of the question, because she is not pretty well. She cannot file a bill of particulars every day, and what resource has she? It is much better to show sympathy in some other way. Be patiently receptive, but not officiously inquisitive of facts. When there is anything of moment you will learn it in one way or another. Ask the doctor, and if he snubs you, reflect that it was best you should be snubbed, and rejoice that you asked one who had a right to do it, and not your friend, who would have been restrained by gratitude.

Especially is it not well to ask the invalid's husband, confidentially, "What *do* you think of her?" adding, by way of consolation, "It does not seem to me she *can* live." In the first place, human nature is the most uncertain thing in the world. A man may dispense with lungs entirely. At least there is a man yet living and in firm health, whose doctors told him twenty years ago that his lungs were gone. A woman who had consumption to the degree of losing her voice for years, and taking leave of her friends, has just set up a boarding-house. People never know what they can live through till they have tried it. Our Creator did not make us stingily. He left a broad margin. We can give up a good many outposts before the citadel must surrender; and the fight is so prolonged, that often by the time it is over, we should have had to yield in the natural course of things.

And suppose your friend cannot live, what is gained by such a remark? Are her chances for life increased? Is she, or are her friends, prepared to meet death with fortitude? Hope is the great opponent of disease; when a man's spirits give way, his strength follows. To dishearten him is to kill him. "He that loses money," says the old Spanish proverb, "loses much; he that loses friends loses more; he that loses his spirits loses all." The sons of the prophets at Jericho heard that Elijah was to be taken up by a whirlwind to heaven, and they came out in great excitement to meet Elisha. "Knowest thou that the Lord will take away thy master from thy head to-day?" "Yea, I know it," answers Elisha, heart-sick; "hold ye your peace." There are things that will not bear to be talked about. Your friend and his sick wife, in the solitude of their own room, before the throne of the Most High, will adjust themselves as best they may, to the conditions of their life. They may even come to speak cheerfully of a separation which they assiduously strive to prevent. They will not weakly shut their eyes to the possible future, while they labor and pray to shape it after their desire. But where each other's touch only soothes and strengthens, a stranger's is torture. What does he think of her? He does not know and if he does, he cannot tell. There is a terrible definiteness in words. He sees the Possibility that stands black and frowning in his path, but shall he limn it for another's gaze? The heart knoweth its own bitterness, and strangers should not intermeddle. He is girding up his loins in the name of the Lord to wade threugh his Slough of Despond. Do not insist upon his measuring it, and giving you its length, breadth, and cubic contents. What you can discuss calmly, is to him fraught with the issues of life. You are walking carefully, sympathetically, it may be, but coolly, over their hearts.

It is not necessary to tell a lie; but also it is not necessary to speak the truth. It only needs to be cheerful. Do not look pitying. Talk about common things in a common way, — the common things that belong to this life and those that touch on all life. Walk softly, and act Christianly in your own sphere, but do not project yourself into your friend's innermost circle where He alone should tread whose form is like the Son of God.

And if your neighbor has a baby who sickens through these wintry days, whose little life quivers on its mother's love, do not jocosely inform the mother, just as you are stepping into the sleigh for a drive, that you expected every day last month to see its death in the papers. If the baby were a French turnip with which your neighbor was trying an experiment, such a mode of speech might be tolerable. Babies, I know, are consumers and not producers, and there are thousands of them all pretty much alike. It may very well be that society does not miss the few who cannot weather the storm; but whatever may be true of babies in general, it is unquestionable that every particular infant lies very near to its mother's heart, and should not be lightly spoken of.

Sometimes babies die. The little lambent light that played so softly and sweetly around the home hearth goes out, and there is a horror of great darkness. Then you will come in your pity and offer consolation. You will begin to explain the mysteries of Providence, and "justify the ways of God to man." But Job did not open his mouth and curse his day till his friends came to comfort him. Lacon says it is often easier to bear our misfortunes than the comments of our friends upon them. Some people like to talk and be talked to in their sorrow. Others do not. They prefer to commune with their own hearts and be still. Go to the former and talk. It will relieve them. But with the latter, hold ye your peace. And try and have a little discernment to find out which is which.

Job had a great deal of trouble. From being the greatest Sheikh in the whole East, the happy father of a goodly family, he was suddenly reduced to poverty and desolation. The Sabeans fell upon his five hundred yoke of oxen and five hundred she-asses; the fire of God smote his seven thousand sheep; the Chaldeans swept off his three thousand camels; a tornado rushed from the wilderness and buried his children under the ruins of their house; and a frightful disease laid hold upon his body; yet through it all Job retained his integrity; and when his wife, with weaker faith, despairingly bade him curse God and die, his meekness and patience quietly answered, "Shall we receive good at the hand of God, and shall we not receive evil?"

But Job had not seen the worst. He was to prove Lacon's statement. Eliphaz the Temanite, and Bildad the Shuhite, and Zophar the Naamathite made an appointment together to come and mourn with him and to comfort him. For seven days and nights none spake a word unto him; for they saw that his grief was very great. It is a pity that they could not have continued so considerate a course; but when Job had once lifted the flood-gate, the love of talking proved too strong for them. None of them spoke well. It would have been better for their reputation if they had not spoken at all; but as Eliphaz, disregarding his better judgment, says apologetically in the beginning, "Who can withhold himself from speaking?" He affirms that Job had always been very helpful to other people when they were in trouble, yet as soon as the trouble came upon him he fainted; but that God would surely deliver him; for who ever perished being innocent? It is rather commonplace, but well-meant and cheery, which is more than can be said of Bildad's remarks. Bildad seems to have been one of those harsh, disagreeable Christians, who pride themselves on having no nonsense about them; who go straight to the mark, regardless of other's feelings; who have no mercy on right-hand fallings-off, or left-hand deflections; who make no allowance for friction in their mechanics, or lack of simple apprehension in their logic. Eliphaz began quietly, "If we assay to commune with thee, wilt thou be grieved?" But Bildad, of coarser grain, walks stoutly into the middle of things, and rudely asks, "How long shall the words of thy mouth be like a strong wind?" Eliphaz reasons, "Job is upright, therefore he will be happy." Bildad, less polite, less catholic, and not more logical, says, "Job is miserable, therefore he must be bad." "Where did you ever know a righteous man cut off?" says Eliphaz. "If thou wert pure and upright, God would make the habitation of thy righteousness prosperous," is Bildad's astute reasoning; but Job still replies meekly, "I know it is so of a truth, but how *should* a man be just with God?" Then Zophar takes up the word, but, instead of copying the polite Eliphaz, he is even more rude than Bildad. "Should a man full of talk be justified? Should their lies make men hold their peace? Know, that God exacteth of thee less than thine iniquity deserveth," which may have been true, but did not belong to Zophar to say. Job's anger is kindled at length. "No doubt," he says, with a fine sarcasm, "but ye are the people, and wisdom shall die with you. But I have understanding as well as you; I am not inferior to you. What ye know, the same do I know also. Ye are forgers of lies, ye are all physicians of no value. O that ye would altogether hold your peace! and it should be your wisdom." Never Job spoke a truer word. The whole manner in which he turns upon them, flinging back their reproaches, probing to the quick the self-complacency which they veil under a flimsy pretence of defending God, avowing a faith in God and a consciousness of sin infinitely stronger than they can have any conception of, yet at the same time meeting their charge of hypocrisy with a proud assertion of his integrity, is admirable. It is a spirited and sensible reply, and an effectual. Bildad and Zophar utter no more officious consolation and self-satisfied reproaches. In fact, they are put on the defensive by Job's dexterous *sortie*, and have enough to do without attacking him. Eliphaz, indeed, who seems to have been a rather weak man and inclined to go with the majority, is somewhat alarmed at finding how much more animated and severe the others are than himself, and tries to make up for it by increased severity, not able to see that he is taking up a weapon which they have thrown down; but Job turns away in disgust. "I have heard many such things before. Miserable comforters are ye all. I also could speak as ye do; if your soul were in my soul's stead, *I* could heap up words against *you*, and shake my head at you. But *I* would strengthen you with my mouth, and the moving of my lips should assuage your grief."

How exquisitely do we see portrayed in this little drama the misery which well-meaning, but shallow friends can impose on a superior soul. Looking only at externals, judging only from their own point of view, they attempt to assuage a grief of which they know nothing. Their scant line cannot fathom its depth, their narrow vision cannot embrace its breadth, their coarse touch has no conception of its quality; they only see that sorrow is there, and feeling it their duty to comfort, and feeling also very likely a sincere desire to comfort, they begin to do something which they call comforting, but which to their victim is anything but comfortable. His sensitive nature is tortured, his motives misunderstood, his acts misconstrued, till his earnest prayer is, "Save me from my friends." They bring forward their threadbare shreds of philosophy, when all philosophy lies at his feet. They proffer homœopathic doses of religion when he keeps his hold on life only by placing his lips close to the life-springs of salvation. Yet they mean well and must not be repulsed, unless, like Job's friends, they impose upon good-nature, and condemn where they are called upon to condole.

But when God speaks, the scene changes. Pettinesses vanish. That self-justification which is sometimes a duty towards man, is not required towards God. He never makes mistakes. "Gird up now thy loins like a man," says the divine voice, and the earthly soul, bowed down with a sudden vision of sin makes lowly answer, "I abhor myself and repent in dust and ashes."

XVI.

DRUNKENNESS AND DRINKING.

WHATEVER may be our views regarding the effects of alcohol upon the system, the propriety of furnishing wine at evening parties, the necessity of total abstinence, the importance of signing the pledge, we are all agreed in thinking that a drunken military commander is the wrong man in the wrong place. If our sons are about to enter the army, we desire them to join a regiment whose colonel is known to be a temperate man. If he has habits of dissipation, we lose all confidence in his ability. We feel that our children will have to encounter other than the ordinary dangers of war, — that their lives may be not sacrificed but wasted. We have no faith that a drunken general will make a skilful disposition of his forces either for attack or defence. Drunkenness, we know, is not favorable to clearness of vision, fineness of observation, soundness of judgment, or rapidity of mental action, and all these are eminently needed on a field of battle, or on one which may become such, without, or in spite of, these qualities. But the bane of our army, and of our army material, seems to have been, and I fear I may say, to be, drunkenness. A regiment leaves for Washington, fully armed and equipped, and its colonel is known as a drunkard, — not, indeed, a rum and gutter drunkard, but a wine and club-room one, which, however superior that may be socially, is, for fighting purposes, the same thing. If a man is drunk, it matters little whether he is drunk at three cents a glass, or eight dollars a bottle, — whether he is lifted into his carriage by his servants, or dragged to the watch-house by a police officer. We hear of a commander of a gunboat, an excellent officer, highly recommended, who has, indeed, but one fault, — drunkenness; but that is the fruitful source of disgrace and disaster. A lieutenant has been educated in military schools, has watched the evolutions of foreign armies, is a fine, noble, patriotic, whole-souled fellow, but he cannot be relied on, he cannot be placed in the situation which wants just such a man as he, because he will occasionally be drunk. The streets of Washington, and the good name of the country, have been disgraced by drunken soldiers. Officers toss off champagne at the hotels, and privates guzzle rum in the saloons. Battles are lost, fortifications surrendered, and brave men slain.

That rum is not considered the natural ally of success, is indicated by the orders to close the dram-shops to which our army had access. Report states that there has since been a great improvement in this respect.

New England is not under martial law. Massachusetts is not under martial law. Shall we then be drunk or sober? It is for ourselves to answer.

We demand, and we have a right to demand, that our army shall be sober. We have a right to demand that they, to whom the defence of the country is intrusted, shall not put themselves in a condition which, for a time, impairs, if it does not destroy their faculties. They may not have much skill, or strength, or courage, but all that they have belongs to the cause under whose banner they have voluntarily ranged themselves; and when they weaken their power, they rob their country. But, on the other hand, they have the same right to demand that we shall be sober. The army does not monopolize the protection of the country. It is not one man's duty to enlist to serve his country, and another man's privilege to stop at home and serve himself. The present responsibility of every American citizen is one and the same. The first earthly work of every American citizen is one and the same, — to see that the Republic receive no harm. You may do it by shouldering a musket and shooting the rebels. A second may do it by making a coat that is to warm you; a third, by managing the bank that is to pay you; a fourth, by writing the paper that is to support you; a fifth, by caring for the family that you have left. But all should work to the same end. All have the same account to render.

If, then, it is the duty of the soldier on the battle-field, for country's sake, to be sober, it is just as much, and just the same, the duty of the farmer in the corn-field, the merchant in the counting-room, the guest at the dinner-table. It amounts to nothing to say that the soldier's post is one of more importance and greater responsibility. God alone knows the extent of responsibility. Every man is responsible for the whole of himself, — no less, no more. Apparent influence is often an entirely different thing from real influence. What seems to be a little, isolated, wrong deed, may have an endless train of stupendous, evil results. What seems to be an insignificant virtue may bear fruit of splendid benefit. It may seem that the general commanding has more influence than he who stays at home, but God alone knows whether he has or not. The keeper at home, by his words or his life, may be influencing a little boy who, under his influence, shall grow up into a greater man than our greatest general. It is not for any one to say to any other, "Your responsibility is great, and you must be virtuous and vigilant. My responsibility is small, and I may be lax and self-indulgent."

All men who are not traitors, or cowardly, ignorantly, and disgracefully indifferent, are either in the army or in the Home Guard, and all are alike under bonds to be sober, to be vigilant, to be brave, to be patriotic.

But while the soldier on the Potomac is under no stronger bonds to be temperate than the citizen in Boston, he is under far stronger temptation to be intemperate. Away from home, deprived of female society, leading an adventurous and roving life, exposed to burning sun and drenching rain, his former habits both of amusement and occupation broken up, hard labor alternating with utter idleness, with but a small variety of food and a slender stock of reading matter, the temptation to one whose appetite for strong drink has ever been awakened, must be almost overpowering. It is not surprising that those who have drank a little at home should drink to excess in the camp. It is not incredible that those who were abstinent at home should be intemperate in the camp. If sore temptation is ever any excuse for any sin, surely the soldiers may plead it for their drunkenness. To keep them in the right path, they need to be surrounded by every inducement, and one of the strongest would be the assurance that the soldiers at home are scrupulously keeping themselves pure from this thing.

Is it not, therefore, the duty of every man and woman who desires that the soldier should be sober, to abstain himself and herself from every form of intoxicating liquor? Is it not eminently selfish and unjust to forbid the wet, tired, footsore soldier a glass of whiskey, and at the same time to sip Roman punch at our own sideboards? If we, with all the luxuries of home, and all the stimulants of society, cannot deny ourselves the accustomed bottle of port or sherry after dinner, with what face can we ask a man who has been drilling five hours, and who has no home to go to but his tent, to deny himself the warm and cheering potency of a glass of grog? I am saying nothing now of the moral right or wrong of abstinence, in the nature of things. I speak not of intrinsic but of relative right; not of duty to God, but duty to country. I appeal to patriotism everywhere to strengthen weak hands, and confirm feeble knees; to show to the soldier that we do not require of him a virtue which we refuse to practise ourselves. It is impertinent to say that, though we drink wine, we do not "get drunk." For military authorities, who ought to know what most conduces to men's efficiency, make no such distinction. It is of the utmost importance that men be in the best condition, and general orders do not say that men may get whiskey, but must not get drunk. They shut up the dram-shops. While the emergency lasts, let us do the same. When the war is over, there will be plenty of time to discuss the innocence and the benefit of moderate drinking; but while our brothers are fighting forty-eight hours on a mouthful of vinegar, let us not be taking advantage of a mooted point to indulge our luxurious tastes. While our men are splitting heads, let us not be splitting hairs. The wide sweep that martial law makes in Virginia, let moral law make in Massachusetts.

A few months ago a party of people, dressed in a good deal of not very brief authority, went down to one of those little villages in which that which is spoken in the ear, — and sometimes a good deal more, — is proclaimed upon the housetops. It was, perhaps, the first time within the memory of the oldest inhabitant, that people of so great distinction had set foot in that quiet village, and of course all the available small boys, and some of the large ones, trotted down to the railroad station to catch such a glimpse of majesty as might be afforded between car and carriage; and if sundry vagrant lads did hang upon the outskirts of the party through the day, is it a thing entirely unheard of in the annals of boys? "And," said one of them, retailing his adventures to a knot of greedy-eared listeners, "when dinner-time come, they sot down on the grass, and had their champagne and their goodies, and by golly! wan't it tall?" So the champagne sparkled from one end of the village to the other.

Now in that village there are mothers whose

sons, — there are wives whose husbands, — there are children whose fathers, — have gone out to breast bayonet and bullet, and who have left at home hearts that ache sore at parting, sorer still because the dear faces may be seen no more, but sorest of all through fear of the work that vice and crime may do on the characters of their loved ones. They give them up cheerfully to death at their country's call, but they have no fortitude to face their degradation. Their daily and constant prayer is, not so much that they may come out of battle unharmed, as that they may come out of the furnace of temptation with no smell of fire upon their garments. They are a simple folk. They know little of the usages of fashionable society, but they know their hearts sink within them when they hear that the habits into which they most dread that their friends shall fall, the habits in which they read the utter extinction of all their hopes and all their joy, receive the sanction of learning, genius and influence. They counsel with an ill-repressed agony of anxiety, and affectionate and generous, yet wayward and thoughtless boys, point to the example of the first men in the State, — and what can the poor mothers say?

Not as a religionist or a reformer, but in the name of loyalty and patriotism, in the name of pity and compassion for the erring, in the name of succor for the weak, and comfort for the sorrowful, in the name of the mothers who have given up their sons, in the name of the young men whose future will be shaped in the encampment, in the name of Him whose loving-kindness forbade to offend the least of His little ones, I appeal to you who sit in high places, — to all whom wealth, or birth, or learning, or genius, has placed in commanding positions, — to all who love your country, and would count it joy to press upon your brows the crown of sacrifice, — to see to it that no liberty of yours prove a stumbling-block to your weak brother for whom Christ died!

XVII.

LANGUAGE.

ONE of the most satisfactory books to the student and lover of his own language is Max Müller's "Lectures on the Science of Language." It takes us where we are, and carries us back to the creation of the world, and that is as far as any reasonable person cares to go. Many books that treat of language are fragmentary. They tell twenty interesting things, but they do not give a thread to string them on, or if they do, they leave it loose at one end. The authors seem to be studying their subject, and the reader studies with them. They are honest and enthusiastic. They give valuable hints, and curious information; but they do not command. One does not feel that they are masters of the situation. They are novices, neophytes, just like himself, — a little farther advanced, but by no means admitted to full priestly orders. This, however, is no neophyte. He takes up the subject like a master. He handles it with confidence, grace, and ability. He is so much at his ease that he has the air of knowing all about it, even when he tells you frankly that he does not know. His enthusiasm is no surface attachment, but based on intimate knowledge of character, and he pursues his subject with a lover's persistency. He has traced language through all its windings and turnings, up, up, up, to where it springs, a tiny fountain, from the unfathomed, mysterious depths of the human soul. And because he knows the way, we follow his lead implicitly and delightedly through devious paths, thridding jungles, scaling mountains, fording rivers, and, it must be confessed, sometimes leaping abysms, because there is nothing for it but to leap or lose the trail. But it is a royal journey, — a triumphal march. New prospects stretch continually before you, — grand and solemn, dainty and picturesque, stately pageants of that dim old world whose echoes tremble, whose shadows glide along the valleys of the new; and all the while, through the opening vistas, under the arching trees, behind the leafy screens, you catch glimpses of the fountain Arethusa which you pursue, and you know that for her there is no escape. No friendly Earth, divinely touched, shall open her bosom to the panting fugitive. You shall snatch her well-guarded secret where first she leaps from hidden caverns fast by the oracles of God.

There are people who regard the subject as a

dry one, but it is of all subjects the one so rich, and juicy, and fruitful, that no awkwardness of treatment can entirely deprive it of its charm. The merest tyro may set up to write a book about it, and all his ignorance and pretension cannot quite obscure the pure gold that glows in his clownish hand. The sweet soul of Cinderella shines through all the soot and ashes of her servitude, and by her gleam the goddess stands confessed. How much more then shall she vindicate her divine descent when she sits in state, apparelled as becomes a daughter of the gods!

The science of language is dry, only because we know so little about it. Just as far as we dissipate the fogs of ignorance, the landscape lies before us, beautiful as the vale of Tempe. We bandy words, tossing them hither and thither, carelessly. They are simply our current coin. They help us to traffic in bread and cheese, love and learning, pity and hatred, devotion and revenge; but they are no more to us than stones. "Only words," we say, and give them no further thought. Only words! The stone is a casket! To him who knows the hidden spring, new worlds reveal themselves. The cold, dead word, holds in its heart the hopes and histories of generations. It is sweet with the breath of spices, and the songs of nightingales. It dazzles with the glare of eternal snow. It thrills with the love of Arab girls. It shudders with the stain of bloody rites. The echoes of martyr-prayers linger still among its cadences, and its secret depths flash out once more the gleam of pirates' steel. Following the certain token of this star in the East, we wander back along the way our fathers trod, — back over the ocean, to that pale, that white-faced shore, that once spurned the fathers to its own dismay, and later spurned their sons with a bitterness that will not soon be forgotten, — back over the German Ocean that our fair-haired ancestors dared in their light sea-skiffs, — farther still, to the

> "Shining hills,
> The steep, wide promontories, where
> They shook their syrcas,
> The garments of battle,
> And thanked God
> That to them the wave-journey
> Had been so easy," —

farther still, over the Austrian mountains, up the steppes of Russia, down through the Golden Horn, — home again at last in the warm old Asian world, the fruitful garden of the earth, the tawny-browed, deep-bosomed mother of us all. And ever along the way there is a resurrection. Under the new forms the old spring into a second life. At the touch of a word, the graves give up their dead, busy cities fade into silence, and the deserts are repeopled. Little children, whose gray hairs have been entombed for centuries, are playing once more among the goats; merchant princes traffic in gold and purple where fishermen spread their nets, and a thousand sinewy hands are fashioning the Sphinx's granite heart. There is no speech nor language, but with the gleam of a magic word the stark statues ring out their Memnon-music down the years, even to these ends of the earth. Who shall say that the age of Fairies and Genii is past, when on such ethereal wings we can behold all the kingdoms of the world and the glory of them.

It is only a chart of this wonderful journey that Müller gives us, but even its points are points of bewildering beauty. He startles us, in the first place, with the assertion that language is one of the physical sciences, as truly as botany or geology; in proof of which he distinguishes so clearly between the growth of language and the history of language, he traces back the former to its germ in the human breast so logically, he points out so unmistakably the fact which commends itself at once to our consciousness, that it is not in the power of men to produce or prevent the ceaseless change in language, — that they can no more control the laws of speech than the circulation of blood, nor invent new words at pleasure than add a cubit to their stature, — that he compels assent. The underlying principle which shapes his researches, the key wherewith he unlocks these secret cells, is that everything in language had originally a meaning. By distinguishing and describing the two processes which comprise the growth of language, viz. Phonetic Decay,—as if, for instance, "Yes, madam," should fade into "Yes, ma'am," and that into "Yes 'm,"—and Dialectical Regeneration, or the continued replenishing of a language from its various dialects, he illustrates his principle with singular success, filling up form with substance, or rather bringing to light the substance which has long lain lost amid the shadows of the form. Thus he shows the origin and meaning of the *d* in *loved*, making the tragic change from love living to love dead. He combats the prevalent idea that dialects are corruptions of a pure, classical language, and insists that they are rather its feeders. He teaches that many dialects originally led a life of republican equality, but those spoken in isolated places having no standard, continually changed, an entire change taking place sometimes in so short a period as the lifetime of a single generation, while those that were more central and consolidated around a literature created by songs, festivals, laws, and occasional intercourse, gradually assumed supremacy. If by any means a literature came to be written, the dialect in which it was written at once swallowed up the rest. But its momentary greatness was atoned for by immediate death. As soon as a tongue becomes fixed, classical, it crystallizes. It is hard, cold,—a dead language, beautiful but unbreathing. All this, however, is quite beyond the control of man. The growth, though not like that of a tree from within, is like that of the crust of the earth, by combinations of given elements according to established, though unknown laws.

The Christian tone of the book is vigorous and refreshing. Scientific men are very apt to patronize the Bible. Müller does not. He never suspects that it must be bolstered up by any clumsy contrivances. He has so much faith in it that he lets it stand on its own ground and pushes his researches without the slightest misgiving of collision. He dates the real beginning of the science from the first day of Pentecost. Christ had to come to teach that mankind were of one blood before the science of mankind and the language of mankind could spring into life. The common origin of mankind and their susceptibility of the highest culture became problems of scientific, because of more than scientific interest. He affirms that the apostles were the pioneers of the science, and their true successors, the missionaries, the most useful allies of the philologer. The translation of the Bible and the Lord's Prayer into every dialect of the world form his most valuable materials. There is a world of good, sturdy, but not very common sense in his way of preventing "not only those who are forever attacking the Bible with arrows that cannot reach it, but likewise those who defend it with weapons they know not how to wield, from disturbing in any way the quiet progress of the science of language." The defence of incompetent friends is much more disastrous than the attack of able enemies.

Without for a moment granting that the subject is dull, we *may* admit that the book is all the more interesting for being enlivened by humor and illustrated by anecdote. It is respectful to its predecessors, — though it cannot help a sly laugh now and then, which does no harm, so long as it is good-humored, — attractive in style, and symmetrical in construction.

XVIII.

CHRIST IN CAROLINA.

EVEN on a very serious subject, one can hardly help being amused at the remarkable logic of Mr. Jefferson Davis in his message to that assembly which call itself the Confederate Congress. The loving-kindness and tender mercy of the slave-owner bubbles over in speaking of "the unfortunate negroes" upon whose sufferings he dwells, and whose grievances he recounts with a pity beautiful to behold; showing the superior benefit to the negroes of slavery over freedom by adding: "By the Northern man, on whose deep-rooted prejudices no kindly restraining influence is exercised, they are treated with aversion and neglect," and in the very next paragraph affirming that "full confirmation is afforded by statements published in the Northern journals by humane persons engaged in making appeals to the charitable for aid in preventing the ravages of disease, exposure and starvation among the negro women and children who are crowded into encampments." That is, he knows the negroes are neglected because of the efforts which are making to take care of them!

But Mr. Jefferson Davis's affirmation that the negroes are very badly off for the comforts and even the necessaries of life, ought not to blind our eyes to the other fact, that they *are* badly off. Over against his assertion, we ought to set the antecedent facts in our possession which would lead us to infer that they must suffer, and the testimony which comes from various sources that they do suffer. If every negro brought within our lines were a swift and cunning workman, abundantly able in the piping times of peace to take care of himself and his family, the suddenness of the change in his situation, the entire absence of any preparation for it, either on his part or our own, would render it wellnigh impossible for him to do so. Added to the floating, fragmentary reports, and the numerous miscellaneous appeals for aid, we have the official action of General Grant in sending chaplains from his army to acquaint Northern people with the sore destitution and need of the freedmen, suffering intensely, as they affirm, from nakedness and want of shelter.

All Christians have desired the extinction of slavery, but slaves are extinguished only by turning them into men, and women, and children, who are at once thrown upon our hands. As slaves, we could do nothing for them, except indirectly. As freedmen, they become at once our solemn trust from God. There is not a man or woman of this country, who is not personally responsible for the comfort and the education of these people. We have prayed that God would undo the heavy burdens, and let the oppressed go free. Now he has undone them. Are we ready to approve ourselves sincere by taking the next step? Are we ready for the consequences of our prayers? Did we pray with the understanding that God should not hear, or that if he did, it was no concern of ours? God having, according to our request, set the slave free, shall we not see to it that his freedom becomes a blessing to him? Under slavery, the slaves were provided for after a fashion; under freedom, shall they be left to perish? We have no excuse of inability. There are very few who are not able to help if they wish to help. What is wanted is common things, — warm clothing for winter, implements of industry for self-help and self-culture, books for instruction, and whatever a slave needs on his journey to independent, intelligent manhood. But the immediate and urgent need seems to be clothing. Now I have no doubt that there is clothing enough in the North, not necessary either to comfort or respectability, to clothe every freedman and freedwoman through the winter. With a nation as rich as ours, there is not the smallest need that the blacks should famish or shiver. If they do, it is owing, not to our poverty, but to our paganism. If the garrets of our farm-houses, if the closets and chests and wardrobes of our well-to-do mechanics, to say nothing of our rich men, could only be made to give up the superfluities which are in them, — the flannels, and the cottons, and the cotton-flannels, the woollen stockings, the old coats, and waistcoats, and trousers, and gowns, and sacks, and shawls, that will not, or need not, be worn, that are lying in wait to be cut over for future fashions, or merely contingent wants, — the blankets, the quilts, the full-puffed bed-spreads, that have been accumulated by a certain New England instinct, but serve the honest pride of the good housewife rather than the necessities of her family, — the wadded and quilted petticoats whose substance has outlived their fashion, and whose fate will ultimately be to go into the depths of chest and chair-covers, — if all these and a great multitude of similar articles could be got at, not a negro need suffer. These ought to be got at. Things ordinarily commendable are not commendable now. The hoards of warm, substantial clothing that have come down to us from those terrible times when a girl was not considered fit to be married till she had knit herself a pillow-case-ful of stockings, and woven herself a chestful of fine-twined linen which the longest life could not wear out, are valuable as heirlooms, and not to be triflingly disposed of. But God has made this generation the depositary of liberty which is the heirloom of the world. To our age is committed the redemption of a race, and in that race all the down-trodden races. Surely all private heirlooms may well be subordinated to this. In no way can the legacies of the past be more sacredly treasured than by devoting them to this sacred cause. Turn the pillow-case upside down, and shake it. Descend into the old chests and bring up the pepper-and-camphor-strewed wealth. One blanket made into clothing may keep several persons warm.

Things more dear than these, I know have been gladly given. Little garments that speak of a lost hope, as well as of tender memories, little hoods that have sheltered tossing curls, little frocks that have covered sweet forms lying under the snow now these many winters, have been drawn forth from the drawers which they consecrated, and sent down with prayer and love for little black babies that had no heritage but love. Was that profanation? Did they profane their purest vestments who cast them in the way for the Blessed Feet to tread? If the infant Christ were cradled now in a manger, on one of the Southern plantations, would it be profanation to wrap his tiny form in the little frocks that once had wrapped your child? But inasmuch as ye have done it unto one of the least of these, my brethren, ye have done it unto me.

Learn a lesson from that noble father of a noble son, whom the powers of Evil "buried with his niggers" for the same purpose that, eighteen hundred years ago, they crucified his Master between two thieves. When a mistaken respect would have brought his body northward for sepulture among his kindred, the father proved himself worthy of his son, and interposed. No pomp of funeral rites, no common burial-place, for him. Such deeds are consecration. The brave beauty, the vigorous youth, the fair name, which he devoted to his grateful country, and to the suffering race, cannot be desecrated; least of all by those he died to save, and who would have died for him. He lies where he fell, with his Guard of Honor around him, and henceforth it is holy ground. So Massachusetts gives to South Carolina best gifts, and by this token the land shall be redeemed. He shall rise again with his warriors, and if the word of God fail not, the King shall say unto him, "Come, ye blessed of my Father, inherit the kingdom prepared for you from the foundation of the world. For I was in prison and ye came unto me."

There is also a foolish feeling of pride against making contributions. People say they have nothing good enough to send. They think their old clothes are too much worn and defaced to be given away. They do not seem quite to divest themselves of the idea that the especial ownership of their mended clothes is going to be obvious all the way down to Vicksburg and the Sea Islands. As a matter of fact, I suppose Mr. Jones's connection with his coat, and Mrs. Jones's with her gown, is generally sundered the moment it is beyond their own door; and past the first stage, even the knowledge of Mr. and Mrs. Jones themselves vanishes away. But suppose not, what harm? If a garment is worth patching, the patch is not a thing to be ashamed of; and I suppose anything that can be mended into decency and a tolerable degree of durability, is worth sending. You can easily ask yourself whether, if you were daily shivering with cold, you would consider it worth sending to you, and if you then doubt whether it will pay for transportation, you can mend it and wear it yourself, and send your strong new garments to the freed people! Appeals, to be sure, are made chiefly for second-hand clothing, but I dare say first-hand would not be refused. It might cost a sacrifice; but not one worthy to be compared with His, who for us left the glory which he had with the Father before the world was, and came down to a manger and a cross.

But after all, it is neither pride nor poverty

which is the chief obstacle, but a certain indifference; the absence of a "realizing sense" of things. We hear as though we heard not; we go our way, one to his farm, another to his merchandise, and think of the matter no more. But when the voice of God calls, "Where is the African, thy brother?" will it be a satisfactory answer to Questioner or questioned, "I know not, — I did not think much about it, one way or another"? We may go on thoughtlessly, but, rigorous and pitiless, winter marches over the freedmen. Whether we hear or forbear, they are suffering from want of food and shelter, and the voice of their blood will surely cry unto God from the ground. To feed the hungry, and clothe the naked, is the imperative duty of this hour. More than ever before, Religion demands to know faith by works. "Bring forth fruits meet for repentance," cried the Baptist; and when people asked, "What shall we do then?" he uttered no abstractions, but "He that hath two coats, let him impart to him that hath none; and he that hath meat, let him do likewise." If Christ Jesus is the same yesterday, and to-day, and forever, the fruits meet for repentance are coats, and cloaks, and stockings for the destitute negroes. And remember, if a brother or a sister be naked, and destitute of daily food, and one of you say unto them, Depart in peace, be ye warmed and filled; I am very sorry for you; I wish you were comfortable; notwithstanding ye give them not those things which are needful for the body; what doth it profit? Let us not so mock the Lord as to pretend to be his followers, if we will not cherish the poor whom, in answer to our prayers, he has given into our hands.

Events have shown the freed slaves to be far superior to what we had any reason to expect. Bravery in battle, fortitude in hardship, skill, ingenuity, industry, loyalty, sagacity, self-control, patience, have been discovered where we should have supposed only the vices and weaknesses of a cowed and abject people. No more heroic deeds illustrate the annals of this war than those which have been performed by negroes. They have been faithful to their light, though it must have shone but dimly. But if they were sottish, brutal, vicious, and lazy, to the last degree, our duty would remain the same. What they are, our race has made them. What they may be, it belongs to us to ascertain. Lazarus may lie at the gate full of sores, desiring only the fallen crumbs; but since they are the sores which our own cruelty has caused, he shall not be turned off with crumbs or crust, but shall have balm for his hurt, wine for his fainting heart, meat for his manhood's wants.

The Sanitary Commission rides on the wave of popular favor. Let us rejoice. It has struck a vein of pure, solid religion. It is the very spirit of Christ, organized into an Institution. Heaven be praised that the prophecy is fulfilled, and kings are its nursing fathers, and queens its nursing mothers; but in caring for our own blood, let us not forget the blood that is not our own, the sad-coursing blood that has flowed through generations of sorrow. We have enough and to spare, and heaven and earth await our action. It is Christ who is an hungered and athirst. In all their affliction, he is afflicted. Shall a man rob God?

XIX.

EDDYKNY-MUR-R-PHY.

THERE is a strange hush and shadow in the air to-day, and the Indian summer is less beautiful than it was. All because a little shining, smiling face is turned towards the sunset, and I see it no more. A little shining face, square and full and healthy, yet delicate and spiritual, two round cheeks, each with its own deep dimple, in which the very spirit of sunshine lurks, two eyes blue, clear, and industrious, shaded by long lovely lashes, a high, broad forehead crowned with fine silken-floss hair, — face and hands, and jacket and trousers, all issuing forth in the morning tidy, spotless, all coming back at night, not to say noon, dingy and dusty and draggled; as why should they not, since the little feet that propelled them have been delving in the dust or digging in the mud all day with unwearied assiduity. If you see a little man answering this description, he will not take it amiss should you ask him his name, but will quite exultantly reply, "Eddykny-*mur*-r-phy," trilling out the *r* with a melody so beautiful, rich, limpid, that you will make him repeat it half a dozen times for joy in the rippling sound. O, but he is a little sunbeam, lighting up every nook and cranny of the old house, and he makes its low rooms lovely with his frisking and questioning and glad odd ways.

His clothes are often old and patched. His father works hard with saw and scythe, his mother harder still over wash-tub and ironing-table; but many a child goes clad in silk and brave with feathers who might take lessons in politeness of my little Irish friend. Indeed I know few American mothers who train their children in the minute but important points of good manners so carefully and constantly as his trim Irish mother.

All the green yard and the broad highway beyond are alive with this wild young life. Yonder wood-pile is his chariot of state. Every morning, long before the dew is gone, out comes he, fresh from sleep and breakfast, fastens his lines to the open gate, mounts that wood-pile, and drives around the world. Just behind it is his garden plot, where, true to his national instinct, he raises innumerable crops of cabbages and potatoes, by the aid of a discarded coffee-pot. With a defunct dripping-pan and a string, he drives a brisk business in the freight and express line. Every day at noon or soon after, there is a lull in the atmosphere, as if the machinery of the earth had somehow stopped, for the space of half an hour. That is because Eddy is on his little bed fast asleep. But in due time he announces to the universe his reassumption of active life by emerging into the yard with a prolonged yell of self-satisfaction, which indeed, with a few slight intervals for eating and drinking, is his normal condition of being. He likes much to be "around" when anything is going on. If a horse stops at the gate, he sits on the bank and gazes at him with steadfast, speechless rapture. He never fails to make his appearance, with unlimited proffers of help, whenever I am at work in the garden. I very well know what the sly little rogue is after. The small rake is lovely in his eyes; the slender hoe is a thing of beauty; but the height and depth of unspeakable happiness dwell in the trowel. It is so manageable for his tiny hands. Earth offers him no greater delight than permission to hold that trowel, and no greater hope than that he may be allowed to use it, — which I sometimes suffer him to do, to the great consternation of the geraniums and other high-born weeds.

There is a muffled bang at the door. It is Eddy's signal. His fingers are not yet equal to the execution of a grown-up knock, and he has improvised a sort of suppressed fisticuff. We answer his summons. It is a little tin two-quart pail of water which he has pumped and brought himself, — a very Herculean labor for him. Never mind that his clean clothes are spattered and soaked as he stands there, the dampest, sweetest little Aquarius one shall see in a long summer day.

"Much obliged," I say, deferentially.

"Much obliged," he repeats, trudging off contentedly, a little confused as to the formulas appropriate to the occasion, but sound in his general principles.

Perhaps it is a different errand: "My mother says will you please to give me your bak-set to get you some apples," or, "My mother is much *oblidged* for your *still-yards.*" We call it a balance, but no matter. Whatever it is, he is always respectful, always courteous.

His mother is going away to work this fine, frosty autumn morning. Little Jemmy is too young to be left behind; but Eddy, at the mature age of four years, must shift for himself. To be sure he will be perfectly happy, for has he not recounted to me the riches which the low cupboard-shelf holds in store for him? "Two *keks* — a junk o' meat — a — junk o' bread 'n butter — a — bowl o' bread 'n milk — a junk o' meat — a — *two keks,*" and so on, with a revolving circle of provisions, in which, after the fashion of his sex, he will find a sufficient solace for all his woes. I observe that his morning is chiefly taken up with jaunts to the cupboard, if one may judge from the frequent appearance of "junks." To spare a remnant for dinner, we invite him in to see us. He accepts with alacrity, even forgetting, in the excitement of the moment, the amenities of life. "Eddy, what *is* that on your head?" A moment of blankness, a flash of memory, and off comes the cap. "And where is your comforter?" He investigates himself with great solemnity. "Do' know." "You have lost it?" "Yes, *Sir!*" "Then you must go at once and find it." He disappears for two minutes, and returns as bright as if successful. "I can't find it. It's lost a mile." Fortunately his mittens cannot be lost, since they are fastened by a long string around his neck, and dangle at his side like two little red paws.

In the house he finds inexhaustible food for thought. The pictures first claim his attention. Then he is exercised on the subject of the books. The bell in the kitchen is an insoluble mystery. Soon he flings himself flat on the floor to inspect the castors on the lounge. A wagon in the house is a thing which was never dreamt of in his philosophy. I am obliged to bid him not talk any more. Obedient as usual, he complies, asking in a loud *whisper*, "What's tham little wheels for?" "You must not talk now, Eddy, because I am reading." "No!" he exclaims, promptly and sonorously, but immediately leans against me, and asks, in a very gentle whisper, "What's tham little wheels for?"

It is a fine clear Sunday, and Eddy has been a dozen miles away to "chur-r-ch," he tells me.

"And what did you do at church?"

"I kneeled down and payed."

"To whom did you pray?"

"Payed to God." I am afraid few of our Yankee children could give so good an account of themselves. Ask the little Protestant four and five-year olds what they did at church, and see what they will say.

He comes in one day whisking a string of brown beads, in high spirits. "What are you going to do with those beads?" "Pay with them. My mother 's got some more." "Play with them?" "No; *pay* with them." "But how can you pray with them?" With the utmost good nature he gives a complete explanation, going through the whole process on the spot, dashing them against his white forehead, and smiting right and left, repeating with more readiness than reverence one of the holy names with each blow; but I trust the God whom he ignorantly worships will declare unto him His peace. Nor will he long worship ignorantly; for his careful mother teaches him the vital points of religion, as his daily life gives ample evidence. "I must not do" this and that, he often says, half to himself; "God won't love me." Once he was ill for several days, and, awaking one night, he told his mother he was going to heaven. She was greatly alarmed, as we are all apt to be at such a prospect; but Eddy persisted that he was going. "Why, Eddy, do you *want* to go to heaven?" "I'd like to go to heaven with Miss Ellen," he replied. To round off the romance he ought to have died; but nothing ever does happen to me out of the common line, and, accordingly, he took a little "whik-sey" and vermifuge, and got well.

And now he has left us. While I write this he is journeying towards the going down of the sun, and I am resolved to set my affections on no more Irish children. The Great West will swallow up this little bubble of life, and I shall never again rejoice in its prismatic, ever-changing light. O fair and fruitful prairie-land, receive my little wanderer tenderly, and entreat him kindly. He comes to you in innocence; restore him, I pray you, in holiness. He comes to you a little child, a fresh young soul, loving and loyal, believing in God, in his father and mother, and in all goodness and purity. What will you do for him?

XX.

MAGAZINE LITERATURE.

TIME was when a book was indeed, as Choate once said, the only immortality. But at present there is a vast amount of transient immortality floating about in the columns of the daily paper, the monthly magazine, and the quarterly review. Scarcely a New England home to which one or more of these messengers does not find access. Whether the extensive prevalence of periodical literature be a benefit or a disadvantage, is not yet fully settled. It has decided opponents, as well as warm advocates. The dissemination of knowledge, say the former, vulgarizes knowledge. A subject which is to be treated in the pages of a monthly magazine cannot be adequately treated. It can neither be probed to its depths, nor grasped in its breadth. Its scope must be diminished to meet the requirements of the case. The first duty of a magazinist is to be readable. He may be profound, logical, systematic, exhaustive, but if he is heavy, or abstruse, it is all over with him. The public is willing to be instructed, but it will be amused. A pill in the sugar if you can smuggle it in, but the sugar at all events. Now sugar is not a wholesome diet. Amusement is not the stamina of great men, — not the material wherewithal nerve and muscle and strength are created.

Moreover, they say, such treatment degrades the subject. Problems that require a lifetime to elucidate, and a volume to express, are treated in twenty pages of a magazine, or sixty of a quarterly, — treated fragmentarily, flippantly, frivolously, but in a sparkling, easy style; and the multitude, because they understand the writer, think they understand the subject, — because they comprehend his views, fancy they comprehend the object viewed, — and, deeming the matter finally disposed of, go on their way self-conceited and satisfied with shallowness, while men who would devote to a theme the time and study of which it is worthy are forestalled by penny-a-liners, and the public is cheated of its due.

The far-reaching periodical literature acts, too, in another way. Old authors that have stood the test of time are summarily set aside for the local gossip, the political scandal, the namby-pamby romance, tinsel rhetoric, crude criticism, and random speculation of the periodicals. Matters of temporary interest and small importance usurp the time that should be devoted to the giants that lived on the earth in former days, and in gaining a knowledge of those secrets which the earth stands waiting to reveal to-day. Small welcome will the greater part of the literature of 1861 receive from 2061. It has neither ballast to steady it, nor sail to carry it down the years. Why, then, should it receive such homage at our hands?

Now there may be truth in these remarks, if it be first proven that amusement is incompatible with benefit; that a subject cannot be partially, and at the same time justly treated, and that the people who write and read magazines would, if there were no magazines, write and read elaborate and exhaustive volumes on the subjects discussed therein. But it is of great importance to have it clearly asserted, and stoutly maintained, that reading is not to be a penance. An object is gained when writers are made to know that bald statements are not enough, that bare reasoning is not enough, that pure mathematics is not enough. The earth softens its granite outlines with verdurous dimples, relieves its bare surface with majestic trees and smiling lakes, flecks its sombre hues with brilliant colors, opens its heart everywhere to the sun's fervid kiss; and the result is, that the earth is not only prettier to look at, but better to live on. But poor human nature is jealous of its pleasures. It has become so accustomed to medicine, that, if its food is not bitter, it immediately suspects sawdust. Yet Macaulay and Motley have shown that the truths of history may be clothed upon with far more fascination than the fictions of the imagination; and Romance in her most gorgeous attire is eclipsed by Science robed only in her native honor. The times of the schoolmen are past. They did yeoman's service in their day, but their day is gone by. The presumption now is, that the writer who is most interesting is the best. The history that is as hard to lay down as a novel or a play, is likely to be the truest history. For the two differ only in this, that history is a portrait, where the novel is a study. The one is a special likeness, but both must have a general likeness. History is a novel "founded on fact."

It is probable that periodical literature, so far from diminishing, really increases the number of "solid" readers; that the great mass of its readers are taken, not from above, but from below its plane. They are people who, without the magazines, would not only not read Bacon and Plato, but would not read anything. The *Ledger*, whose vast circulation was a thorn in the sides of so many of its more cultivated contemporaries, need have given little anxiety. It was seen in the hands of those who read nothing else, and doubtless they were elevated and improved by it. The avowed object of the proprietor was to awaken a taste for reading in classes where such taste did not exist. It was a noble and humane object, and in a degree successful. From the *Ledger* the gradation is easy to the magazines, and from the magazines to the quarterlies, and from the quarterlies to the classics. Certainly these periodicals bring the old authors to the knowledge and notice of thousands who would otherwise never hear of them. It was Addison's criticisms of Milton that reintroduced Milton to the English public, and Macaulay's criticisms of Addison have led throngs back to the *Spectator*. Many who cannot afford to buy books may get a tolerable knowledge of their contents from an able review. Without the review, it would not be that they would buy the book, but they would have no knowledge of it whatever. There are also books which one does not care to read as a whole, but of which one wants a bird's-eye view, so that the synopsis of a judicious reviewer is often more valuable than the book itself; while the necessity of presenting a condensed, yet comprehensive, an interesting, and, at the same time, valuable view of a subject, benefits the writer. The amount of thought, study, research, genius, spread out, or rather concentrated, weekly, monthly, quarterly, before the public, is astonishing. It is true that future investigations may make mischief with many of our closely-reasoned conclusions. The brilliant discovery of to-day may be thrown entirely into the shade by the brilliant discoveries of distant to-morrows; but such a *shall be* will be only the counterpart of many a *has been.* The arguments of the fifty-paged quarterly reviewers cannot be more entirely refuted than those of the many-volumed mediæval philosophers. Indeed, if truth could be *precipitated* like a metal held in solution, we question whether a single number of a modern monthly, bought for twenty-five cents, does not sometimes contain as much of it as whole book-shelves of the old fine-drawn ecclesiastics.

At the same time, there is danger lest reading conduce to frivolity. A diet composed exclusively of Lady's Books and Gentleman's Magazines is only one remove from starvation. A man is not necessarily intelligent because he reads his county newspaper. He who stops there will scarcely be rewarded for having begun. The only difference between some readers of newspapers, and those who read nothing, is that the former know the gossip and scandal of the country, while the latter know only the gossip and scandal of their own village. The only difference between some readers of magazines and those who read nothing, is that the former have filled their lives with milk-and-water romancing, and unmitigated snobbery, while the latter have never deviated from the bread and butter of their homely circle; and though the snob is unquestionably higher than the clod, both are so far below the true man, that the difference between them is scarcely perceptible.

But for any danger that may happen to literature, no one need give himself the smallest concern. Literature was made for man, not man for literature. Whatever ministers to human needs has a right to live. Whatever innocently amuses, comforts, instructs, strengthens, has its justification in its work. There is no divine right in the twelve books of the epic which does not equally inhere in the Poet's Corner of the village newspaper. The ponderous volume whose immortality consists in lying in state "in every gentleman's library," may have less influence in building up a noble manhood than the vigorous leader in Tuesday's paper, which nobody reads on Wednesday. The book which solaces the weary mother while rocking the cradle, or from which the household drudge catches a page of sunshine or sympathy while standing over the cooking-range, waiting for the milk to boil, — the book in which the day-laborer finds an assurance of human brotherhood, or the humble mourner a glimpse of the silver lining of his cloud, — does just as high a service and makes just as good an excuse for being, as the "standard work" whose name is on the tongue of every would-be critic, and whose contents are perhaps mastered by a hundred scholars in a hundred generations. The ennobling of man is a better thing than the ennobling of literature. The ennobling of man, first or last, *is* the ennobling of literature. The process may be hidden, but the result is sure. The streams run underground, but they mingle. No good thing is cast into the river of humanity but it shall rise again, in some far-off fountain of song or saga. The book which leaves its mark on the human soul, helping to fashion it for the indwelling of the Holy Spirit, or to deform it into a haunt for devils, is the immortal book, whether its name go securely down the centuries or pass away with spring's first violets.

XXI.

WORDS FOR THE WAY.

WHEN any patriotic person groans under the pressure of the war, he may find his account in reading such a book as Fanny Kemble's Journal of her Plantation Life in Georgia, or in looking at certain well-authenticated photographs of the backs of negro slaves who have come into our lines, — photographs taken and exhibited for the purpose of giving infallible proofs of the tender mercies of slavery as seen in welt and scar. The book can scarcely be called pleasant summer reading, and as specimens of art the pictures may not compare favorably with the "Heart of the Andes," or Bierstadt's "Rocky Mountains"; but as a specific for heart-sickness contracted by hope of victory long deferred, I know nothing better. The war for which three months seemed an age, has dragged its slow length along three years and more. Good people there are, lovers of their country, but lovers also of quiet, haters of strife and bloodshed, weary with waiting for the grand "movement" which is to crush rebellion, and bring back to us the dear placidity of old days; people who desire their country's honor to be defended, her integrity preserved, and her slaves emancipated, but who long with an irrepressible longing for the time which shall stay the effusion of blood, are sometimes tempted to say within themselves, "Where is the promise of his coming?" But when we read and see such portrayals of the abominations of slavery, when we remember that these unspeakable outrages have been endured by millions of people, not for three years, but for a time that can be reckoned by generations, — endured without the hope that ever so patient endurance, or ever so heroic valor, should lighten the burden or avert the future woe, — endured without seeing in any quarter the dawn of a release; thinking of this, we should reckon the sufferings of this present war not worthy to be compared with those under which the African race has so long groaned, being burdened. All the pangs of parting, all the torture of wounds, all the agonies of death, every bitter measure which has been meted out to us, would not balance the physical pain, the mental woe, which we have dealt to the slave; nor have we anything to offset the spiritual degradation to which we have confined, if not reduced him. We, too, have the great content of being free agents; he only bent to an inexorable necessity.

In the natural sequence of events, which is but another name for Divine law, slavery and the war stand to each other in the relation of cause to effect. There may be for both a deeper cause, but this is the immediate connection. Now since there is for nations no redemption, no atonement, but only the natural law, eye for eye, tooth for tooth, hand for hand, foot for foot, burning for burning, wound for wound, stripe for stripe; until we have suffered, in mind, body, and estate, as much as the negro race has suffered at our hands, we have no reason to think it strange concerning the fiery trial which is trying us, as though some strange thing happened unto us. Nay, as under the Hebrew law, ordained of God, for the stolen ox five oxen should be restored, and four sheep for a sheep; since the prophet of old time was not commanded to speak comfortably unto Jerusalem that her warfare was accomplished, until she had received of the Lord's hand double for all her sins; since in Apocalyptic vision the voice from heaven cried, "In the cup which she hath filled, fill to her double," we have, at least, indication that we may not look for deliverance till the shame and sorrow of the subject race have been twice and thrice poured out upon our own heads. I do not say that it will be so with us, that this is the invariable Divine mode of procedure; but that it is the only thing we have a right to expect, and that if peace comes before we have drunk the dregs of the cup of retribution, it will be of mercy, and not of law.

The innocence of individuals is no plea for immunity. It is but "done as others use," to suffer, to fight, to die for the freedom of the negro whom we have not enslaved, and for the defence of the Union which we have always upheld, and whose honor we have never violated. Individuals cannot escape the penalty, even if they escape the contamination of the society to which they belong, and our society is verily guilty concerning our brother. Through the good hand of our God upon us, in war and its confusions, we have been led to a partial view of the error of our ways; but we are not yet fully aroused to do justly. Was it a Northern or a Southern Congress that, but a few months ago, refused to give the people an opportunity to abolish slavery according to the Constitution? Ever since the war began, the footsteps of justice have been through fire and flood, and we would have it so.

Another consideration should have weight. The unvarying testimony concerning our army proclaims its spirit invincible. Chaplains, surgeons, delegates of the Christian Commission, wounded soldiers returning on furlough, bear witness to the courage, the heart, the "pluck" of the men. A brother, himself wounded, just come from his brother's grave, writes home: "I lost a dear friend when Charley died, but, thank

God, he died a brave soldier. Live or die, we must not give up the war till the rebellion is crushed." A boy of eighteen, brought into the hospital, speechless and bleeding, writes on a slip of paper to the by-standers to have "Rally round the flag, boys," sung, and waves his bloody arms above his head in jubilant chorus. A wounded negro standard-bearer wraps the flag around his body, crawls on his hands and knees a mile and a quarter to where his comrades are, and cries to them, "Take it, boys, take it! *It has n't touched the ground!*" From the extreme Southwest, from Virginia, from the front all along the lines, comes the same note of courage and unflinching purpose; and if they, who bear all the hardship, and brave all the danger, keep a stout and even a merry heart, does it become us at home to exceedingly fear and quake? The one complaint from the soldiers is an indignant and bitter denunciation of Northern Rebel sympathizers. It is a fire in the rear against which they are not armed, and with which they have, justly enough, no patience. Let those who are not Rebel sympathizers beware lest an unmanly and unwomanly faint-heartedness put them in the wrong category.

For the matter of high prices, let it not be so much as named among us! So far as it is the result of greed, it is to be denounced and resisted. May every man who has added one iota to his country's perplexity that he might fill his own pockets, find his gains to be as rottenness in his bones. But, as one of the hardships of the war, high prices are to be nothing accounted of. Suppose sugar *is* thirty cents a pound, molasses a dollar a gallon, beef sold by the square inch, cotton cloth sixty cents a yard, and gold at two hundred and eighty the dollar. How long has it been since a man's life consisted in the abundance of sweets which he could swallow? If sugar is three times as high as it used to be, use one third as much of it, and the equilibrium is at once restored. Even at that we shall probably have as much as the soldiers have. If St. Paul would agree to eat no meat while the world standeth, lest he make his brother to offend, cannot Christian men and women forego beefsteak for a year, or two, or three, or twenty, that a nation perish not? If cambric and linen are expensive, are we all princes and princesses that we must have twelve dozen of everything, the wardrobe through? Pull out the bureau drawers and use their contents unflinchingly, regardless of the future, where the honor of *now* is imperative. Attack the old linings with scissors and needle, and "gar auld claes look amaist as weel 's the new." Ask for black buttons at the shops, and then see what an inexhaustible mine of black buttons your old boots at home are, and walk away without purchasing, at a clear gain of forty-two cents. Make your loaf-cake of dried apples and molasses, and affirm resolutely that nobody could tell the difference, till people are silenced if not convinced! Economy can be made as interesting as a mathematical problem, and as merry as a July picnic. And having economized carefully and successfully, consider that the pleasure and the privilege of it are enough for your share, and send the money saved to the relief of wounded soldiers, or of the freed people.

It may be said that this does not take into account the really poor people; but, so far as I have observed, the fearful looking for is not among the really poor people. It is not those who are threatened with absolute want, but those who fear a curtailment of luxuries, a diminution of dividends, an increase of expenditure, who have the most anxiety.

Let it not be forgotten that all these calamities are trying this nation as never nation before was tried. There is a popular use of the word "trial" which is not strictly correct. We often make it synonymous with affliction. "To try," not seldom means to annoy, to provoke, to weary, to harass, to exasperate. But we confound result with process. To try, is to test. All afflictions are trials, but all trials are not afflictions. A fretful child tries, that is, tests, the mother's temper. Her temper does not stand the test. She too becomes fretful and impatient. It may be her fault or the fault of circumstances. It may be that her temper is not under as firm control as it should be, or that the test is severer than it ought to be, or both; at any rate, she does not stand the test, and it becomes an annoyance. Another person is tried by a lovely child. She falls into a weak idolatry and pride, and her test becomes her sin. The fact that trial has so largely come to mean sorrow, grief, annoyance, is a strong indication that trials generally do not bring out well-tempered metal. Let them reveal comprehensive minds and serene hearts; let a man possess his soul in patience; be just as benevolent and self-respectful, whether he be raised from poverty to affluence, or cast down from affluence to poverty, and trials will presently come to mean blessings.

Ever since Thomas Paine, we have talked about the times that tried men's souls, not, as a general thing, perhaps, having any very definite idea of what we were talking about. We meant the days of the Revolution, and were referring to their straits, and suffering, and bloodshed; but the days on which we have fallen are sounding the hitherto unfathomed depths of many an abysmal word on whose fair and beautiful surface we have pleasantly floated, not dreaming of the gems held in its silent caverns. Patriotism, loyalty, truth, honesty, courage, victory, defeat, disaster, cowardice, rebellion, treason, — what revelations have these last years made! We saw only the green boughs and sprays and vines that overarched, concealing, granite gates. The drum-beat of war has been an open sesame, throwing back the unsuspected portals, and discovering vista upon vista stretching down measureless distances till the solemn aisles lose themselves in the inward fastnesses of humanity.

Times that try men's souls! We have fallen on such times. We are all in the crucible.

> "We wait beneath the furnace blast
> The pangs of transformation."

In common days we go on pleasantly together. We lift ourselves to gentle heights. We slide, unastonished, into easy depths. The war comes slowly at first, and not severe. It is a toy, brilliant and sonorous, with just enough of danger to make it piquant, fascinating, exhilarating. It stirs our sluggish blood to heroic, joyful pulses. We watch it with eager eyes, but a smile on the lips. It rolls along, furrowing for itself a deeper groove in our lives, our homes, our hearts. It is no longer a toy; it has grown into a fearful engine. We cannot toss it away. We cannot control it. We can but imperfectly guide it. It whirls on, now slowly, now swiftly, always terrible, crushing a nation's hearts beneath its iron wheels. Inexorable, pitiless, we fling ourselves in vain against those ponderous sides, and tears and sobs and moans are powerless to hinder its career. The smile dies out of our lips. Shall they become tremulous with fear, pallid with despair, distorted with base entreaty, or shall they be firm with manly purpose?

This is the test, the trial. This shall show what manner of people we are. The way in which we bear ourselves through the lingering and disastrous days of this war, shall be our proof to ourselves and to our children. We can be weak, impatient, querulous, driven about by every wind of rumor, now desponding, now exultant, complaining, foreboding, lamenting, regretting. We can be hopeful, cheerful, trustful, patient, learning to wait as well as to labor, drawing from history, from philosophy, from religion, consolation under defeat, caution in judgment, industry after victory, energy after disaster, and wisdom in all things.

We can see in numerous instances how these times have tried men's souls. Here and there they "shine in the sudden making of splendid names." Men who walked unknown along the plains of peace, have risen above the wild surgings of these war-waves "in shape and gesture proudly eminent." There have been unfolded calm souls, clear to see, and strong to grasp the opportunity. The fire that lay hidden in many a heart has flashed out into flame, consuming the gathered dross of drowsy years, and refining the latent gold. Among the living and the dead, we count up names that will never die. We have seen, too, sadder sights. Men that did run well, hindered,—men that stood in angel guise whispering softly into the world's slumberous ear, changed by the touch of these glittering war-spears into loathsome shapes,—men who were thought to have attained the fulness of the ideal manhood, weighed in the balance and found wanting,—hopes that did mount gloriously, coming down in utter darkness.

The nation has been tried,—tried by domestic rebellion, by foreign threats, by the frightful incapacity of its leaders,—and the trial is still going on. Its courage, its persistence, its magnanimity, its resolution, its humanity,—almost every quality that a nation should possess,—has been tried by the exigencies of this war, and is yet in the furnace heat. What the result will be, God alone knows.

Insatiable ambition, insatiable avarice, struck deep into the nation's life, this war has brought to light. But there has also been developed an eagerness for sacrifice, an unselfish devotion, a trust in God, which is the basis of noble character. God will decide the issue. He knows whether there is virtue enough in the land to redeem it. If it is worth saving, it will be saved. If it is not worth saving, it is better that it should be destroyed. He doeth His pleasure among the inhabitants of earth as well as in the armies of heaven. Our part is to work with might and main; to strain nerve and muscle to put down the rebellion on the one side, and to raise our own standard, and the standard of all men, to the moral heights which God requires, on the other. We sigh for a great man, but it may be the will of God — it certainly is so far — that we shall not have a great man. We must do the work ourselves. A great man is not in accordance with the "spirit of our institutions." We are a democracy, and it is the people that must save the country. We must work with such material as we have. And while we are doing with our might whatsoever our hands find to do, we must, if we are faithful, besiege the throne of Heaven with an importunity that will not be resisted; in all places and at all times making supplication unto God for the help that he never refuses; beseeching him to take the leadership, and so to guide us that our cause shall be His cause, and our prayer for national unity, and peace, and freedom, one with "Thy kingdom come, Thy will be done."

XXII.

"OUT IN THE COLD."

FOR many years the great bugbear of this country has been Disunion. Lovejoy was shot in Alton; Dr. Bailey was mobbed in Washington; Judge Hoar was driven out of Charleston; and Garrison was dragged through the streets of Boston with a rope around his neck, to placate this implacable monster. Books were tampered with, traffic was tainted, printing-presses thrown into the river, and pulpits so polluted that they ought to have been; nothing was held too precious, too sacred, to be offered on his shrine. Free speech, free press, free action, were all tossed into his ravenous maw. Statesmen, tradesmen, merchants, ministers, saints, and sinners, all went down on their knees, and agreed that black was white, if so he might be fended off. Nay, they not only agreed to it, — they argued it; they swore to maintain it, and henceforth to tolerate no doubt, and suffer no agitation on the subject, lest the dragon should rear his horrid front again.

But there is an end of that. We shall probably never — certainly not for this generation — have any more Southern menaces of disunion. No right will have to be postponed, no wrong allowed, because the South threatens to withdraw. If she accomplishes her purposes, there will be no occasion for a renewal of her threat; and if she does not, no possibility. But the resources of Satan are infinite; and, having ridden one horse to death, he has now slipped upon the back of another to take an airing through the North. Finding that his bugbear is going to be transfixed and analyzed, and all that is bug hooted, and all that is bear throttled out of existence, he sets up a new and fresh one. Slavery, not being able to drag the South out of the Union, is now making a frantic effort to push New England out. Having tried in vain to fix a great gulf along Mason and Dixon's line, she next undertakes to chip off Plymouth Rock. But slavery will find no more profit to herself in stone-cutting than in ditch-digging. Plymouth Rock was cut out of the mountain without hands, and hands cannot prevent it from becoming a great mountain, and filling the whole earth. Suppose New England were thrust out of the Union, had Zimri peace who slew his master? Would the principles that have made New England what she is be any less forceful because she was no longer called America? A rose by any other name is just as sweet. If New England were baptized New Zealand, righteousness would still go up a sweet savor unto the Lord.

Is it said that such expulsion would be her ruin, — that henceforth her name would be but a memory? What then? Is civilization shut up in Boston State-House? Whom the gods will destroy, they first make mad. Are men mad enough to suppose that, at this late day, truth crushed to earth will not rise again? that, because John Brown's body lies a-mouldering in the grave, his soul is mouldering with it? Plymouth Rock is no bit of quartz or feldspar, but a principle; and principles will live and reign though New England be not only left out in the cold, but thrust down into the ocean depths forever. Every church, every school-house, every town-house, from the Atlantic to the Pacific, has Plymouth Rock for its foundation-stone. Every man in every land who opens his mouth for truth, stands on Plymouth Rock. Wherever Freedom aims a musket, or plants a standard, or nerves an arm, or sings a song, or makes a protest, or murmurs a prayer, there is Plymouth Rock. Cows may meander, as of old, along Washington Street; but the hands shall not go back on the dial-plate of God. Boston may be grass-grown, and New England forgotten, but love of life and love of liberty shall never die out of the hearts of men. Let Southern traitors and their Northern abettors arrange things as they will. Let them eject New

England, sheathe the sword, stifle discussion, inaugurate Jefferson Davis, annul the freedman, and perpetuate the slave; is that the end? Will they so find rest? Will cotton once more resume sway, and right be forever held in abeyance? Never, so long as there is a conscience in man, or a God in heaven! They may make themselves a new Pandora's box, filled with peace, and commerce, and wealth, and every blessing, but this evil at the bottom shall poison every good. They cannot bind it to quietude. They may resolve and legislate and menace; Jefferson Davis and all his kind may bear down upon it with their whole force; but the divinely appointed unrest of iniquity will heave and throb till the vexed lid fly up with a rebound that shall hurl them to irrevocable doom. Men forget that ethics is not mechanics. They forget the divine power of truth,— the divine nature of humanity. God made man in his own image; in the image of God created he him; male and female created he them. And can it be supposed that male and female, created in God's own image, are to remain eternally passive under the weight of hell's oppression, or, worse than this, are to be the ever patient agents of hell's iniquity? If the programme of these lewd fellows of the basest sort, these Northern men, who, of their own free will and taste, souse their hands into the filth amid which their Southern comrades were most innocently born; if their programme could be carried out; if New England could be quietly disposed of; if the cry of three millions of slaves could be hushed, and the voice of nineteen millions of freemen stilled, and a dead silence reign throughout the land,—the woe to the African would be a thousand and a thousand fold less than the woe to his Caucasian oppressor. But this cannot be, because the good in man can no more be ignored than the evil; because there is implanted in him a divine spark, which is ever springing up into flame. Whoever makes laws or frames plans, without taking into account the action of this irrepressible agent, will find his laws and his plans blown finally to a thousand fragments, by its checked and accumulated forces.

Meanwhile, let us possess our souls in patience. The cry of separation between North and South is, it seems, to be superseded by the cry of separation between East and West. If we are to be cut off, so be it; but do not let us die a thousand deaths through fear of one. Dread of Southern separation has sat at our council-boards for a lifetime; if this fresh one is to supplant it, the little finger of the new tyrant will be thicker than the loins of the old. The best way is to do justly, love mercy, and walk humbly before God, precisely as if nothing had been said. If it happens, we shall be no worse off for having slept o' nights; and if it does not happen, we shall be a great deal better. Let no New England voice be lifted against the measure, for, apart from law and loyalty, dignity seems to require that New England's defence shall come from other lips than her own, as it certainly does come through all the North and West, with unequivocal and generous reverberations. But above all things, as we value our birthright, and the charge intrusted to us by our fathers, let no New England voice be *lowered* to meet this new-found threat. Though, as an American, one should bewail such a catastrophe in dust and ashes, as a New Englander, he should exult. America would wear her decree of divorce forever branded on her brow; but New England would inscribe it highest on her banner of the light; for the separation would not be because of her usurpation of power, but her inflexibility of principle; not for what is bad in her, but for what is good. So may she live only so long as life and honor are one; and if die she must, let her go down grandly, like the Cumberland, firing her last broadside at the foe, flinging her last flag to the breeze, knowing of a surety that the dead which she shall slay at her death will be more than they which she slew in her life.

XXIII.

INTERRUPTION.

I SAT down to write, but through the noonday air, calm and still as midsummer, though in the heart of winter, comes the boom of distant cannon. In another latitude it might be a tone of terror and agony; but over our quiet valleys the besom of destruction has never swept, the voice of carnage has not sounded, the "feverish lips" of cannon, save in one mad hour, have spoken only summons to battle and shouts of victory. When, early in the war, the vexed air quivered with its fiery freight, it used to raise high hopes. Eager eyes answered to eager lips. Was Richmond taken? Was Beauregard defeated? Was Davis captured? Was the land avenged, and peace restored? But we have learned wisdom since then, and patience. Still the guns boom, deafening enough in their places, no doubt, but to us, afar off, deadened down to a sturdy rumbling; and a sweeter sound mingles with the deep reverberation. The clangor of bells is softly heard. Beginning at the west it ripples along to the south; one and another take up the joyful strain, and ring out happy chimes. So faint, so far, the little chords of melody give forth, as it were, the echoes of some Æolian harp stirred by a light-winged zephyr. Tiny wavelets strike out from tiny centres of sound, and all along the southern horizon meet and mingle in harmonious confusion, till the fairy-like music steals into our hearts. The drum-beat adds its solemn undertone, and far, far beyond that line of southern hills, crowned with its Procession of the Pines, I know there are thousands of hearts beating with wild tumult of joy, thousands of hearts throbbing with rapturous gladness. For — do you know? Not a child in the village street but can tell you wherefore the village bells are ringing so merrily. It is the returning regiments.

The returning regiments! How long it is since the April morning that left a stain on the pavements of Baltimore! How long before us stretched the three strange, terrible months — months menacing us with unknown perils and shadowy terror — to which our early volunteers were called! Could that excitement, that indignation, that new and ominous roar of approaching battle, endure three months? Could we endure it? Bear for three months the anxiety, the uncertainty, the raging thirst for victory and vengeance, the "dull, deep pain and constant anguish of patience?" It is three and thirty months since then, and still our battle-flag remains unfurled, and still an outraged nation waits to be avenged.

Seventy-five thousand men! Where could the beloved land find foes to withstand a host like that? we asked, in our simplicity. They laughed in Montgomery. They had measured their strength better than we. They knew their iniquitous purpose. Our grand army was but a stripling come out to fight a giant with smooth stones from the brook. They knew themselves, but there was a strength of which they never dreamed. They did not know that our seventy-five thousand men were but the first rain-drops from the cloud not yet ripe for showers. The prince of the powers of darkness had marshalled his minions well, as we presently learned. Then the cloud spread up the sky. It gathered thick, and thundered loud, and the rent heavens rang with the shout, the solid earth shook with the tread of ten hundred thousand men.

And now they have come back to us. They have fulfilled their high promise. They have acquitted themselves like men. They rushed to the breach, when the foe came in like a flood, and stayed the desolation. There are men who dare to sneer at patriotism, and talk of the attractive power of thirteen dollars a month. To such a talker, one is moved to say: "Your testimony is conclusive as far as it goes; but it goes no farther than your solitary self. You may know that *you* would give up wife, and child, and life for thirteen dollars a month, but you are not authorized to say that all men would do the same. As like naturally seeks like, it is very possible that the clique to which you belong, and from which you generalize your unworthy laws, are impelled by such petty considerations. But a clique does not establish laws for humanity."

No one supposes that men, in becoming soldiers, become angels. Pay, pension, promotion, of course, have their influence, and they are all honorable motives, — closely entwined with

> "The graces and the loves that make
> The music of the march of life,"

but in the breasts of our brave soldiery there is somewhat broader, deeper, higher than these. He is blind who does not see it.

I was reading, the other day, the funeral sermon of a young man of Michigan, Major Noah Henry Ferry, of the Fifth Michigan Cavalry. He fell at Gettysburg, swept away by treason's highest wave. His is only one of the many names written in "living light," and for every name we see, there are, doubtless, scores that we see not. But every name, every record of a hero's life and a martyr's death, is as fresh and fair as if his name alone illumined our country's annals. In a letter to his mother, shortly before his departure from Washington, Major Ferry writes: "If by the accident of war I should find my end upon the field . . . . you will have the comfort of knowing that I have, by dying in such a cause, not lived in vain; and that (I can tell it to you) no impure motive had a voice in bringing me here; nor is there in my history anything of which my friends need feel ashamed."

That he was not impelled by love of glory, or any personal ambition, is constantly seen. To a younger brother, chafing under the necessity of remaining at home, he writes, "Why, Ned, when I read of your work at home, and hear you talk of discontent, because you are not doing more for your country, I feel guilty in staying here. You are doing manifold more than I am. Your place cannot be vacated without being felt by very many, while mine would hardly be missed." In another letter he writes "If I go to war, I want to fight; if I go to play, I want to play." And what says the father of this young soldier, when the tidings came from Gettysburg? "Not one son, but *all*, if need be; rather than that this unholy rebellion triumph. If my country must fall, welcome the annihilation of every temporal interest and the destruction of life itself: for I do not desire to survive my country's ruin." While such words are spoken, while such fire burns in heroic hearts, and such dust mingles with the soil, who is he that dares to sit by the fireside from which he has never stirred and prate his malign insinuations?—

They have come back to us, but not as they went away. For boys tenderly reared and carefully watched, for men with soft hands and sheltered lives, we have a band of bronzed and scarred, war-worn and weather-beaten veterans. Two years may have been twenty for the sinewy manliness to which they have grown. We hoped that on their return we should

"hear the bells of cheer
Ring peace and freedom in,"

but it was not to be. Their feet are shod only with the *preparations* of the gospel of peace: still the trumpet sounds to arms, but they are undismayed. They have come back only for one breathing-space, and they will rally yet again around the dear old flag. Let their home-sojourn be filled to the brim with pleasant things, and their after-life crowded with pleasant memories. Give, first of all, thanks unto the Lord, for he is good. Enter into his gates with thanksgiving, and into his courts with praise. Let the voice of social love greet them, and the hand of friendship clasp theirs. O maidens, bring to them your sweetest smiles; mothers, unfold your deepest tenderness; and crow your lustiest, round-eyed babies, voicing a joy you do not understand. Spread, blue and clear above their heads, ye wintry skies. Lie white and hard beneath their feet, ye hills of snow. Let sleigh-bells jingle merrily, let the lamp be brightly trimmed, and the red firelight dance. Let friends and neighbors meet to give them hearty welcome. Bring down to the spit the king of the turkeys, cram the puddings with pulpy plums. Marshal the pumpkins and the cranberries, and the spicy, multifarious mixtures for all manner of unwholesome edibles that men delight in; they can stand it for a month, and on distant camping-grounds, when hard-tack shall have resumed its sway, it may delight them to remember these things.

They have come back to us, but not all. The still deadliness of malaria and "the thunder-storm of battle" have made sad havoc here. We have but thinned and shattered ranks for the gallant regiments that went

> "Marching along, fifty score strong,
> Great-hearted gentlemen."

They come back tens, who went out hundreds. Their graves are green in many a valley, and the breezes whisper softly where they lie. Under the waters and above the clouds they rest in dreamless slumber. Some sleep among their kindred, in the shade of marble monuments, and some sleep just as peacefully whose sepulchres no man shall ever know. God help the hearts whose wounds will this day bleed afresh.

The sounds have ceased. The cannon's low

roll is hushed, and the bells are still. Now the crowds are dispersing, the civic greeting is over, and the doors of happy homes open, — and close again. The angel of the Lord descend and crown them with his blessing.

XXIV.

ANNO DOMINI.

IT is right and fitting that this nation should cherish a peculiar gratitude and render especial thanksgiving to the Most High. Through all its existence it has rejoiced in the sunshine of Divine favor; but never has that favor been so benignly and bountifully bestowed as in these latter days. For the unexampled material prosperity which has waited upon our steps, — for blessings in city and field, in basket and store, in all that we have set our hand unto, it is meet that we should render thanks to the Good Giver; but for the especial blessings of these last four years, — for the sudden uprising of manhood, — for the great revival of justice, and truth, and love, without which material prosperity is but a second death, — for the wisdom to do, the courage to dare, the patience to endure, and the godlike strength to sacrifice all in a righteous cause, let us give thanks; for in these consists a people's life.

To every nation there comes an hour whereon hang trembling the issues of its fate. Has it vitality to withstand the shock of conflict and the turmoil of surprise? Will it slowly gather itself up for victorious onset? or will it sink unresisting into darkness and the grave?

To this nation, as to all, the question came: Ease or honor, death or life? Subtle and savage, with a bribe in his hand, and a threat on his tongue, the tempter stood. Let it be remembered with lasting gratitude that there was neither pause nor parley when once his purpose was revealed. The answer came, — the voice of millions like the voice of one. From city and village, from mountain and prairie, from the granite coast of the Atlantic to the golden gate of the Pacific, the answer came. It roared from a thousand cannon, it flashed from a million muskets. The sudden gleam of uplifted swords revealed it, the quiver of bristling bayonets wrote it in blood. A knell to the despot, a pæan to the slave, it thundered round the world.

Then the thing which we had greatly feared came upon us, and that spectre which we had been afraid of came unto us, and, behold, length of days was in its right hand, and in its left hand riches and honor. What the lion-hearted warrior of England was to the children of the Saracens, that had the gaunt mystery of Secession been to the little ones of this generation, an evening phantom and a morning fear, at the mere mention of whose name many had been but too ready to fall at the feet of opposition and cry imploringly, "Take any form but that!" The phantom approached, put off its shadowy outlines, assumed a definite purpose, loomed up in horrid proportions, — to come to perpetual end. In its actual presence all fear vanished. The contest waxed hot, but it wanes forever. Shadow and substance drag slowly down their bloody path to disappear in eternal infamy. The war rolls on to its close; and when it closes, the foul blot of secession stains our historic page no more. Another book shall be opened.

Remembering all the way which these battling years have led us, we can only say, "It is the Lord's doing, and it is marvellous in our eyes." Who dreamed of the grand, stately patience, the heroic strength, that lay dormant in the hearts of this impulsive, mercurial people? It was always capable of magnanimity. Who suspected its sublime self-poise? Rioting in a reckless, childish freedom, who would have dared to prophesy that calm, clear foresight by which it voluntarily assumed the yoke, merged its strong individual wills in one central controlling will, and bent with haughty humility to every restraint that looked to the rescue of its endangered liberty? The cannon that smote the walls of a Sumter did a wild work. Its voice of insult and of sacrilege roused the fire of a blood too brave to know its courage, too proud to boast its source. All the heroism inherited from an honored ancestry, all the inborn wrath of justice against iniquity, all that was true to truth sprang up instinctively to wrest our Holy Land from the clutch of its worse than infidels.

But that was not the final test. The final test came afterwards. The passion of indignation burned out as passion must. The war that had been welcomed as a relief bore down upon the land with an ever-increasing weight, became an ever-darkening shadow. Its romance and poetry did not fade, but their colors were lost under the sable hues of reality. The cloud hung over every hamlet; it darkened every doorway. Even success must have been accompanied with sharpest sorrow; and we had not success to soften sorrow. Disaster followed close upon delay, and delay upon disaster, and still the nation's heart was strong. The cloud became a pall, but there was no faltering. Men said to one another, anxiously: "This cannot last. We must have victory. The people will not stand these delays. The summer must achieve results, or all is lost." The summer came and went, results were not achieved, and still the patient country waited, — waited not supinely, not indifferently, but with a still determination, with a painful longing, with an earnest endeavor, less demonstrative, but no less definite, than that which Sumter roused. Moments of sadness, of gloom, of bitter disappointment and deep indignation, there have been; but never from the first moment of the Rebellion to this its dying hour has there been a time when the purpose of the people to crush out treason and save the nation has for a single instant wavered. And never has their power lagged behind their purpose. Never have they withheld men or money, but always they have pressed on, more eager, more generous, more forward to give than their leaders have been to ask. Truly, it is not in man that walketh thus to direct his steps!

And side by side, with no unequal step, the great charities have attended the great conflict. Out of the strong has come forth sweetness. From the helmeted brow of War has sprung a fairer than Minerva, panoplied not for battle, but for the tenderest ministrations of Peace. Wherever the red hand of War has been raised to strike, there the white hand of Pity has been stretched forth to solace. Wherever else there may have been division, here there has been no division. Love, the essence of Christianity, self-sacrifice, the life of God, have forgotten their names, have left the beaten ways, have embodied themselves in institutions, and have lifted the whole nation to the heights of a divine beneficence. Old and young, rich and poor, bond and free, have joined in offering an offering to the Lord in the persons of his wounded brethren. The woman that was tender and very delicate has brought her finest handiwork; the slave, whose just unmanacled hands were hardly yet deft enough to fashion a freedman's device, has proffered his painful hoards; the criminal in his cell has felt the mysterious brotherhood stirring in his heart, and has pressed his skill and cunning into the service of his countrymen. Hands trembling with age have steadied themselves to new effort; little fingers that had hardly learned their uses have bent with unwonted patience to the novelty of tasks. The fashion and elegance of cities, the thrift and industry of villages, have combined to relieve the suffering and comfort the sorrowful. Science has wrought her mysteries, art has spread her beauties, and learning and eloquence and poetry have lavished their free-will offerings. The ancient blood of Massachusetts and the youthful vigor of California have throbbed high with one desire to give deserved meed to those heroic men who wear their badge of honor in scarred brow and maimed limb. The wonders of the Old World, the treasures of tropical seas, the boundless wealth of our own fertile inland, all that the present has of marvellous, all that the past has bequeathed most precious, — all has been poured into the lap of this sweet charity, and blesseth alike him that gives and him that takes. It is the old convocation of the Jews, when they brought the Lord's offering to the work of the tabernacle: "And they came, both men and women, and brought bracelets, and ear-rings, and rings, and tablets, all jewels of gold; and every man that offered offered an offering of gold unto the Lord. And every man with whom was found blue and purple and scarlet and fine linen and goats' hair and red skins of rams and badgers' skins brought them. And all the women that were wise-hearted did spin with their hands, and brought that which they had spun, both of blue and of purple and of scarlet and of fine linen. And the rulers brought onyx-stones, and stones to be set, and spice, and oil for the light. The children of Israel brought a willing offering unto the Lord, every man and woman."

Truly not the least of the compensations of this war is the new spirit which it has set astir in human life, this acknowledged brotherhood which makes all things common, which moves health and wealth and leisure and learning to brave the dangers of the battle-field and the horrors of the hospital for the comfort of its needy comrade. And inasmuch as he who hath done it unto one of the least of these his brethren has done it unto the Master, is not this, in very deed and truth, Anno Domini, the year of our Lord?

And let all devout hearts render praises to God for the hope we are enabled to cherish that He will speedily save this people from their national sin. From the days of our fathers, the land groaned under its weight of woe and crime; but none saw from what quarter deliverance should come. Apostles and prophets arose in North and South, prophesying the wrath of God against a nation that dared to hold its great truth of human brotherhood in unrighteousness, and the smile of God only on him who should do justly and love mercy and walk humbly before Him; but they died in faith, not having obtained the promises. That faith in God, and consequently in the ultimate triumph of right over wrong, never failed; but few, even of the most sanguine, dared to hope that their eyes should see the salvation of the Lord. Upright men spent their lives in unyielding and indignant protest, not so much for any immediate result as because they could do no otherwise, — because the constant violation of sacred right, the constant defilement and degradation of country, wrought so fiercely and painfully in their hearts that they could not hold their peace. Though they expected no sudden reform, they believed in the indestructibility of truth, and knew, therefore, that their word should not return unto them void, but waited for some far future day when happier harvesters should come bringing their sheaves with them. How looks the promise now? A beneficent Providence has outstripped our laggard hopes. The work which we had so summarily given over to the wiser generations of the future is rapidly approaching completion beneath the strokes of a few sharp, short years of our own. Slavery, which was apologized for by the South, tolerated by the North, half recognized as an evil, half accepted as a compromise, but with every conscientious concession and every cowardly expedient sinking ever deeper and deeper into the nation's life, stands forth at last in its real character, and meets its righteous doom. Public opinion, rapidly sublimed in the white heat of this fierce war, is everywhere crystallizing. Men are learning to know precisely what they believe, and, knowing, they dare maintain. There is no more speaking with bated breath, no more counselling of forbearance and non-intervention. It is no longer a chosen few who dare openly to denounce the sum of all villanies; but loud and long and deep goes up the execration of a people, — the tenfold hate and horror of men who have seen the foul fiend's work, who have felt his fangs fastened in their own flesh, his poison working in their own hearts' blood. Hundreds of thousands of thinking men have gone down into his loathsome prison-house, have looked upon his obscene features, have grappled, shuddering, with his slimy strength; and thousands of thousands, watching them from far-off Northern homes, have felt the chill that crept through their souls. The abhorrence of slavery that fills the heart of this people it is impossible for language to exaggerate. It is so strong, so wide-spread, so uncompromising, so fixed in its determination to destroy, root and branch, the accursed thing, that even the forces of evil and self-seeking, awed and overpowered, are swept into the line of its procession. Good men and bad men, lovers of country and lovers only of lucre, men who will fight to the death for a grand idea and men who fight only for some low ambition, worshippers of God and worshippers of Mammon, are alike putting their hands to the plough which is to overturn and overturn till the ancient evil is uprooted. The very father of lies is, perforce, become the servant of truth. That old enemy which is the Devil, the malignant messenger of all evil, finds himself, — somewhat amazed and enraged, we must believe, at his unexpected situation, — with all his executive ability undiminished, all his spiritual strength unimpaired, harnessed to the chariot of human freedom and human progress, and working in his own despite the beneficent will of God.

Unspeakably cheering, both as a sign of the sincerity of our leaders and as a pledge of what the nation means to do when its hands are free, are the little Christian colonies planted in the rear of our victorious armies. In the heart of woods are often seen large tracts of open country gay with a brilliant purple bloom which the people call "fire-weed," because it springs up on spots that have been stripped by fire. So, where the old plantations of sloth and servitude have been consumed by the desolating flames of war, spring up the tender growths of Christian civilization. The filthy hovel is replaced by the decent cottage. The squalor of slavery is succeeded by the little adornments of ownership. The thrift of self-possession supplants the recklessness of irresponsibility. For the slave-pen we have the school-house. Where the lash labored to reduce men to the level of brutes, the Bible leads them up to the heights of angels. We are as yet but in the beginning, but we have begun right. With his staff the slave passes over the Jordan of his deliverance; but through the manly nurture and Christian training which we owe him, and which we shall pay, he shall become two bands. The people did not set themselves to combat prejudices with words alone, when the time was ripe for deeds; but while the Government was yet hesitating whether to put the musket into his hand for war, Christian men and women hastened to give him the primer for peace. Not waiting for legislative enactments, they took the freedman as he came all panting from the house of bondage; they ministered to his wants, strengthened his heart, and set him rejoicing on his way to manhood. The Proclamation of Emancipation may or may not be revoked; but whom knowledge has made a man, and discipline a soldier, no edict can make again a slave.

While the people have been working in their individual capacity to right the wrongs of generations, our constituted authorities have been moving on steadfastly to the same end. Military necessity has emancipated thousands of slaves, and civil power has pressed ever nearer and nearer to the abolition of slavery. In all the confusion of war, the trumpet-tones of justice have rung through our national halls with no uncertain sound. With a pertinacity most exasperating to tyrants and infidels, but most welcome to the friends of human rights, Northern Senators and Representatives have presented the claims of the African race. With many a momentary recession, the tide has swept irresistibly onward. Hopes have been baffled only to be strengthened. Measures have been rejected only to be restored. Defeat has been accepted but as the stepping-stone to new endeavor. Cautiously, warily, Freedom has lain in wait to rescue her wronged children. Her watchful eyes have fastened upon every weakness in her foe: her ready hand has been upraised wherever there was a chance to strike. Quietly, almost unheard amid the loud-resounding clash of arms, her decrees have gone forth, instinct with the enfranchisement of a race. The war began with old customs and prejudices under full headway, but the new necessities soon met them with fierce collision. The first shock was felt when the escaping slaves of Rebel masters were pronounced free, and our soldiers were forbidden to return them. Then the blows came fast and furious, and the whole edifice, reared on that crumbling corner-stone of Slavery, reeled through all its heaven-defying heights. The gates of Liberty opened to the slave, on golden hinges turning. The voice of promise rang through Rebel encampments, and penetrated to the very fastnesses of Rebellion. The ranks of the army called the freedman to the rescue of his race. The courts of justice received him in witness of his manhood. Before every foreign power he was acknowledged as a citizen of his country, and as entitled to her protection. The capital of our nation was purged of the foul stain that dishonored her in the eyes of the nations, and that gave the lie direct to our most solemn Declaration. The fugitive-slave acts that disfigured our statute-book were blotted out, and fugitive-slave-stealer acts filled their places. The seal of freedom, immediate, unconditional, and perpetual, was set upon the broad outlying lands of the Republic, and then came that crowning act which in its results shall make slavery forever impossible, and liberty the one supreme, unchangeable law in every part of our domains.

What we have done is an earnest of what we mean to do. After nearly four years of war, and war on such a scale as the world has never before seen, the people have once more, and in terms too emphatic to be misunderstood, proclaimed their undying purpose. With a unanimity rarely equalled, a people that had fought seven years against a tax of threepence on the pound, and that was rapidly advancing to the front rank of nations through the victories of peace, — a people jealous of its liberties and proud of its prosperity,— has re-elected to the chief magistracy a man under whose administration burdensome taxes have been levied, immense armies marshalled, imperative drafts ordered, and fearful sufferings endured. They have done this because, in spite of possible mistakes and short-comings, they have seen his grasp ever tightening around the throat of Slavery, his weapons ever seeking the vital point of the Rebellion. They have beheld him standing always at his post, calm in the midst of peril, hopeful when all was dark, patient under every obloquy, courteous to his bitterest foes, conciliatory where conciliation was possible, inflexible where to yield was dishonor. Never have the passions of civil war betrayed him into cruelty or hurried him into revenge; nor has any hope of personal benefit or any fear of personal detriment stayed him when occasion beckoned. If he has erred, it has been on the side of leniency. If he has hesitated, it has been to assure himself of the right. Where there was censure, he claimed it for himself; where there was praise, he has lavished it on his subordinates. The strong he has braved, and the weak sheltered. He has rejected the counsels of his friends when they were inspired by partisanship, and adopted the suggestions of opponents when they were founded on wisdom. His ear has always been open to the people's voice, yet he has never suffered himself to be blindly driven by the storm of popular fury. He has consulted public opinion, as the public servant should; but he has not pandered to public prejudice, as only demagogues do. Not weakly impatient to secure the approval of the country, he has not scorned to explain his measures to the understanding of the common people. Never bewildered by the solicitations of party, nor terrified by the menace of opposition, he has controlled with moderation, and yielded with dignity, as the exigencies of the time demanded. Entering upon office with his full share of the common incredulity, perceiving no more than his fellow-citizens the magnitude of the crisis, he has steadily risen to the height of the great argument. No suspicion of self-seeking stains his fair fame; but ever mindful of his solemn oath, he seeks with clean hands and a pure heart the welfare of the whole country. Future generations alone can do justice to his ability; his integrity is firmly established in the convictions of the present age. His reward is with him, though his work lies still before him.

Only less significant than the fact is the manner of his re-election. All sections of a continental country, with interests as diverse as latitude and longitude can make them, united to secure, not any man's continuance in power, but the rule of law. The East called with her thousands, and the West answered with her tens of thousands. Baltimore that day washed out the blood-stains from her pavement, and free Maryland girded herself for a new career. Men who had voted for Washington came forward with the snows of a hundred winters on their brows, and amid the silence and tears of assembled throngs deposited their ballot for Abraham Lincoln. Daughters led their infirm fathers to the polls to be sure that no deception should mock their failing sight. Armless men dropped their votes from between their teeth. Sick men and wounded men, wounded on the battle-fields of their country, were borne on litters to give their dying testimony to the righteous cause. Dilettanteism, that would not soil its dainty hands with politics, dared no longer stand aloof, but gave its voice for national honor and national existence. Old party ties snapped asunder, and local prejudices shrivelled in the fire of newly-kindled patriotism. Turbulence and violence, awed by the supreme majesty of a resolute nation, slunk away and hid their shame from the indignant day. Calmly, in the midst of raging war, in despite of threats and cajolery, with a lofty, unspoken contempt for those false men who would urge to anarchy and infamy, this great people went up to the ballot-box, and gave in its adhesion to civil liberty and universal freedom. And as the good tidings of great joy flashed over the wires from every quarter, men recognized the finger of God, and, laying aside all lower exultation, gathered in the public places, and, standing reverently with uncovered heads, poured forth their rapturous thanksgiving in that sublime doxology which has voiced for centuries the adoration of the human soul: —

> "Praise God, from whom all blessings flow,
> Praise Him, all creatures here below,
> Praise Him above, ye heavenly host,
> Praise Father, Son, and Holy Ghost!"

So our country to the world gives greeting. So a free people meets and masters the obstacles that bar its progress. So this young republic speaks warning to the old despotisms, and hope to the struggling peoples. Thus with the sword she seeks peace under liberty. Striking off the shackles that fettered her limbs, emerging from the thick of her deadly conflict, with many a dint on her armor, but with no shame on her brow, she starts on her victorious career, and bids the suffering nations take heart. With the old lie torn from her banner, the old life shall come back to her symbols. Her children shall no longer blush at the taunts of foreign tyrannies, but shall boldly proclaim her to be indeed the land of the free, as she has always been the home of the brave. Men's minds shall no longer be confused by distinctions between higher and lower law, to the infinite detriment of moral character, but all her laws shall be emanations from the infinite source of justice. Marshalling thus all her forces on the Lord's side, she may inscribe, without mockery, on her silver and gold, "In God we trust." She may hope for purity in her homes, and honesty in her councils. She may see her growing grandeur without misgiving, knowing that it comes not by earthly might or power, but by the Spirit of the Lord of Hosts; and the only voice of her victory, the song of her thanksgiving, and her watchword to the nations shall be, "Glory to God in the highest; and on earth peace, good-will toward men."

XXV.

A RAMBLE IN THE OLD PATHS.

THE earliest known inhabitants of Great Britain were the Britons, or Celts. The literature which they left is comprised in a few words, chiefly names of lakes, rivers, and mountains.

About 55 B. C., the Romans, under Julius Cæsar, invaded and occupied England. They preserved their own nationality, and did not coalesce with the Britons. They built excellent military roads, — still represented by the chief roads of England, — and substantial military stations, where stand now some of the most important towns. They also left a few names and terminations of names.

About 449 A. D., the Angles and the Saxons, with other Gothic tribes from Central Northern Europe, now Germany, took possession of England in what, if they were not our ancestors, we should call a decidedly piratical manner. But as they gave up their piratical craft after they had landed, and took kindly to what civilization the Romans had left in Britain, let bygones be bygones. The Romans, and for the greater part the Britons, disappeared; the Angles, who gave her name to England, the Saxons, and perhaps the Scandinavians or Danes, intermingled, are generally considered to be the chief founders of the present English nation, although its early history is involved in obscurity.

The conversion of the islanders to Christianity had been attempted and professedly accomplished, in the first century; but we find Augustine beginning at the beginning again, in the sixth or seventh century. Literature advanced hand in hand with Christianity, but it was chiefly in possession of the clergy, and written in the Latin language. The Anglo-Saxon was not supposed to be dignified enough for writing. The "Venerable Bede" translated a part of the Bible into Anglo-Saxon, and wrote a valuable Ecclesiastical History of England. He, with Alcuin, his pupil, the friend and tutor of Charlemagne, Aldhelm, Johannes Erigena, and others, less distinguished, wrote Commentaries on the Bible, Homilies, Lives of the Saints, treatises on Grammar, Music, Orthography, the Body and Blood of our Lord, and other themes little known to modern readers.

A few Anglo-Saxon poems remain to us, — the most interesting of which is a narrative poem by Caedmon, from which Milton is supposed to have borrowed some of the ideas of "Paradise Lost." Literature received inestimable advantages from the patronage and active exertions of King Alfred the Great, who lived in the ninth century. Suffering constantly from painful disease, he wrote books of his own, translated those of others, encouraged literary men, fought his country's battles, and left, as he desired, to the men that lived after him, his remembrance in good works.

In 1066, England was conquered again by the Normans. Norman-speech (French) affected the language somewhat, but the English of to-day is, in its structure, Saxon. The Normans held themselves a superior race to the Saxons, and made French the fashionable language. But if the Normans were proud, the Saxons were steadfast, as they generally are, and finally carried their point, as they generally do. The English aristocracy traces its descent chiefly from the Normans, but English literature has a Saxon framework. The twelfth century devoted itself mostly to the classics, and may be summarily dismissed. The thirteenth gave to Englishmen and Americans the Great Charter of their liberties. The Gesta Romanorum, a motley collection of fables, legends, parables, and anecdotes, written in Latin, came into somewhat general circulation at this time, particularly among the monks. Shakespeare, Parnell, and others, owe to the Gesta sundry of their plots and incidents. The Fabliaux, and Chivalrous

Romances, wherein figure King Arthur and his Knights of the Round Table, Sir Lancelot, Sir Galahad, and the Holy Grail, were translated into English and England, during this century. Some of them are supposed to have originated in England, but to have been written in French to give them the court stamp, and insure their reception by "the best society." One of them, "Havelok," is the story of the orphan child of a Danish king, whose faithless guardian sets him adrift on the open sea. He drifts to some purpose, however, as he is finally picked up on the eastern coast of England, by a fisherman named Grim. After he is grown up, the wicked guardians of a beautiful princess, supposing him to be nothing but a fisherman, force her to marry him, that she may become nothing but a fisherman's wife, and they obtain her kingdom. After the marriage, Havelok informs her that she has not made so bad a match after all, recovers both kingdoms by battle, and lives happily ever after; which was doubtless very satisfactory to them, but not so interesting to us as the fact that General Havelock of the Sepoy rebellion immortality descended in a direct line from this valiant soldier, and the white linen things which our soldiers wear on their heads, to do the work which their hats ought to do, descended from him. If any one does not believe this story, he can go to England and visit the very town Grimsby, or he can go to Washington and see the soldiers under their Havelocks.

The fourteenth century gave us a foretaste of the Reformation in John Wycliffe. He is known through the boldness with which, being a priest, he attacked priestly abuses and Papal supremacy, as well as through his literary works. He inveighs against the "fair hors, and jolly and gay sadeles and bridles ringing by the way, and [the priest] himself in costly clothes and parure," while "Beneficed priests kennen not the Ten Commandments, ne read their sauter, ne understand a verse of it." "Capped priests that had bean cleped masters of divinity have their chamber and service as lords and kings, and senden out idiots full of covetise to preache not the Gospel, but chronicles, fables, and lesings, to please the people and to rob them." Wycliffe was befriended by the king's son, John of Gaunt, or it would have gone hard with him. His most valuable work is his translation of the Bible, in 1380. It is not only our first entire English Bible, but is among our earliest Saxon prose books.

The very oldest is Sir John Mandeville's account of his travels, published in 1355. Among the marvellous things which he saw in his Eastern travels was a palace, in the hall of which was "a vine made of gold that goeth all about the hall, and it hath many bunches of grapes. Some are white, . . . and the red are rubies." One of the emperors whom he visited "hath in his chamber a pillar of gold in which is a ruby and carbuncle a foot long, which lighteth all his chamber by night." He gave to Becket's shrine in Canterbury Cathedral a glass globe containing an apple brought from the East in good preservation, and to the altar of St. Albans Abbey Church, a patera from Egypt, still preserved in London.

Contemporary with Wycliffe, and like him a friend of Prince John, was Geoffrey Chaucer, student, man of the world, soldier, courtier, ambassador, traveller, but greater than all, and best known to us, as poet, and the "Father of English Poetry." Ruddy, and of a beautiful countenance, so that the Countess of Pembroke used to tell him that his silence was more agreeable to her than his conversation (which, by the way, most of us would consider a questionable compliment), of graceful figure and polished manners, familiar with the splendors of the most splendid court of Europe, and on terms of intimacy with her finest gentlemen, Chaucer led a life such as few poets have led; though, towards the end of it, he is supposed to have shared the common lot, and to have suffered from poverty and neglect. He not only enriched our literature by his direct contributions, but he crystallized the language, which at that time was fluctuating and uncertain. People clung to old Saxon forms after the substance had faded, and rejected any improvements from the hated Normans. But Chaucer, in close intimacy with them, had no such scruples, and he introduced a multitude of French words which are now a part of our daily speech. It is of him that Spenser speaks as the "well of English undefyled." Before his time, the language could hardly be called English at all. His poetry, as might be supposed, deals with men and women rather than with nature, yet it is sweet-scented everywhere with the breath of the May-time. He joins his contemporaries in the hue and cry raised against priestcraft, and has thousands of sharp, shining arrows for the fashionable vices and weaknesses of society. His principal work is the Canterbury Tales. Some of them bear date after his sixtieth year, and the whole work lay upward of seventy years in the manuscript, when Caxton made it one of the earliest productions of his press. It consists of stories told by thirty persons who are on a pilgrimage to Canterbury. Each is to tell one story in going, and one in returning; but he did not complete his design, as there are only twenty-four stories in all. They are prefaced by a pen-portrait of each one of the company, which is the best part of it. He gives us admirable pictures of the life and manners of the Englishmen of the day, from highest to lowest. He is genial, manly, shrewd, full of sly, or keen, or broad humor. His observation is minute and accurate. His outlines are firm and full. His men and women are real, living, English human beings, acting just as fourteenth-century Englishmen would be supposed to act. Nothing of its kind in English literature has surpassed it. Merrie England never before or since sat for her portrait to such a master of his art. His healthy good humor, his own manifest enjoyment of his work, his nice sense of the ridiculous and his inimitable skill in taking advantage of it, his tenderness of feeling, his gentle pathos, the little dew-drops of Nature, that sparkle throughout, the lofty, romantic, chivalrous, and even heroic tone of a great part, make us overlook much coarseness, some of which is attributable to the age, and not to the writer.

It is marvellous that we do not read Chaucer more. The language presents no difficulties that may not be overcome by a little practice, and Chaucer modernized is Chaucer about as good as spoiled. It destroys his simplicity, and the exquisite olden flavor, while the ancient form gives us at a glance the history of numerous words, and is a quarry of interesting lore.

What with French wars, insurrectionary wars, and civil wars, Merrie England seems to have had a very pretty time of it during the fifteenth century; and since people that are fighting cannot always stop to write, literature languished during this and the first half of the next century. Some of our best old ballads, however, which came in as the Chivalrous Romances died out, and were to the common people what these had been to the nobility, are referable to this period.

Sir Thomas More, too, lived his noble life, died his honorable death, and produced the work of genius of his age. He has been said to be the first English writer whose prose is good. "Utopia," written in Latin, is an account of a commonwealth planted on an island newly discovered in the Atlantic. The principles on which it is founded put to shame the boasting nineteenth century. His republic recognizes the importance of religious toleration, popular education, and the prevention rather than the punishment of crime. He will have no lawyers in it, and men who do not believe in a future state are ineligible to office, but not punished, "because a man cannot make himself believe what he please," and he "will not drive men to dissemble." He even goes so far as to punish persecutors by banishment or slavery. In its design it suggests Plato's "Republic," and in style Swift's "Gulliver's Travels." It is a romance, — serious enough to express his views, which were far in advance of his age, — and having enough the air of a jest and satire to be passed off as such in case its free-thinking should bring him under the ban of Henry the Eighth. Utopia is a word of Greek derivation, and means "nowhere." Its chief river, Anyder, means "waterless," and its nomenclature is arranged chiefly after the same fashion.

Roger Ascham, the beloved tutor of the lovely and ill-fated Lady Jane Grey, and a fine classical scholar, somewhat later than More, wrote excellent English and excellent sense. His most interesting work is "The Schoolmaster," in which he promulgates his ideas of teaching, — ideas that have even now much value. It is in this work that we find Lady Jane Grey reading Greek while her family are out hunting. He prophesies also a failure in the attempt to naturalize hexameters, — a prophecy which seems to have been true, notwithstanding "Evangeline."

Henry Howard, Earl of Surrey, courteous, chivalrous, and accomplished, — beheaded at the age of thirty-one by Henry the Eighth for being a kinsman of Katherine Howard, — transplanted the Sonnet from Italy to England, polished the language to greater refinement, and gave the first blank verse to English poetry in his translations of Virgil.

The first series of private letters known to exist in Europe are called "The Paston Letters," and date back to this century. They are sprightly and interesting familiar letters, by and to different members of a rich and respectable family of English gentry.

The sixteenth century dragged heavily at first, under the feet of a bloody and brutal king, but after Elizabeth ascended the throne, in 1558, the soul of the nation came up like a lion from the swelling of Jordan, and made that century, and the first part of the next, memorable. Patriotism, kindled by Spanish menace, the Spirit of Freedom evoked by Luther, joined hands with the lingering Romance of the past, and life and vigor and beauty burst everywhere into bloom. The virgin queen surrounded herself with men, any one of whom would have made a reign illustrious.

Francis Bacon, born and bred in the sunshine of her court, and, in his childhood, playfully called by her her young Lord Keeper, was at once the glory and the shame of his time, — a man who, with undying fame in his grasp, cringed for court favor, with all future ages at his feet, sold his integrity for a bawble, and who by his intellect secured an immortality which his character can only deprecate. Politics was his business, and it left him a disgraced and broken-hearted old man. Philosophy was his amusement, and it crowned him with glory, honor, and immortality. "I have taken all knowledge to be my province," was the sublime watchword of the youthful philosopher. "I do plainly and ingenuously confess that I am guilty of corruption. I beseech your lordships to be merciful to a broken reed," is the pathetic wail of the aged Chancellor. His great work is *Instauratio Magna*, "The Great Restoration" (of Philosophy). He inaugurated a new era. The old philosophers revered Science as a goddess, but Bacon made her the handmaid of man. They would have deemed the telegraph a degradation of electricity. He would have deemed it a new gem in its crown. So he honored man and labored for his good. The *Instauratio Magna* is divided into six parts, of which the second, the *Novum Organum*, is perhaps the most celebrated, certainly the most quoted, especially the first book, which its aphoristic style facilitates. Bacon also wrote a romance, "The New Atlantis," but he is most popularly known by his Essays, which are written in every-day language, on every-day subjects, and, to use his own words, "come home to men's business and bosoms." Few modern books are so well worth reading. He is replete with wit and wisdom, concise and concentrated, often imaginative, often poetical, always suggestive, always peerless.

Edmund Spenser, the friend of Leicester and Raleigh, named in his epitaph, with no "obituary falsehood," "prince of poets in his tyme," —

> "Sweet Spenser, moving through his clouded heaven
> With the moon's beauty and the moon's soft pace,"

shines upon us still with a white radiance that no years can dim. His principal work, "The Faerie Queene," is a chivalrous romance. We walk in a marvellous land, — a land of enchanted forests, and mystical gardens, and golden palaces, of valiant knights, and lovely ladies, and light-footed naiads, of witches, and hags, and elves, and satyrs. But more is meant than meets the eye. Under the surface-story lies an allegory, and perhaps somewhat of traditional history. With or without allegory, the poem — especially the first book, which is a poem by itself — is resplendent with genius and spotless in purity. Written in the full flush of his prime, there is an exquisite delicacy and harmony of language, a luxuriance of imagination, a tenderness of feeling, a religious fervor, a sweet and serious simplicity, which justify his title, "Poet of poets." His "Epithalamion," or Marriage Song, a

> "Song made in lieu of many ornaments
> With which my love should duly have been dect,"

is a gush of melody, an "intoxication of ecstasy." Never, surely, were maiden brows wreathed with a chaplet so fair.

Of Shakespeare it is needless to speak.

> "He was not of an age, but for all time."

Over the remote past and the remote future, he waved his wand, and they became instinct with life. The world of reality and the realm of Faerie were alike laid under subsidy. In creative power, in knowledge of the human heart, and in his all-comprehensive philosophy, the "myriad-minded man" stands alone,

> "Not one, but all mankind's epitome.'

Of the man Shakespeare we hardly know more than of Melchisedec. The poet Shakespeare was the legacy of his age to all future generations.

In connection with Shakespeare, it may be mentioned that the early theatres in England were under the direction of the clergy, who often wrote the plays, and were not unfrequently the actors. They found that people insisted on being amused by vulgar and pernicious exhibitions at the country fairs, and they very wisely took the matter into their own hands, and made themselves friends of the mammon of unrighteousness. Under their auspices, the Drama became a source not only of amusement, but of instruction. The plays (known as Mysteries) were religious, and were founded on Bible narratives or saintly legends, and called Miracle-Plays, in distinction from a later class which grew out of them, called Moral Plays, which were made instructive by personifying abstract qualities. Subsequently, these two were confounded into Mixed Plays, or Interludes. It was not till the middle of the sixteenth century that the Drama was divided into Comedy and Tragedy. Nicholas Udall wrote the earliest known Comedy, "Ralph Roister Doister," at a date earlier than 1557. He was master of Eton, and wrote several Latin plays to while away the long winter evenings of his boys, who acted them. Thomas Norton and Lord Buckhurst (Thomas Sackville, son of Sir Richard Sackville, who prompted the composition of Ascham's "Schoolmaster") wrote the first Tragedy, "Gorboduc," and first applied blank verse to dramatic composition, about 1567.

Among the most celebrated minor dramatic writers, contemporary, or nearly so, with Shakespeare, may be reckoned Marlowe, solemn and stately, yet in his tragic frenzy "tearing and rending his way through his verse."

> "His raptures were
> All air and fire."

Ben Jonson, of the noted epitaph, (O rare Ben Jonson!) the burly bricklayer, Shakespeare's friend and admirer, Camden's pupil, Fuller's "Spanish great galleon," in artistic merit has been ranked next to Shakespeare. Poignant, sarcastic, and learned, — at once strong and delicate, — he deserves special mention for preserving moral purity in the midst of licentiousness.

Beaumont and Fletcher, twins in genius and associates in life, barely escaped greatness. With much elevation of sentiment, much wealth of imagination, much fineness of feeling and exquisite poetic diction, their works are grievously marred by the indecency of their age.

The melancholy Massinger, whose tombstone only records "Philip Massinger, a stranger," vigorous, original, romantic, graceful, majestic; Ford, working out horrible plots with pathos and effect; Webster, delighting in the charnel-house; Chapman, chiefly known for his Homeric translation of Homer, — are all that I have space to mention. The style of all seems to us somewhat stiff and uncouth. They affected antiquated or obsolete phrases, and far-fetched conceits, but the worst fault is their immorality.

What had been mere coarseness of language and manners sunk gradually into the grain of life and society, and literature in the seventeenth century and under the reign of Charles the Second became frightfully depraved, although the heroic and life-giving impulse of the sixteenth extended to the first half of the succeeding century. Among the prose-writers of that period, Sir Philip Sidney, brightest ornament of Queen Elizabeth's court, the gentleman and hero among a race of heroes, "a warbler of poetic prose," wrote a "Defence of Poesy," rather eloquent than lucid, and whose existence is his strongest argument. His Arcadia is a voluminous romance, said to have been written to please his sister, the Countess of Pembroke, extremely popular in its day, but now little read. Sir Walter Raleigh, in the Tower of London, under sentence of death, wrote a huge history of the world, full of learning, serious and devout in tone, as it well might be, and less read, perhaps, than from its eloquence it deserves to be. Among theologians, Hooker's famous "Ecclesiastical Polity" ably discusses the principles on which the Reformed English Church was established, and is strenuous for popular government to the verge of democracy. Grave and elevated in style, it is said to be, in point of eloquence, the noblest monument in our language.

Hall, a generation later than Hooker, is clear, logical, shrewd, practical, pedantic, erudite, — often, in his sermons, colloquial even to punning. He has been called the English Seneca. His "Contemplations" is his most celebrated work.

Jeremy Taylor, his contemporary, is imaginative, fanciful, rhetorical to a degree which sometimes disfigures his style, impassioned, gentle, and charitable. His sermons abound in classical and other quotations, and his imagination sometimes bears him aloft beyond the vision of a commonplace audience. His "Holy Living," "Holy Dying," and "Life of Christ," are more familiar to the present generation than "The Golden Grove," — so named from the place where it was written, the house of his neighbor and patron, the Earl of Carberry. His "Liberty of Prophesying" is the first direct and able plea for religious toleration. Written during his own forced silence and retirement in Wales for his religious opinions, it may well have been earnest. He affirms that the very fact that wise and good men differ about certain doctrines indicates that those doctrines are not revealed in the Bible, — that the fundamental truths can be placed in very small compass, — in fact, embrace no more than the Apostles' Creed.

Baxter (who died in 1691) wrote for use, not for reputation, amid sickness and persecution. He is careless of style, careful only for matter, bold, acute, impetuous, often homely, and even coarse in his determination to be intelligible and impressive. His "Saint's Everlasting Rest," and his "Call to the Unconverted," are widely known.

Fuller, of marvellous memory and inexhaustible wit, eccentric, kind-hearted, and pious, overflowing with "quips, and cranks, and wanton wiles," has been called "the very strangest writer in our language." Wandering up and down in England, he preached sermons so interesting, so attractive, so irresistible, that it has been said he was accustomed to have two audiences at every discourse; the one seated in the church, the other listening eagerly through the open windows. Sometimes his words cleft the scholarly air of Cambridge; then he went down into the fruitful and beautiful valley-lands of Dorsetshire; up again presently into the thick of London life; but wherever he went, his fame went before him, and lingered behind him. Dry-as-dust, in the Cambridge archives, lifted his eyes from his fragrant and beloved tomes, roused into animation by that cheery, hearty voice; Colin, fresh from his sheepfold, felt its persuasive power; and above all the din and roar of the angry crowd in the great city, it rang out its trumpet-notes of no uncertain sound. A civil war shook the land. Lovers of liberty, then as now, left home and quiet, child and wife, buckled on armor, and rushed joyfully to battle and to death. Amid many a lurid sacrifice, set on fire of hell, gleamed over all the land the heavenly light of burnt-offerings acceptable unto the Lord. Among it all, with watchful eye and undaunted heart, this man walked; no partisan,—too firm a believer in the divine right of kings for the one side, too loyal a supporter of the divine right of the people for the other,—but respected for his worth, courted for his wit, and admired for his wisdom. On whichever side he spoke, men believed in his sincerity, and his lofty aims. Over a nation, surging with love and rage, he endeavored to pour the oil of peace and patience; yet on occasion, he could fire a beleaguered garrison to heroic and successful resistance. Never suffering himself to be carried beyond the control of reason and right, he evinced the serene self-poise of his character by enforcing the claims of religion, and the duty of moderation in the midst of civil war; and was yet so joyous, so light-hearted, so full of infinite jest and most excellent humor, that it seemed "He scarce could ope his mouth, but out there flew" an anecdote, a pun, a sarcasm,—something witty and winged for a straight flight to the mark. Indeed, Lamb says, "Such was his natural bias to conceits, that I doubt not upon most occasions it would have been going out of his way to have expressed himself out of them." His lively imagination was aided by a marvellous memory. Five hundred words, entirely unconnected, in different languages, he could repeat, after hearing them twice read.

Passing down one side, and up the other, of one of the busy streets of London, he could repeat, in their order, every sign on both sides. A whole sermon, after one reading, he could repeat word for word. An anecdote is told corroborative at once of his memory, his wit, and his benevolence. The Committee of Sequestrators, at one of their sittings, were speaking of his great memory; he offered to give them an example of it; they accepted the motion, and he immediately mentioned a poor parson, his neighbor, who had been deprived of his living, and committed to prison, to the great distress of his family; adding, "If you will please to release him out of prison, and restore him to his parish, *I will never forget the kindness while I live!*" Travelling to and fro as chaplain in the army, gathering from every old woman and every rustic such snatches of local history and tradition as they could furnish, and storing them away in the vast halls of his memory, re-creating through his imagination, he made his mind an inexhaustible repertory, from which he brought forth at command things new and old. Quaint and sensible, learned and lively, witty and genial, religious and humane, he has never wanted, through all these years, his coterie of enthusiastic admirers; but time and books have interposed between him and a large audience.

Among the lay writers may be mentioned John Lyly, whose "Euphues" is worthy of note more for its influence than for its intrinsic worth. It is pompous and pedantic, but it pleased his readers, and was for a time fashionable. Selden's "Table-Talk" is the precursor of Boswell. Burton's "Anatomy of Melancholy," an "undigested farrago," was the only book, Johnson says, that took him out of bed two hours before he wished. Sir Thomas Browne is quaint, somewhat cumbrous, paradoxical, brilliant, and full of interest.

The muster-roll of the gods closes with the name of John Milton. Here it becomes us to walk with unsandalled feet, for we tread on holy ground. His whole life was an exposition of his noble words,—"that he who would not be frustrate of his hope to write well hereafter in laudable things, ought himself to be a true poem; that is, a composition and pattern of the best and honorablest things; not presuming to sing high praises of heroic men, or famous cities, unless he have in himself the experience and the practice of all that which is praiseworthy." In the bloom of his beautiful youth, he wrote "L' Allegro," "Il Penseroso," and "Lycidas." The first is an invocation to Mirth, the second to Melancholy. In the one, Nature is a country lass, cheerful, ruddy, and buxom. In the other, she is a pale-browed Madonna, saintly and pure. "Lycidas" is a monody on the death of his young friend King, drowned in the Irish Sea. It is a memorial of dignified sorrow, to which only Tennyson's "In Memoriam" is second. His "Ode on the Nativity" is simple, calm, majestic, self-poised above comment. While he was drinking in the loveliness of Italy, basking in the sunshine of her appreciative homage, and strengthening himself for his life-work, a sound of battle in his native land broke harshly upon the soft Italian air. Already the gleam of his great song had shone upon him, but at the call of patriotism he put off his garland and singing-robes and went home to do knightly duty. His pen wrought mightily for England and liberty. His polemical writings were of course chiefly of local and temporary interest. His style is always elaborate, inverted, to us unnatural, and often harsh; but alike in prose and in poetry, his wonderful learning is poured out with unstinted prodigality, and ever and anon the grand soul of the poet bursts forth resplendent and sublime. His "Areopagitica," a plea for unlicensed printing, is a noble, glowing, and eloquent tribute to Truth, such as any age might be proud to claim. He loved liberty with an immortal love. Assured by his physicians that the completion of his "Defence of the English People" would result in total blindness, he still believed his duty unchanged, finished the work, and took leave forever of the sweet sunshine. The sacrifice which he made in turning aside from poetry and literature to controversy, is one which few have the ability to make. His own account of it has a manly modesty and sublime self-confidence,—the loftiness, and breadth, and majesty which stamps alike his writings and his life. "For although a poet, soaring in the high reason of his fancies, with his garland and singing-robes about him, might, without apology, speak more of himself than I mean to do; yet for me sitting here below in the cool element of prose, a mortal thing among many readers of no empyreal conceit, to venture and divulge unusual things of myself, I shall petition to the gentler sort, it may not be envy to me. I must say, therefore, that after I had for my first years, by the ceaseless diligence and care of my father, (whom God recompense!)" studied and written "the style, by certain vital signs it had, was likely to live. But much latelier in the private academies of Italy, whither I was favored to resort, perceiving that some trifles which I had . . . . composed at under twenty or thereabout, met with acceptance above what was looked for. . . . . I began thus far to assent both to them and to divers of my friends here at home, and not less to an inward prompting which now grew daily upon me, that by labor and intense study, ... joined with the strong propensity of nature, I might perhaps leave something so written to after times, as they should not willingly let it die. . . . . Neither do I think it shame to covenant with any knowing reader, that for some few years yet I may go on trust with him toward the payment of what I am now indebted, as being a work not to be raised from the heat of youth, or the vapors of wine; . . . . but by devout prayer to that Eternal Spirit, who can enrich with all utterance and knowledge, and sends out his Seraphim, with the hallowed fire of his altar, to touch and purify the lips of whom he pleases. . . . . Although it nothing content me to have disclosed thus much beforehand, but that I trust hereby to make it manifest with what small willingness I endure to interrupt the pursuit of no less hopes than these, and leave a calm and pleasing solitariness, fed with cheerful and confident thoughts, to embark in a troubled sea of noises and hoarse disputes. . . . . But were it the meanest under-service, if God by his secretary conscience enjoin it, it were sad for me if I should draw back." So, a Cavalier and a poet by taste, a politician and a Roundhead by principle, his days went grandly by. When the Republic vanished, and Charles the Second had introduced the age of moral degradation,

"His soul was like a star, and dwelt apart."

He was blind, poor, despised, forsaken, but his groping fingers wandered over the sacred keys, and drew thence "a sevenfold chorus of songs and harping symphonies." The glories of heaven passed in stately procession before the eyes that were closed to earth, and his epic life blossomed in that flower of a thousand centuries, "Paradise

Lost." His dust consecrates the chancel of St. Giles Church; his spirit is passed beyond our ken; his memory is the heritage of his race.

John Dryden is the only other poet of the seventeenth century who need be mentioned in a general sketch, and he is remembered more for his ability than for his achievements. He displays great vigor of reasoning and the utmost felicity of expression. The characters of his dramas are unnatural, and their talk is harangue. His panegyrics are stilted and full of conceits. His renderings of Chaucer are easy and pleasant, but, compared with Chaucer, verbose. His Ode on St. Cecilia's Day is animated and picturesque. His Satires are condensed, discriminating, and terribly severe. His command of language is admirable, — he says what he undertakes to say; and he did much for the improvement of style. Had he only been able to stand aloof, like Milton, whom he admired, from the venality of his time, he might have left a great name; but he chose the applause of a vile present, to the approval of the purer future. He deemed it

"Better to reign in hell than serve in heaven,"

and he stooped to conquer. By pandering to licentiousness, he led the licentious herd, and — lost the prize! Yet he deserves pity rather than scorn. The miserable husband of an Earl's daughter, — who despised him for a plebeian, but who yet must not be unduly blamed, since it was not her fault that she was born a Howard and a fool, — a wretched home gave him no comfort, and his brain was his only resource for bread. But it must be a profound and lasting regret

> "that a ribald king and court
> Bade him toil on to make them sport;
> Demanded for their niggard pay,
> Fit for their souls, a looser lay,
> Licentious satire, song, and play;
> The world defrauded of the high design,
> Profaned the God-given strength and marred the lofty line."

Among the lesser lights of this period is Samuel Butler, author of "Hudibras," a rhymed satire on the Puritans; keen-scented for cant, homely even to coarseness, keeping up a steady fire of wit, surpassingly ingenious in the manufacture of humorous rhymes, pungent, and Anglo-Saxon, he is excellent for condiment, but too spicy for the chief dish. Izaak Walton, gentle, quaint, courteous, graceful, is still the tutelar divinity of anglers, in virtue of his "Complete Angler," a half professional, half æsthetic, and wholly charming conversational treatise on the sport he loved.

John Bunyan, the Bedford Tinker, has been called the Father of English Novelists. Unhampered by learning, he struck out a path for himself, and wrought in Bedford Jail his "Pilgrim's Progress," equally the delight of young and old. Robert South, the "shrewdest, sharpest, bitterest, wittiest of English divines," bedaubed a vile king with flattery, mauled everybody else, and devoted his income to the charity which was a stranger to his tongue. Barrow, said at the time of his nomination to the headship of Trinity College to be the best scholar in England, second only to Newton in mathematics, and second to nobody, it is to be hoped, in the length of his sermons, which were never less than an hour and a half, and sometimes over three hours, long; Burnet, whose heterodoxy in maintaining that the story of Eden was an allegory, and that punishment was finite, stood in the way of his preferment; Owen, a Nonconformist against the blandishments of king and court,—the former of whom sent for him, talked with him two hours, and finally gave him a large sum of money to distribute among the persecuted poor, —an estimable man, a learned and an eloquent writer, whom, however, Robert Hall said he never could read with patience, and of whom somebody —it sounds like Johnson—said, "He is a double Dutchman, floundering in a continent of mud,"—all belong to this age.

The eighteenth century will be rather pressed for elbow-room, but then it is a mean kind of a century. It finished the work of Dryden, and carried neatness, clearness, and elegance of expression to an unprecedented height. But it was a cold, sneering, finical, critical, didactic age. Of course this is not true of every writer from 1700 to 1800. There are no exact dividing lines in mind to correspond with those of time, and the short, sad, passionate life of one who stirs the profoundest depths of the human heart falls wholly within this century. But the genius of the age was the legitimate offspring of the moral baseness which preceded it. It has no faith. It is earnest about nothing. It is trim, epigrammatic, sparkling, well-bred, self-possessed, but it never thrills you, possesses itself of you. Its passion is simulated. Its imagination is ingenious rather than strong and soaring. It has nothing heroic, nothing sublime. It never rises into rapture. It often sinks into coarse spitefulness, and sometimes into something worse. I am talking of the time, but I believe I am thinking of Pope, who is perhaps its best exponent. His mechanism is wonderful. His diction is unsurpassed. His versification is rarely at fault, and in a slovenly age his finish is worthy of study. But he and his contemporaries thought less of substance than of form. They burnished their flies' wings exquisitely, but they made nothing but flies. Pope touched nothing which he did not adorn, but he touched only small things. His finest poem, "The Rape of the Lock," is founded on a quarrel caused by a gentleman's slyly snipping a lady's tress. It is a mock-heroic, incomparable in its kind, full of wit, keen satire, and of flowing harmony, to be fully appreciated only by those who are familiar with real heroic poems. His "Dunciad" is an elaborate ridicule of his co-writers, ill-natured and bitter, but very clever. But the game was not worth the candle. His satire is the Valhalla of dunces. Many of those whom he transfixes would be completely forgotten but for being thus transfixed. When he rises higher, he writes Essays on Criticism and on Man, containing a great deal of terse sense, but there seems to be no especial reason why they should be written in verse. His epistle from Eloise to Abelard is intended to be intense and pathetic, and is — *ratherish*, as Charles Lamb would say. His letters, both in prose and verse, are very readable, yet hardly like real letters. Of him and his contemporaries it may be said, in general, that they conceived meanly and executed finely.

We approach Addison, the gentle, shy, modest, courteous, benevolent man whom Pope hated and satirized, with feelings nearer akin to tenderness. He too, like Dryden, "married discord in a noble wife," and domestic unhappiness helped to fix almost the only stain that sullies his fair name. His poetry would hardly have rescued his name from oblivion, though his hymns are still sung in all our churches; but, not great himself in poetry, he illustrated the greatness of others. It was his criticisms that led people back to Milton. He showed the treasures that lay hidden in our old ballads, and did much to arouse once more the spirit of true poetry. But his name is inseparably connected with the rise of periodical literature. In 1709 Richard Steele, a warm-hearted, good-natured, dissipated, troublesome friend of Addison's, of excellent principles and execrable practices, himself a writer of no small merit, began to issue "The Tatler," which in 1711 was succeeded by "The Spectator,"—a combination of novel, newspaper, quarterly review, and monthly magazine. To both, Addison contributed a large, and by far the most valuable part. It is here that he shines out in the fulness of his soft splendor. His nice observation, his delicate humor, his playful wit, the beautiful grotesqueness of his conceptions, the full outline and warm coloring of his portraits, the combination of a keen sense of the ridiculous with the largest charity and the profoundest reverence, the singular grace, ease, and refinement of his style, the purity and nobleness of his sentiments, the sincerity and depth of his religious feeling, have given him a place in our respect and affections second to few, and have placed the Spectator in the honorable rank of the English classics.

Very different from Addison in tone and temper is the sour, severe, Ishmaelitic Jonathan Swift, a clergyman whose errant life, and especially whose conduct toward women, and particularly towards the two who sacrificed life and peace to him, can be excused and even accounted for only on the supposition of insanity, or some constitutional moral deformity, — a coarse, shrewd, masculine, ferocious writer. His "Gulliver's Travels" is the story of a shipwrecked sailor who finds himself cast away in Liliput, a land whose inhabitants are so small that he strides without difficulty over their loftiest edifices, and has to walk with the greatest care to keep from crushing the people by the dozen. Another shipwreck leaves him in Brobdignag, to whose inhabitants he is as small as the Liliputians were to him. The relation of his experience in these two countries is a keen and amusing satire on the follies of mankind. By taking from their setting many of the points about which men have disputed with the utmost intensity, and by representing them among his little people, he shows their real frivolity. His "Battle of the Books" is a satire upon a fierce controversy waged upon the respective merits of ancient and modern writers in general, and upon the genuineness of the "Epistles of Phalaris" in particular. "The Tale of a Tub" casts similar ridicule upon ecclesiastical disputes, and stood sadly in the way of his promotion. One characteristic of his odd inventions is the air of reality which he gives them. He is perfectly grave, earnest, and circumstantial. He speaks with as much apparent accuracy, reflectiveness, and philosophy, as if he were relating the most momentous history. His polemical writings had great weight, and affected the destinies of Europe.

Boswell, Mrs. Thrale, and Madame d'Arblay, have made us better acquainted with Samuel Johnson than we are with most of our neighbors. Johnson the man is far more interesting than Johnson the writer. His verses are remembered for his sake, and not he for his verses' sake. His Dictionary, the fruit of eight years' toil, was valuable in its day, but has been superseded. His "Rasselas" is said to have been written to defray the expenses of his mother's funeral. It comes under the head of Romance, but would be rather heavy to the romance-readers of the present day. "The Rambler," a periodical paper, somewhat after the fashion of the Spectator, was conducted and mostly written by Johnson. It lacks the sprightliness and versatility of the Spectator, but it has a certain imposing stateliness. His "Tour to the Hebrides" is as favorable to the Scotch as could have been expected from one who hated, or pretended to hate them, so thoroughly. His "Lives of the Poets" reveals his prejudices in the selection, rejection, and treatment of his subjects, — though the selection is perhaps the work of the bookseller rather than his own, — and is not always trustworthy, but was received with great favor, and is still read. His style is elaborate, Latinized, and inverted, and has been greatly imitated and ridiculed; but there is something pleasing in the pompous, balanced, antithetic roll of his sentences. His talk is incomparable. Everybody says a good thing occasionally, but Johnson kept saying good things all the time. He would drop pearls enough at the breakfast-table to make common people brilliant for a year. His conversation was as finished and as well arranged as his writings. His power of repartee, his sarcasm, his wit and weight, his preparedness, his felicity and fertility of illustration are astonishing. His life was a romance. In his youth, he was miserably poor and proud. In his maturity, he was the lawgiver and king of the literary world. He married a coarse, ugly, and frivolous woman, twice as old as himself, and was devoted to her. He was an upright and a sincere Christian, yet through fear of death was all his lifetime subject to bondage. When he was rich enough to have a house, he filled it with blind, poor, and impotent folks, and endured all their fretfulness, and dramatized their fights. For the rest, how huge, ugly, short-sighted, awkward, rude, dogmatic, superstitious, prejudiced, cowardly, brave, independent, slovenly, fastidious, tender-hearted, he was, — how he lorded it over Boswell, and lectured Chesterfield, and petted Fanny Burney, and bullied Fanny Brown, and brushed the books with his eyelashes, and hated to go to bed, and made people sit up half the night to talk to them, and ground out doggerel rhymes on the tea, and browbeat, protected, and *mothered* Goldsmith, — is it not all, and a great deal more, written in the chronicles aforesaid?

Goldsmith follows naturally in the wake of Johnson, though utterly unlike him; — Goldsmith, the gentle, generous, thriftless, warm-hearted, simple, blundering, bashful Irishman, "who wrote like an angel and talked like poor Poll"; who would give all his blankets away to poor people, and then rip open his feather-bed and creep inside to get warm; who knew no better way to put out his candle than to throw his slipper at it; who had to keep his hat with him at parties to cover up the stain on his peach-bloom coat. Laughed at by the wits, living always from hand to mouth, with a legion of poor relations behind him, the drudge and slave of the booksellers, he preserved throughout, his unvarying sweetness. His writings have a finish and elegance that would hardly be expected from him, and which did surprise his superficial contemporaries so much that they laid the merit at Johnson's door, and poor Oliver bungled, and confirmed the suspicion. His "Traveller" and "Deserted Village" are gently, tearfully, archly, and naturally charming. "The Vicar of Wakefield" is a unique little gem, full of Goldsmith; though Johnson berated it, after having read and sold it to keep Goldsmith out of prison. His miscellaneous writings are numerous. He touched upon science, history, literature, life, and manners; and everything which he touched he adorned. His satire is good-natured, his amiability inexhaustible, his style easy, natural, and pleasing.

James Thomson, the day-star of Wordsworth, the admired of school-girls and school-boys, wrote "The Seasons," and took his descriptions first-hand from Nature, wherefore his poem is likely to live. It is in parts well known, and widely admired, as its noble diction and catholic and truly pious spirit deserve. A shorter poem, "The Castle of Indolence," is written in the Spenserian measure and manner, and has much of the spirit of Spenser, combined with a grand, energetic manliness.

Edward Young wrote "Night Thoughts" occasioned by the death of his wife and two children. It is divided into nine books, eight of which, I can depose and say, leave only a general, dismal impression; yet there does not seem to be so much real grief in it as in Tennyson's little four stanzas, —

> "Break — break — break —
> On thy cold gray stones, O sea."

Thomas Gray is polished, classical, artistic, scholarly, and sometimes a little stiff, though he *could* unbend in prose, and occasionally in verse. His "Bard" is spirited and stirring. The "Elegy in a Country Churchyard" is a mosaic, — not to be improved. He and Collins wrote but little, but on that little their fame rests securely. Nothing passed carelessly through their fastidious hands. Collins has more fire, and tenderness, and pathos than Gray. His Odes stand high, though they are probably read by very few. "To Liberty" is a splendid poem.

Chatterton,

> "The marvellous boy,
> The sleepless soul that perished in his pride,"

drained the cup of misery to the dregs, and dashed it down in passionate despair. In all literature can scarcely be found a story more profoundly sad than his. Wandering, a little child, in the beautiful old church of St. Mary Redcliffe, of which his ancestors had been the sextons for many generations, images of the past thronged in upon his soul, and peopled the dim galleries and the solemn aisles. From the strange, dreamy, isolated life of his childhood, there came forth a series of poems, which he professed to have discovered in an old chest in the church, in the manuscript of one Thomas Rowley, a priest of the Middle Ages. These poems are now generally believed to have been written by himself, and, as the productions of a boy, are wonderful. A succession of forged documents — poems, histories, chronicles — issued from the fabulous chest, and astonished the good people of Bristol. Flushed with success, he went up to London to try his fortunes in the great world, but the great world knew him not. Four months of brilliant hopes and small fruition, of incessant and wonderful writing and little money, of boyish boasting and generous gifts to mother and sister at home, and genius, poverty, obscurity, and starvation for himself in London, — and one summer morning closed the scene. Impatient of fate, and but vaguely acquainted with God, he swallowed poison and died, August 24, 1770, at the age of seventeen years, nine months. He was buried among paupers in a nameless grave. A few days after, a distinguished literary gentleman went down to Bristol to inquire into his case and provide for him. But he had taken his case into his own hands.

A softer sadness hangs around the name of Cowper, whose sweet hymns have made that name a household word. Sensitive and shrinking as a woman, yet without effeminacy, the ways of the world were too rough for him, and angels came and ministered unto him. During a large part of his life he was afflicted with a settled melancholy, which more than once deepened into positive insanity; but friendly hands tended him with motherly love and care, and kept the clouds apart for the sunshine to drift through. Human nature never looks more lovable than when we see it ever

"Beside him, true and loving."

Mrs. Unwin's long devotion, Lady Austin's and Lady Hesketh's more playful but not less tender attention, the Throckmortons' delicate kindness, — all this and much more not only relieves the gloom of Cowper's life and memory, but encircles them with a soft and saintly glory. So, surrounded by gentle ministrations, God gave his beloved sleep.

His poetry has enjoyed a rare popularity. A warm, sincere, genial, catholic, joyous, religious sentiment pervaded it. It is alike inspired with a love of God, of Nature, and of man. Yet he is capable of honest and trenchant indignation. Though gentle, he has no namby-pambyism. The tenderest and deepest sympathy and pity are found in connection with a brilliant wit and sharp satire. In style, he is clear, vigorous, and idiomatic; nor is he removed either in matter or manner from the sphere of common life. Throwing off the ornate and elaborate fashion which Pope had established, he set up a new, trusting Nature, and became the forerunner of the nineteenth century. His letters are unaffectedly simple, playful, wise, and delightful.

And yet another name adorns the annals of this age, —

> "A name
> That calls, when brimmed her festal cup,
> A nation's glory and her shame
> In silent sadness up."

With a genius whose scope and strength his short life scarcely more than essayed, Robert Burns stood up, self-assertive, before the world, and the world — made him an exciseman. Battling with the wolf which stood always at his door, he found in poetry a solace for toil, anxiety, insult, and misery, — nay, a rapt delight which raised him above it all; and so, in spite of grinding poverty and stinging neglect, he

"Walked in glory and in joy,
Following his plough along the mountain-side."

Inexhaustibly rich in all that makes a man; "dowered with the hate of hate, the scorn of scorn, the love of love," yet often overborne by the violence of his passions, and often overwhelmed with remorse for their indulgence, he bound the hearts of his countrymen to himself with a bond which time only tightens and strengthens. His songs came up fresh and glowing from his great, tender, honest, fiery heart, and go deep into the heart of humanity. The indwelling dignity of man was the first article of his creed, and he maintained it with all the force of his sturdy, glorious nature. But every chord of the heart thrills to his touch, and the eye fills or the cheek flames at his will. In other poetry than songs, he is great. "The Cotter's Saturday Night" is a Dutch painting for accuracy and minuteness of detail, with the Burns spirit shining through it, and diffusing a golden atmosphere. "Tam O'Shanter" is without a rival.

The reign of the novelists began in the eighteenth century.

Daniel Defoe, dying in 1731, wrote many pamphlets and novels, only one of which, the inimitable and immortal "Robinson Crusoe," is extensively read; but that is read enough to make up for the oblivion of the others.

Harry Fielding added the unsophisticated Parson Adams, Amelia, Squire Western, and Joseph Andrews to the picture-gallery of literature, and poured out in his novels wit enough, and power enough to stock a score of modern ones of the common type.

Clarissa Harlowe and Sir Charles Grandison stalked statelily through Richardson's novels, and roused an interest which they can never again awaken.

Laurence Sterne's "Sentimental Journey," and "Tristram Shandy," are whimsical, indescribable books, with their irregular chapters, some only three or four lines long, and some beginning or ending in the middle of a sentence. A good deal of his sentiment is lackadaisical, especially when one knows that he was a bad, hard-hearted man.

Sly little Fanny Burney hid in a corner and wrote a novel which blocked up with ducal coaches the streets that led to the circulating library, made such men as Burke and Reynolds sit up all night to read the adventures of "Evelina," and was the forerunner of the more natural and purer novels of our own time.

Horace Walpole, the aristocratic tenant of Strawberry Hill, wrote "The Castle of Otranto," an Italian romance, — more pretentious than his sharp, malicious, witty, gossiping, *blasé* Letters, but not half so readable. Mrs. Radcliffe terrified the nervous with impossible horrors, Hannah

More sent out "Cœlebs in Search of a Wife," and the Eighteenth Century was gathered to its fathers, and the Nineteenth reigned in its stead.

Now, if you knew all this before, you will read it with great delight; if you did not know it, it may perhaps serve your turn in lack of a better guide.

XXVI.

A COUNTERCHARM.

T has been said that the very best time to offer your love to a woman is directly after her own love has been trifled with by a third person. When a graceless fellow, who had possessed himself of the gem which he had not the soul to appreciate, who had esteemed carelessly, and worn lightly, what you would give your life to win, has at length tossed it away, or suffered it to fall from him, then, say the philosophers, is your time. The tendrils of a heart, rudely rent from the strength which they had clasped, will close with blind, instinctive clinging around the first support that offers.

In a matter like this, there is a great deal to be said on both sides; but I rather think it is so. Here is our Columbia, this fair young land, whose name is breathed first in our morning and evening prayer; who is entwined now with all that is high and holy in life; whose very dust is dear to us; whom in prosperity we berated soundly, but over whom now, in an agony so fearful that in the morning we say, Would God it were even! and at even, Would God it were morning! we bend with a sacred furor of tenderness; — this lovely and beloved daughter of the nations has been scorned and spurned by England. And turning away in the passion of our disappointment, we behold over against her France, *la belle* France, sunny land of apple-orchards and olive-groves and vine-clad hills; land of Trouveur and Troubadour; of sweet Provence song and wild minstrel music; of rivers whose names are a tinkling waterfall; of valleys all a-quiver with golden-throated birds; — unhappy France, that rose up maddened from her humiliation, unfurling her silken banners but to trail them in the dust, flashing aloft her golden lilies too quickly fouled with crimson stains, wild for revenge and drunk with blood, whelming in a common ruin the monuments of her degradation, the castles of her despair, the altars of her faith, and the pillar of her hopes; — suffering, sad-eyed France, to whom Liberty came, a Nemesis, with flaming eyes and fierce, fixed lips, driving her chariot of fire over the writhing limbs and throbbing hearts of her own worshippers; — faithful France, wooing an idea through seventy years of fruitless endeavor, loving not wisely but too well, now putting forth all her strength in one frantic effort, then sinking into the torpor of utter weariness and despair; — wayward and graceful France; —

blind and beautiful France, that now in a strong, unrelaxing grasp lies panting and prostrate, yet with an awful vitality which no chains can confine, no threats intimidate, no blood subdue, biding her time.

Now I do not know whether it would be quite safe to throw ourselves unhesitatingly into the arms of France; but surely, if she has many more such men as Tocqueville and Gasparin, it would be no leap in the dark. Is there another nation on the earth that has produced a single mind with the sagacity to discern, and the ability to expound, the spirit of our institutions as these two men have done? Long may Gasparin's memoir remain unwritten. Tocqueville has already "gone over to the majority," and a loving hand has penned a brief and beautiful record of his pure, noble life. I do not design to give even a synopsis of his book, "Democracy in America," or his Memoir, but only to call attention to a few striking points in them, because both seem eminently fit for the times on which we have fallen.

It is little to know that Alexis de Tocqueville was born in Paris, July 29, 1805, or that his father was Prefect of Metz, and Peer of France. We are more interested to read that he set out early in search of truth. Disheartened in his boyhood by the impotence of human reason, he writes sadly: "If I were desired to classify human miseries, I should do it in this order:—1. Sickness. 2. Death. 3. Doubt." It was in pursuit of truth that he made his ever-memorable visit to America. There are many still living who will remember the interest that was awakened by the two young Frenchmen, well-born and highly educated, who undertook a thirty-five days' sea-voyage for the purpose of exploring our public archives, watching the practical working of our laws, threading the stone passages of our prisons, and penetrating the almost impenetrable forests of wild Michigan, — making, in fact, a *reconnoissance* of this Western world; at once investigating the experiments of a novel civilization, and laying bare their souls to the sublime solitude where Nature had not yet bowed before the hand of man. Stronger than any impression made by the visit of these young men, is the recollection of the book which one of them wrote after his return, — a book of whose wisdom every day is adding fresh proofs, whose sagacity seems sometimes to have been almost inspiration, whose prophecies of 1835 are the history of 1862. It is most refreshing to turn aside from the "weak, washy, everlasting flood" of egotistic trash, with which British tourists have deluged us, to the calm, philosophic, statesmanlike work of Tocqueville's "Democracy in America." He was impelled by other motives than theirs. He had no prejudices to strengthen, no pique to gratify, no vanity to flatter. He never stooped to unmanly and frivolous motives; he never descended to personal details; he did not care to build up a flimsy fame by flattering his countrymen and ridiculing his hosts. He did not travel to confirm a theory or to decide a question of beef-steak with or without butter. France was then in the mid-agony of that long revolution which, beginning before he was born, is not finished now that he has passed away. He saw that she was surely drifting toward a democracy for which he feared that she was unprepared. The problem was, how to unite liberty with equality, — how to prevent democracy from one day throwing itself into the arms of despotism, as a last refuge against anarchy. In this New World was a democracy in the full tide of experiment, and he came over to study it for France. America was the subject of his book, but France was continually in his heart. While he watched us, he silently adjusted our institutions to France, and pointed out their fitness or unfitness for her. He had neither motive nor inclination to magnify our faults, or to ignore our virtues. He spoke the language neither of eulogy nor of slander.

Striving not to dogmatize or despise, but to learn and teach, he saw, as perhaps no other ever did, the real character and bearings of this grand democratic "experiment," and, returning to his beloved France and "secluding himself during these two years from society, spending the day-time, in order to avoid interruption, in a lodging, the secret of which was known only to very few of his friends, sustained by the flattering dreams which always visit a young author, and by the attachment which he had already formed to the lady whom he was soon to marry, he gave himself up to the intoxication which generally attends the continuous creative action of mind."

As a result, he has left alike in the land which he visited and in the land for which he visited, a monument more durable than brass. Aiming only at the highest, he gained all honors. Although he was collating, comparing, inferring, presenting, with a single eye to the welfare of his country, America holds his name in a veneration which France may equal, but can hardly excel. His book passed through fourteen editions at Paris, and has been translated into nearly all the languages of modern Europe. Its author was adjudged the Monthyon prize by the French Institute, — a prize given annually for the work of the highest moral utility that has been produced during the year; and in this case, to mark a special distinction, the prize was increased from six thousand francs, its usual amount, to eight thousand.

The reception which it met with in America shows that we can bear censure if it be kind and judicious. We are not so "thin-skinned" but that we can tolerate the keen knife in a skilful and friendly hand. What frets us is the villanous little gad-flies that sting here, and stab there, teasing everywhere, but with not the dimmest perception as to whether they have thrust their lancets into a vein or an artery, and generally in a state of profound and placid ignorance as to the existence of both veins and arteries.

Tocqueville is everywhere observant, discriminating, just. His mistakes are marvellously few. He knows what is incident, and what is essence, — what is peculiar to us, and what is common to the race. His work is perhaps the best exhibition of our institutions that has ever been given. Nowhere else can "Young America" find, within so brief a compass, a *résumé* so exhaustive, and an exposition so lucid. He sees as clearly into the genius of the country as a native, and looks upon it as impartially as if it were an antiquity. He is consequently free from all pettiness, — broad, and deep, and high.

The book should be read and studied much more than it is in America, and we welcome every effort to bring it before the people, whether its beauty be made to appeal to the eye, or its cheapness to the purse. Our people need more sound political information. A self-governing people should be a self-understanding people. The work should be made a text-book in colleges, that at least no graduate should lack a familiar acquaintance with its large truths. Nowhere else do we find so calm, unprejudiced, and impartial a statement of the principles which constitute, the dangers which beset, and the opportunities which await Democracy. Here our people may learn the origin and meaning of many usages with whose workings they are familiar, but of whose spirit they are profoundly ignorant. Here they may discern the dangers between which society oscillates, — of despotism on the one side, and anarchy on the other; the evils which threaten, and the measures which may avert, the destruction of our Republic. Religion, education, literature, commerce, universal suffrage, municipal and local authority, are here discussed, in their relation to government, with a comprehensiveness and candor which cannot fail to impart somewhat of their own elevated nature to him who shall pass them in review. A knowledge of this book is not so much a matter of taste as of national life. Read backward, it gives the interior history of our rebellion; and it was written thirty years ago. The causes which wrought then are working still, and the better we understand a democracy, the better we shall enact it. It is only by a full knowledge of its possibilities that we can be saved from disaster. The lesson that we must learn — and from no human source can we learn it better than from this book — is, that a people which would govern itself wisely must be a people intelligent, virtuous, and honorable.

Tocqueville's character was intrinsically noble. He was elevated to the heights of abstract goodness. His unselfishness was chivalrous. He read to his friend and travelling companion, Beaumont, a charming little work, "A Fortnight in the Wilderness," who at once, unthinkingly, predicted for it a far greater success than that attained by his own novel, laid in similar scenes. "At the time, Tocqueville said nothing; but he had made up his mind, and nothing could ever induce him to publish what might trespass upon the ground chosen by his friend, or appear as a rival to his work." That friend, worthy of a generosity so delicate, now prints, for the first time, this withheld manuscript.

Eminent by birth, fortune, and intellect, Tocqueville surprised the worldly-wise by marrying a young English lady, who, apparently, could in no wise advance his worldly interests. The wisdom of his course, his letters to his most intimate friends indicate. It may be supposed that the sweetness of the honey-moon still lingered around his pen when, a year after his marriage, he wrote: "I cannot tell you the inexpressible charm which I have found in living so continually with Marie, nor the treasures which I was perpetually discovering in her heart. You know that in travelling, still more than at other times, my temper is uneven, irritable, and impatient. I scolded her frequently, and almost always unjustly" (this particular trait is not held up for imitation; though women would not generally object strenuously to a little unjust husbandly scolding, *if* the husband were Tocqueville! Cases alter circumstances); "and on each occasion I discovered in her inexhaustible springs of tenderness and indulgence. . . . . Although I have great power over her mind, I see with pleasure that she awes me; and as long as I love her as I now do, I am sure that I shall never allow myself to be drawn into anything wrong." But twenty-five years later, when Madame de Tocqueville, worn out by fatigue and grief consequent upon his continued illness, herself fell ill, and was confined to a darkened room, "such was his tender love for her, and so impossible was it for him to live without her, and away from her, that, as she could no longer sit by his bed of suffering, he succeeded in dragging himself to hers. But the deep gloom of her room increased his illness, and, yielding to a sort of physical instinct, he escaped to the sunshine, which alone revived him. It was a sad fate for two beings so necessary to each other, to be able no longer to live together or apart. In fact, in a few minutes, Tocqueville returned to his wife's bedside, and said, 'Dear Marie, the sunshine ceases to do me good, if to enjoy it I must give up seeing you.'" Surely the moon must have had a honey-spring to well up sweetness so long.

His ambition was pure and lofty,—"an ambition which, in a free country, is the first of public virtues; an ambition which is patriotism, which is eagerness for the grandeur of the country which it aspires to govern through the struggles which belong to liberty, by efforts never suspended, and by successes due only to merit and to talent." The sensitiveness of his purity could not admit the shadow of a stain. He lost an election rather than permit an official recommendation from the Prime Minister, who was his kinsman. When his friend Kergorlay had compromised himself with the government, Tocqueville, who had joined it, rushed to his support, "and zealously defended him; not as one would generally defend a person under accusation, but as one would plead for a loved and honored friend." How different from the course which Bacon pursued towards Essex!

His "death was that of a Christian, as had been his life. His mind was always much disturbed by doubt. . . . . But in the midst of his greatest perplexities, he never ceased to be sincerely Christian. This sentiment amounted in him to a passion, and was even a part of his political creed; for he believed that there could be no liberty without morality, and no morality without religion. . . . . The great problem of the destiny of man impressed him with daily-increasing awe and reverence; more and more piety, and gratitude for the Divine blessings, entered every day into his actions and feelings."

He died on the 16th of April, 1859.

The pictures of domestic life, and of mature, manly, and almost romantic friendship, with which his Memoir abounds, are pure, delightful, and elevating. With such hearts and homes in France, surely her redemption draweth nigh.

The letters, whose publication a death so recent would admit, with some extracts from Mr. Senior's journal relating Tocqueville's "Table Talk," make up the whole of the second, and a part of the first volume, and are extremely interesting and valuable. The "Tour in Sicily," "A Fortnight in the Wilderness," "Visit to Lake Oneida," "France before the Revolution," and "The Consulate," are appended to the Memoir. There is throughout the book, alike in the writings of the subject and of the author of the Memoir, an indescribable nobleness, an atmosphere of refined and lofty purity, of delicate generosity, of something beyond and above the materialism of commonplace, selfish life, such as men might have breathed in the Golden Age.

XXVII.

THE NEW SCHOOL OF BIOGRAPHY.

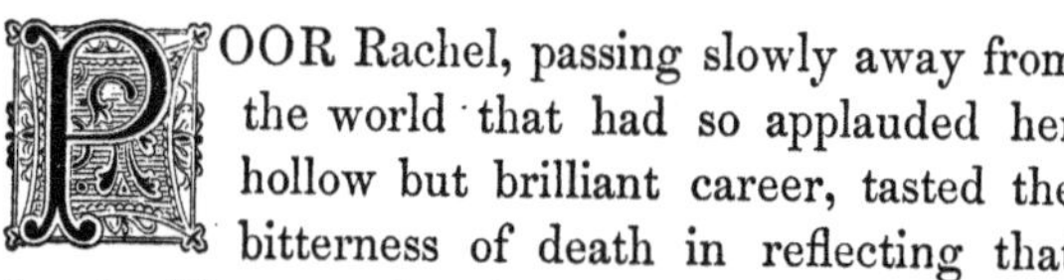

POOR Rachel, passing slowly away from the world that had so applauded her hollow but brilliant career, tasted the bitterness of death in reflecting that she should so soon be given over to the worms and the biographers. Fortunate Rachel, resting in serene confidence that the two would be fellow-laborers! It is the unhappy fate of her survivors to have reached a day in which biographers have grown impatient of the decorous delay which their lowly coadjutors demand. They can no longer wait for the lingering soul to yield up its title-deeds before they enter in and take possession; but, fired with an evil energy, they outstrip the worms and torment us before the time.

Curiosity is undoubtedly one of the heaven-appointed passions of the human animal. Dear to the heart of man has ever been his neighbor's business. Precious in the eyes of woman is the linen-closet of that neighbor's wife. During its tender, teething infancy, the world's sobs could always be soothed into smiles by an open bureau, with large liberty to upheave its contents. As the infant world ascended from cambric and dimity to broadcloth and crinoline, its propensity for investigation grew stronger. It loved not bureaus less, but a great many other things more. What sad consequences might have ensued, had this passion been left to forage for itself, no one can tell. But, by the wonderful principle of adaptation which obtains throughout the universe, the love of receiving information is met and mastered by the love of imparting information. As much pleasure as it gives Angelina to learn how many towels and table-cloths go into Seraphina's wedding-outfit, so much, yea, more, swells in Cherubella's bosom at being able to present to her friend this apple from the tree of knowledge. The worthy Muggins finds no small consolation for the loss of his overcoat and umbrella from the front entry in the exhilaration he experiences while relating to each member of his ever-revolving circle of friends the details of his loss, — the suspicion, the search, the certainty, — the conjectures, suggestions, and emotions of himself and his family.

Hence these tears which we are about to shed. For, betwixt the love of hearing on the one side, and the love of telling on the other, small space remains on which one may adventure to set the sole of his foot and feel safe from the spoiler.

There is of course a legitimate gratification for every legitimate desire, — the desire to know our neighbor's affairs among others. But there is a limit to this gratification, and it is hinted at by legal enactments. The law justly enough bounds a man's power over his possessions. For twenty-one years after his generation has passed away, his dead hand may rule the wealth which its living skill amassed. Then it dies another death, sinks into a deeper grave, and has henceforth no more power than any sister-clod. But, except as a penalty for crime, the law awards to a man the right to his own possessions through life; and the personal facts and circumstances of his life have usually been considered among his closest, most inalienable possessions.

Alas that the times are changed, and we be all dead men so far as concerns immunity from publication! There is no manner of advantage in being alive. The sole safety is to lie flat on the earth along with one's generation. The moment an audacious head is lifted one inch above the general level, pop! goes the unerring rifle of some biographical sharp-shooter, and it is all over with the unhappy owner. A respectable and well-meaning man, suffering under the accumulated pains of Presidentship, has the additional and entirely undeserved ignominy of being hawked about the country as the "Pioneer Boy." A statesman whose reputation for integrity has been worth millions to the land, and whose patriotism should have won him a better fate, is stigmatized in duodecimo as the "Ferry Boy." An innocent and popular Governor is fastened in the pillory under the thin disguise of the "Bobbin Boy." Every victorious advance of our grand army is followed by a long procession of biographical statistics. A brave man leading his troops to victory may escape the bullets and bayonets of the foe, but he is sure to be transfixed to the sides of a newspaper with the pen of some cannibal entomologist. We are thrilled to-day with the telegram announcing the brilliant and successful charge made by General Smith's command; and according to that inevitable law of succession by which the sun his daily round of duty runs, we shall be thrilled to-morrow with the startling announcement that "General Smith was born in ——," etc., etc., etc.

Unquestionably, there is somewhere in the land a regularly organized biographical bureau, by which every man, President or private, has his lot apportioned him, — one mulcted in a folio, the other in a paragraph. If we examine somewhat closely the features of this peculiar institution, we shall learn that a distinguishing characteristic of the new school of biography is the astonishing familiarity shown by the narrator with the circumstances, the conversations, and the very thoughts of remarkable men in their early life. The incidents of childhood are usually forgotten before the man's renown has given them any importance; the few anecdotes which tradition has preserved are seized upon with the utmost avidity and placed in the most conspicuous position; but in these later books we have illustrious children portrayed with a Pre-Raphaelitic and most prodigal pencil.

Take the opening scene in a garden where "Nat" — we must protest against this irreverent abbreviation of the name of that honored Governor whose life in little we are about to behold — and his father are at work.

"'There, Nat, if you plant and hoe your squashes with care, you will raise a nice parcel of them on this piece of ground. It is good soil for squashes.'

"'How many seeds shall I put into a hill?' inquired Nat.

"'Seven or eight. It is well to put in enough, as some of them may not come up, and when they get to growing well, pull up all but four in a hill. You must not have your hills too near together, — they should be five feet apart, and then the vines will cover the ground all over. I should think there would be room for fifty hills on this patch of ground.'

"'How many squashes do you think I shall raise, father?'

"'Well,' said his father, smiling, 'that is hard telling. We won't count the chickens before they are hatched. But if you are industrious, and take very good care indeed of your vines, stir the ground often and keep out all the weeds and kill the bugs, I have little doubt that you will get well paid for your labor.'

"'If I have fifty hills,' said Nat, 'and four vines in each hill, I shall have two hundred vines in all; and if there is one squash on each vine, there will be two hundred squashes.'

"'Yes; but there are so many *ifs* about it, that you may be disappointed after all. Perhaps the bugs will destroy half your vines.'

"'I can kill the bugs,' said Nat.

"'Perhaps dry weather will wither them all up.'

"'I can water them every day, if they need it.'

"'That is certainly having good courage, Nat,' added his father; 'but if you conquer the bugs, and get around the dry weather, it may be too wet and blast your vines, — or there may be such a hail-storm as I have known several times in my life, and cut them to pieces.'

"'I don't think there will be such a hail-storm this year; there never was one like it since I can remember.'

"'I hope there won't be,' replied his father. 'It is well to look on the bright side, and hope for the best, for it keeps the courage up. It is also well to look out for disappointment. I know a gentleman who thought he would raise some ducks,'" etc., etc., etc.

We are told that this scene was enacted about thirty-five years ago, and, as if we should not be sufficiently lost in admiration of that wonderful memory which enabled somebody to retain so long, and restore so unimpaired, the words and deeds of that distant May morning, we are further informed that the author is "obliged to pass over much that belongs to the patch of squashes"! "Is it possible?" one is led to exclaim. We should certainly have supposed that this report was exhaustive. We can hardly conceive that any further interest should inhere in that patch of squashes; whereas it seems that the half was not told us. Nor is this the sole instance. Records equally minute of conversations equally brilliant are lavished on page after page with a recklessness of expenditure that argues unlimited wealth, — conversations between the Boy and his father, between the Boy and his mother, between the Boy's father and mother, between the Boy's neighbors about the Boy, in which his numerous excellences are set in the strongest light, exhortations of the Boy's teacher to his school, play-ground talk of the Boy and his fellow-boys, — among whom the Boy invariably stands head and shoulders higher than they. We fear the world of boys has hitherto been much demoralized by being informed that many distinguished men were but dull fellows in the school-house, or unnoticed on the play-ground. But we have changed all that. The Bobbin Boy was the most industrious, the most persevering, the most self-reliant, the most virtuous, the most exemplary of all the boys of his time. So was the Ferry Boy, and the Pioneer Boy so. "Nat" — we blame and protest, but we join in the plan of using this undignified *sobriquet* — Nat was the one that swam three rods under water; Nat astonished the school with the eloquence of his declamation; it was Nat that got all the glory of the games; it was of no use for any one to try for any prize where Nat was a competitor. And as Nat's neighbors thought of Nat, so thought Abe's — we shudder at the sound — Abe's neighbors of Abe, the Pioneer Boy. Of what Salmon's neighbors said about Salmon we are not so well informed; but we have no doubt they often exclaimed one to another, —

> "Was never Salmon yet that shone so fair
> Among the stakes on Dee!"

Nor are the Boys backward in having a tolerably good opinion of their own goodness.

"Never swear, my son," says Abe's mother to the infant Abe.

"I never do," says Abraham.

"Boys are likely to want their own way, and spend their time in idleness," says the mother of a President, upon another occasion.

"I sha'n't," responds virtuous Abraham.

"Always speak the truth, my son."

"I do tell the truth," was "Abraham's usual reply."

"When a boy gets to going to the tavern to smoke and swear," says Nat's mother, "he is almost sure to drink, and become a ruined man."

"I never do smoke, mother," replies Nat, pouring cataracts of innocence. "I never go to the stable nor tavern. I don't associate with Sam and Ben Drake, nor with James Cole, nor with Oliver Fowle, more than I can help. For I know they are bad boys. I see that the worst scholars at school are those who are said to disobey their parents, and every one of them are poor scholars, and they use profane language."

Virtue so immaculate at so tender an age seems to us, we are forced to admit, unnatural. The boys that have fallen in our way have never been in the habit of making profound moral reflections, and we cannot resist the unpleasant suspicion that Nat had just been playing at marbles for "havings" with Cole, Fowle, and both the Drakes at the village inn, and, having found this savory repast too strong for his digestion, went home to his mother and wreaked his discomfort on edifying moral maxims. Or else he was a prig.

The unusual and highly exciting nature of the incidents recorded in these biographies must be their excuse for a seeming violation of privacy. When a rare gem is in question, one must not be over-scrupulous about breaking open the casket. What puerile prejudice in favor of privacy can rear its head in face of the statement which tells us that at the age of seven years our honored President "devoted himself to learning to read with an energy and enthusiasm that insured success"? — such success that we learn "he could read *some* when he left school."

At the age of nine he shot a turkey!

Soon after, — for here we are involved in a chronological haze, — he began to "take lessons in penmanship with the most enthusiastic ardor."

Subsequently, "there, on the soil of Indiana, ABRAHAM LINCOLN WROTE HIS NAME, WITH A STICK, in large characters, — a sort of prophetic act, that students of history may love to ponder. For, since that day, he has 'gone up higher,' and written his name, by public acts, on the annals of every State in the Union."

He wrote a letter.

He rescued a toad from cruel boys, — for, though "he could kill game for food as a necessity, and dangerous wild animals, his soul shrunk from torturing even a fly." Dear heart, we can easily believe that!

He bought a Ramsay's "Life of Washington," and paid for it with the labor of his own hands.

He helped to save a drunkard's life. "He thought more of the drunkard's safety than he did of his own ease. And there are many of his personal acquaintances in our land who will bear witness, that, from that day to this, this amiable quality of heart has won him admiring friends."

He took a flat-boat to New Orleans, and defended her against the negroes, who, poor fellows, were not prophetic enough to see that they were plotting against their Deliverer.

He "always had much *dry* wit about him that kept *oozing* out!"

We have given a bird's-eye view of the main incidents of his boyhood, for we cannot quite agree with our author in thinking that his "old grammar laid the foundation, in part, of Abraham's future character," seeing that he had "become the most important man in the place" before he studied grammar; and we have the same writer's authority for believing that "the habits of life are usually fixed by the time a lad is fifteen years of age." Nor can we admit that this grammar even "taught him the rudiments of his native language," when we have been having proof upon proof, for two hundred and eighty-six pages, that he was already familiar with its rudiments. We are equally sceptical as to whether it really "opened the golden gate of knowledge" for him: we should certainly say that this gate had stood ajar, at least, for years. Indeed, that portion of his history which relates to grammar seems to us by far the most unsatisfactory of all. In his honesty, in his penmanship, in his kindness of heart, in his wit, dry or damp, we feel a confidence which not even the shock of political campaigns has been able to move. But in respect of grammar we find ourselves in a state of the most painful uncertainty. We have never regarded it as our beloved President's strong point, but we have considered any verbal defect more than atoned for by the hearty, timely, sturdy, plain sense which appeals so directly and forcibly to the good sense of others. This book calls up a distressing doubt, and a doubt that strikes at vital interests. "Grammar," our President is reported to have said before he had cast the integuments of a grocer's clerk, "Grammar is the art of speaking and writing the English language with propriety!" Is this definition, we sorrowfully ask, becoming an American citizen? It has, indeed, in many respects the qualities of a perfect definition. It is accurate; it is exhaustive; but it is *not* loyal. Coming from the lips of a subject of Great Britain, it would not surprise us. An Englishman undoubtedly believes that grammar is the art of speaking and writing the English language with propriety. All the grammatical research that preceded the establishment of his mother-tongue was but the collection of fuel to feed the flame of its glory; all that follows will be to diffuse the light of that flame to the ends of the earth. Greek, Latin, Sanscrit, were but stepping-stones to the English language. Philology *per se* is a myth. The English language in its completeness is the completion of grammatical science. To that all knowledge tends; from that all honor radiates.

So claims proud Britain's prouder son. But can an American tamely submit to such a monopoly? Is not grammar rather, or at least quite as much, the art of speaking and writing the *American* language correctly, and shall he sit calmly by and witness this gross outrage upon his dearest rights? But, as our author would say, we "must not dwell," and most gladly do we leave this unpleasant branch of a very pleasant subject, inwardly supplicating, that, whatever disaster is yet to befall us, we may be spared the pang of suspecting that our honored President, so stanch against the Rebels, so unflinching for the Slave, is in danger of lowering his lofty crest to the rampant British lion! In view of such a calamity, one can only say in the words of that distinguished British citizen who, living in England in the full light of the nineteenth century, must be supposed to have reached the summit of grammatical excellence, —

"Gin I mun doy I mun doy, an' loife they says is sweet,
But gin I mun doy I mun doy, for I couldn abear to see it."

The life of the Ferry Boy was scarcely less adventurous than that of the Pioneer Boy, and was, indeed, in some respects its counterpart. As the latter learned to write on the tops of stools, so the former learned to read on bits of birch-bark. At an early period of his existence he broke a capful of eggs. He owned a calf. He caught an eel. He put salt on a bird's tail and learned his first lesson of the deceitfulness of the human heart. He walked to Niagara Falls from Buffalo. He got lost in the woods. He went to live with his uncle in Ohio, where he displayed spirit and killed a pig. Here also occurred a "prophecy" almost as striking as the Pioneer Boy's writing his name with a stick. "Salmon" wished to go swimming. "The Bishop said, 'No!' adding, 'Why, Salmon, the country might lose its future President, if you should get drowned!' This was the first time his name had ever been mentioned in connection with that high office; and the remark, coming from the grave Bishop's lips, must have made a strong impression on him. Was it prophetic?" Let us assume that it was, although it must for the present be ranked with what is theologically called "unfulfilled prophecy." We cannot, at any rate, be too thankful that the only occasion on which it was ever hinted to an American boy that he might one day become President has not been suffered to pass into oblivion, but has found in this little volume a monument more durable than brass. To go on with our inventory. A whole flock of thirteen pigeons shot by the Ferry Boy answered through their misty shroud to the Pioneer Boy's turkey which called to them aloud. He taught school two weeks, and then had "leave to resign." He went to Washington and said his prayers like a good boy: we trust he has kept up the practice ever since.

From such a record there is but one inference: if the man is not President, he ought to be!

One great element in the success which these little books have commanded, the one fact which, we are persuaded, accounts for the quiet, but significant "twenty-sixth thousand" that we find on the title-page of one of them, is the pains which their authors take to make their meaning clear. They do not, like too many of our modern authors, leave a book half written, forcing the reader to finish their work as he goes along. They are instant, in season and out of season, with explanation, illustration, reflection, until the idea is, so to speak, reduced to pulp, and the reader has nothing to perform save the act of deglutition.

"When he ['Nat'] was only four years old, and was learning to read little words of two letters, he came across one about which he had quite a dispute with his teacher. It was INN.

"'What is that?' asked his teacher.

"'I-double n,' he answered.

"'What does i-double n spell?'

"'Tavern,' was his quick reply.

"The teacher smiled, and said, 'No; it spells INN. Now read it again.'

"'I-double n — tavern,' said he.

"'I told you that it did not spell tavern, it spells INN. Now pronounce it correctly.'

"'It *do* spell tavern,' said he.

"The teacher was finally obliged to give it up,

and let him enjoy his own opinion. She probably called him obstinate, although there was nothing of the kind about him, as we shall see. His mother took up the matter at home, but failed to convince him that i-double n did not spell tavern. It was not until some time after that he changed his opinion on this important subject.

"That this instance was no evidence of obstinacy in Nat, but only of a disposition to think 'on his own hook,' is evident from the following circumstances. There was a picture of a public-house in his book against the word INN, with the old-fashioned sign-post in front, on which a sign was swinging. Near his father's, also, stood a public-house, which everybody called a *tavern*, with a tall post and sign in front of it, exactly like that in his book; and Nat said within himself, 'If Mr. Morse's house [the landlord*] is a tavern, then this is a tavern in my book.' He cared little how it was spelled; if it did not spell tavern, '*it ought to*,' he thought. Children believe what they *see*, more than what they hear. What they lack in reason and judgment they make up in eyes. So Nat had seen the *tavern* near his father's house again and again, and he had stopped to look at the sign in front of it a great many times, and his eyes told him it was just like that in the book;

* The meaning of this is, that Mr. Morse was the landlord, not the house. Of course a house could not be a landlord; still less could it be a landlord to itself. — *Note by Reviewer.*

therefore it was his deliberate opinion that i-double n spelt tavern, and he was not to be beaten out of an opinion that was based on such clear evidence. It was a good sign in Nat. It was true of the three men to whom we have just referred,—Bowditch, Davy, and Buxton. From their childhood they thought for themselves, so that, when they became men, they defended their opinions against imposing opposition. True, a youth must not be too forward in advancing his ideas, especially if they do not harmonize with those of older persons. Self-esteem and self-confidence should be guarded against. Still, in avoiding these evils, he is not obliged to believe anything just because he is told so. It is better for him to understand the reason of things, and believe them on that account."

Would our Parks, our Palfreys, our Prescotts, our Emersons, have expounded this matter so clearly? Most assuredly not. They would have left us in the Cimmerian darkness of dreary conjecture regarding the causes of Nat's strange opinion, and the lessons to be drawn from it. Or if they had condescended to explanation, it would have been comprised in a curt phrase or two. No boundary-line between a virtue and its corresponding vice would have been drawn so that a wayfaring man, though a fool, should not err in following it. This author has struck the golden mean. There is just enough, and not too much.

Again,—

"'I should rather be in prison, than to sit up nights studying as you do.'

"'I really enjoy it, David.'

"'I can hardly credit it.'

"'Then you think I do not speak the truth?'

"'Oh, no! . . . . I only meant to say that I cannot understand it.'

"Allusion is here made to an important fact. David could not understand how Abraham could possess such a love of knowledge as to lead him to forego all social pleasures, be willing to wear a threadbare coat, live on the coarsest fare, and labor hard all day, and sit up half the night, for the sake of learning. But there is just that power in the love of knowledge, and it was this that caused Lincoln to derive happiness from doing what would have been a source of misery to David. Some of the most marked instances of self-forgetfulness recorded are connected with the pursuit of knowledge. Archimedes was so much in love with the studies of his profession, that, etc., etc. Professor Heyne, of Göttingen," etc., etc., etc.—A clearer explanation than this we have rarely met with outside the realm of mathematical demonstration.

A shorter example of the same judicious oversight we have when "in rushed Nat, under great excitement, with his eyes 'as large as saucers,' to use a hyperbole, which means only that his eyes looked very large indeed." The impression which would have been made upon the rising generation, had the testimony been allowed to go forth without its corrective, that upon a certain occasion *any* Governor's eyes were really as large as saucers, even very small tea-saucers, is such as the imagination refuses to dwell on.

This exuberance of illustration increases the value of these books in another respect. To use a homely phrase, we get more than we bargained for. Ostensibly engaged with the life of the Bobbin Boy, we are covertly introduced to the majority of all the boys that ever were born and came to anything. The advertised story is a kind of mother-hen that gathers under her wings a numerous brood of biographical chicks. Quantities of recondite erudition are poured out on the slightest provocation. Nat's unquestioned superiority to his schoolmates evokes a disquisition for the encouragement of dull boys, in which we are told that "the great philosopher, Newton, was one of the dullest scholars in school when he was twelve years old. Doctor Isaac Barrow was such a dull, pugnacious, stupid fellow, etc., etc. The father of Dr. Adam Clarke, the commentator, called his boy, etc. Cortina," (vernacular for Cortona, probably,) "a renowned painter, was nicknamed, etc., etc. When the mother of Sheridan once, etc., etc. One teacher sent Chatterton home, etc. Napoleon and Wellington, etc., etc. And Sir Walter Scott was named," etc., etc., etc. All of which makes very pleasantly diversified reading. Nat's kindness of heart paves the way to our learning, that, "at the age of ten or twelve years, John Howard, the philanthropist, was not distinguished above the mass of boys around him, except for the kindness of his heart, and boyish deeds of benevolence. It was so with Wilberforce, whose efforts, etc., etc., etc. And Buxton, whose self-sacrificing heart," etc., etc., etc. While Nat is swimming four rods under water, we on shore are acquiring useful knowledge of the Rothschilds, of Samuel Budget, Sir Joshua Reynolds, Buxton again, Sir Walter Scott again, and the Duke of Wellington again. Nat walks to Prospect Hill, and is attended by a suite consisting of Sir Francis Chantrey, "the gifted poet Burns," "the late Hugh Miller," etc., who also loved to look at prospects. Nat organized a debating-society, (which by the way was, "in respect of unanimity of feeling and action, a lesson to most legislative bodies, and to the Congress of the United States in particular." Congress of the United States, are you listening?) and "such an organization has proved a valuable means of improvement to many persons." Witness "the Irish orator, Curran," with biography; "a living American statesman," with biography; "the highly distinguished statesman, Canning," more biography; "Henry Clay, the American orator," with autobiography; and a meteoric shower of lesser biographies emanating from Tremont Temple. Nat carried a book in his pocket, and "Pockets have been of great service to self-made men. A more useful invention was never known, and hundreds are now living who will have occasion to speak well of pockets till they die, because they were so handy to carry a book. Roger Sherman had one when he was a hard-working shoemaker, etc., etc., etc. Napoleon had one in which he carried the Iliad when, etc., etc., etc. Hugh Miller had one, etc., etc., etc. Elihu Burritt had one," etc., etc., for three pages, to which we might add, from the best authority, the striking fact which our author, notwithstanding the wide range of his reading, seems unaccountably to have missed, —

> "Lyddy Locket lost her pocket,
> Lyddy Fisher found it,
> Lyddy Fisher gave it to Mr. Gaines,
> And Mr. Gaines ground it."

Allusion is here made to an important fact. *Mr. Gaines was a miller!*

Yet, with all this elucidation, we take shame to ourselves for admitting that there are points which, after all, we do not comprehend. They may be trivial; but in making up testimony, it is the little things which have weight. Trifles light as air are confirmation strong as proofs of Holy Writ, and confutation no less strong. When, as a proof of Nat's ardor in the pursuit of knowledge, we are told that he walked ten miles after a hard day's work to hear Daniel Webster, and then *stood* through the oration in front of the platform, because he could see the speaker better,—and when, turning to the next page, we are told that he was so much interested that he "would have *sat* entranced till morning, if the gifted orator had continued to pour forth his eloquence,"—what are we to believe? When we are bidden to "listen to the gifted orator, as the flowing periods come burning from his soul on fire, riveting the attention," etc., is it a river, or is it a fire, or is it a hammer and anvil, that we have in our mind's eye, Horatio? When Nat "waxed warmer and warmer, as he advanced, and spoke in a flow of eloquence and choice selection of words that was unusual for one of his age," did he come out dry-shod? We are told of his visit to the Boston book-stores,—that he examined the books "outside before he stepped in. *He read the title of each volume upon the back, and some he took up and examined*, but we have no explanation of this extraordinary behavior. "It was thus with" Abraham. "The manner in which Abraham made progress in penmanship, writing on slabs and trees, on the ground and in the snow, anywhere that he could find a place, reminds us forcibly of Pascal, who demonstrated the first thirty-two propositions of Euclid in his boyhood, without the aid of a teacher." We not only are not forcibly reminded of Pascal, but we are not reminded of Pascal at all. The boy who imitates on slabs mechanical lines which he has been taught, and he who originates mathematical problems and theorems, may be as like as my fingers to my fingers, but — alas that it is forbidden to say! — we do not see it. When Mr. Elkins told Abraham he would make a good pioneer boy, and "'What's a pioneer boy?' asked Abraham," why was Mr. Elkins "quite amused at this inquiry?" and why did he "exercise his risibles for a minute" before replying? When Mr. Stuart offered young Mr. Lincoln the use of his law-books, and young Mr. Lincoln answered, — very properly, we should say, — "You are very generous indeed. I could never repay you for such generosity," — why did Mr. Stuart respond, "shaking his sides with laughter"? We do not wish to be too inquisitive, but few things are more trying to a sensitive person than to see others overwhelmed with merriment in which, from ignorance, he cannot share.

Want of space forbids us to do more than touch lightly upon the many excellences of these books. We have given extracts enough to enable our readers to see for themselves the severe elegance of style, the compactness and force of the narrative, the verisimilitude of the characters, the unity of plan, and the cogency of the reasoning. We trust they will also perceive the great moral effect that cannot fail to be produced by them. Such books are specially adapted to meet a daily increasing want. Our American youth are too apt to value virtue for its own sake. They are in imminent danger of giving themselves over to integrity, to industry, perseverance, and single-mindedness, without looking forward to those posts of usefulness for which these qualities eminently fit them. Fired with the love of learning, they are languid in claiming the honors which learning has to bestow. Eager to become worthy of the highest places, they make no effort to secure the places to which their worth points them. Political supineness is the bane of our society. The one great need is to rouse the ambition of boys, and wake them to political aspiration. To such objects such books tend; and who would hesitate at any sacrifice of his prejudices in favor of privacy, when such is the end to be obtained? Breathes there the man with soul so dead who would not lay upon the altar his father, his mother, his sisters, not to say his uncles and cousins, nay, the inmost sanctities of his home, to enable American boys to fasten their eyes upon the White House? Would he refuse, at the call of patriotism, to spread before the public the very secrets of his heart, the struggles of his closet, his communion with his God?

As a collateral result of this new school of biography, we can but admire the new form in which Nemesis appears. The day of rich relations is gone by. No longer can stern Uncle Bishops lord it over their obscure nephews, for ever before their eyes will flaunt the possible book which will one day lay open to a gazing world all their weakness and their evil behavior. Let not wicked or disagreeable relatives imagine henceforth that they may safely indulge in small tyrannies, neglects, or other peccadilloes; for no robin-redbreast piously will cover them with leaves, but that which is done in the ear shall be proclaimed upon the house-tops, nor can they tell from what quarter the sound shall come. The unkempt boy, the sullen girl in the chimney-corner, may be the Narcissus or nymph in whose orisons all their sins shall be remembered.

> You that executors be made,
> And overseers eke
> Of children that be fatherless,
> And infants mild and meek,
> Take you example by this thing,
> And yield to each his right,
> Lest God with such like misery
> Your wicked minds requite."

In view of which benefits, and others "too numerous to mention," we humbly beg pardon for the petulance which disfigures the commencement of our paper, and desire to use all our influence to induce all persons of distinction meekly and humanely to lay open to the dear, curious world their lives, their fortune, and their sacred honor.

But, however beneficial and delightful it is for a friend to impale a friend before the public gaze, a man would generally not desire that his adversary should write a book about him. In the motives that prompted, in the grace of the doing, in the good that will result, we can forgive the deed when friend portrays friend; but we cannot be lenient when a hostile hand exposes the life to which we have no right. We would fain borrow the type and the energy of Reginald Bazalgette to enforce our opinion that it is "ABBOMMANNABEL," and the innocence of Pet Marjorie to declare it "the most Devilish thing." Yet in a loyal, respectable, religious newspaper we lately saw a biography of Mr. Vallandigham which puts to blush all previous achievements in the line of contemporary history. It is not so much that we are let into the family secrets, but the family secrets are spread out before us, as the fruits of that species of domestic taxation known as "the presents" are spread out on the piano at certain wedding-festivals. We are led back to first principles, to the early married life of the parent Vallandighams. The mother is portrayed with a vigorous feminine pencil, and certainly looks extremely well on canvas. Clement's behavior towards her is shown to be exemplary. There is excuse for this in the attacks which have been made upon him in the relation of son. But upon what grounds are Clement's sisters' homes invaded? Because a man is disloyal and craven, shall we inform the world that his brother was crossed in love? Still more shall his wife be taken in hand, and receive what even the late Mr. Smallweed would have considered a thorough "shaking-up?" "If they were all starving," declares the energetic narrator, "she could not earn a cent in any way whatever, so utterly helpless is this fine Southern lady. She will not sleep, unless the light is kept burning all night in her room, for fear 'something might happen'; and when a slight matter crosses her feelings, she lies in bed for several days." Tut, tut, dear lady! surely this once thy zeal hath outrun thy discretion. Clement L. Vallandigham's public course is a proper target for all loyal shafts, but prithee let the poor lady, his wife, remain in peace,—such peace as she can command. It is bad enough for her to be his wife, without being overborne with the additional burden of her own personal foibles. One can be daughter, sister, friend, without impeachment of one's sagacity or integrity; but it is such a dreadful indorsement of a man to marry him! Her own consciousness must be sufficiently grievous; pray do not irritate it into downright madness. Nay, what, after all, are the so heinous faults upon which you animadvert? She cannot earn a cent: that may be her misfortune, it need not be her fault. Perhaps Clement, like Albano, and all good husbands, "never loved to see the sweet form anywhere else than, like other butterflies, by his side among the flowers." She will keep a light burning in her room, forsooth. Have we not all our pet hobgoblins? We know an excellent woman who once sat curled up in an arm-chair all night for fear of a mouse! And is it not a well-understood thing that nothing so baffles midnight burglars as a burning candle? "When a light matter crosses her feelings, she lies in bed for several days." Infinitely better than to go sulking about the house with that "injured-innocence" air which makes a man feel as if he were an assaulter and batterer with intent to kill. Blessings rest upon those charming sensible women, who, when they feel cross, as we all do at times, will go to bed and sleep it away! No, let us everywhere put down treason and ostracize traitors. It is lawful to suspend "*naso adunco*" those whom we may not otherwise suspend. But even traitors have rights which white men and white women are bound to respect. We will crush them, if we can, but we will crush them in open field, by fair fight, — not by stealing into their bedchambers to stab them through the heart of a wife.

XXVIII.

PICTOR IGNOTUS.

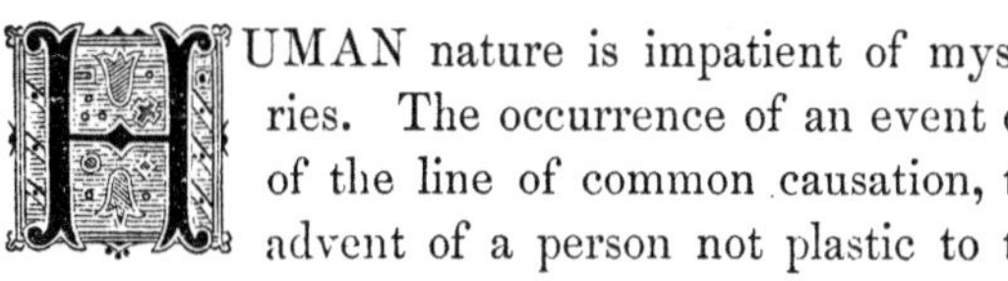

HUMAN nature is impatient of mysteries. The occurrence of an event out of the line of common causation, the advent of a person not plastic to the common moulds of society, causes a great commotion in this little ant-hill of ours. There is perplexity, bewilderment, a running hither and thither, until the foreign element is assigned a place in the ranks; and if there be no rank to which it can be ascertained to belong, a new rank shall be created to receive it, rather than that it shall be left to roam up and down, baffling, defiant, and alone. Indeed, so great is our abhorrence of outlying, unclassified facts, that we are often ready to accept classification for explanation; and having given our mystery a niche and a name, we cease any longer to look upon it as mysterious. The village-schoolmaster, who displayed his superior knowledge to the rustics gazing at an eclipse of the sun by assuring them that it was "only a phenomenon," was but one of a great host of wiseacres who stand ready with brush and paint-pot to label every new development, and fancy that in so doing they have abundantly answered every reasonable inquiry concerning cause, character, and consequence.

When William Blake flashed across the path of English polite society, society was confounded. It had never had to do with such an apparition before, and was at its wits' end. But some Daniel was found wise enough to come to judgment, and pronounce the poet-painter mad; whereupon society at once composed itself, and went on its way rejoicing.

There are a few persons, however, who are not disposed to let this verdict stand unchallenged. Mr. Arthur Gilchrist, late a barrister of the Middle Temple, a man, therefore, who must have been accustomed to weigh evidence, and who would not have been likely to decide upon insufficient grounds, wrote a life of Mr. Blake, in which he strenuously and ably opposed the theory of insanity. From this book, chiefly, we propose to lay before our readers a slight sketch of the life of a man who, whether sane or insane, was one of the most remarkable productions of his own or of any age.

One word, in the beginning, regarding the book before us. The death of its author, while as yet but seven chapters of his work had been printed, would preclude severe criticism, even if the spirit and purpose with which he entered upon his undertaking, and which he sustained to its close, did not dispose us to look leniently upon imperfections of detail. Possessing that first requisite of a biographer, thorough sympathy with his subject, he did not fall into the opposite error of indiscriminate panegyric. Looking at life from the standpoint of the "madman," he saw how fancies could not only appear, but be, facts; and then, crossing over, he looked at the madman from the world's standpoint, and saw how these soul-born facts could seem not merely fancies, but the wild vagaries of a crazed brain. For the warmth with which he espoused an unpopular cause, for the skill with which he set facts in their true light, for the ability which he brought to the defence of a man whom the world had agreed to condemn, for the noble persistence with which he forced attention to genius that had hitherto received little but neglect, we cannot too earnestly express our gratitude. But the greater our admiration of material excellence, the greater is our regret for superficial defects. The continued supervision of the author would doubtless have removed many infelicities of style; yet we marvel that one with so clear an insight should ever, even in the first glow of composition, have involved himself in sentences so complicated and so obscure. The worst faults of Miss Sheppard's worst style are reproduced here, joined to an unthriftiness in which she had no part nor lot. Not unfrequently a sentence is a conglomerate in which the ideas to be conveyed are heaped together with no apparent attempt at arrangement, unity, or completeness. Surely, it need be no presumptuous, but only a tender and reverent hand that should have organized these chaotic periods, completing the work which death left unfinished, and sending it forth to the world in a garb not unworthy the labor of love so untiringly bestowed upon it by the lamented author.

To show that our strictures are not undeserved, we transcribe a few sentences, taken at random from the memoir: —

"Which decadence it was led this Pars to go into the juvenile Art-Academy line, *vice* Shipley retired."

"The unusual notes struck by William Blake, in any case appealing but to one class and a small one, were fated to remain unheard, even by the Student of Poetry, until the process of regeneration had run its course, and, we may say, the Poetic Revival gone to seed again: seeing that the virtues of simplicity and directness the new poets began by bringing once more into the foreground, are those least practised now."

"In after years of estrangement from Stothard, Blake used to complain of this mechanical employment as engraver to a fellow-designer, who (he asserted) first borrowed from one that, in his servile capacity, had then to copy that comrade's version of his own inventions — as to motive and composition his own, that is."

"And this imposing scroll of fervid truisms and hap-hazard generalities, as often disputable as not, if often acute and striking, always ingenuous and pleasant, was, like all his other writings, warmly welcomed in this country."

Let us now go back a hundred years, to the time when William Blake was a fair-haired, smooth-browed boy, wandering aimlessly, after the manner of boys, about the streets of London. It might seem at first a matter of regret that a soul full of all glowing and glorious fancies should have been consigned to the damp and dismal dulness of that crowded city; but, in truth, nothing could be more fit. To this affluent, creative mind dinginess and dimness were not. Through the grayest gloom golden palaces rose before him, silver pavements shone beneath his feet, jewelled gates unfolded on golden hinges turning, and he wandered forth into a fair country. What need of sunshine and bloom for one who saw in the deepest darkness a "light that never was on sea or land?" Rambling out into the pleasant woods of Dulwich, through the green meadows of Walton, by the breezy heights of Sydenham, bands of angels attended him. They walked between the toiling haymakers, they hovered above him in the apple-boughs, and their bright wings shone like stars.

For him there was neither awe nor mystery, only delight. Angels were no more unnatural than apples. But the honest hosier, his father, took different views. Never in all his life had that worthy citizen beheld angels perched on tree-tops, and he was only prevented from administering to his son a sound thrashing for the absurd falsehood, by the intercession of his mother. Ah, these mothers! By what fine sense is it that they detect the nascent genius for which man's coarse perception can find no better name than perverseness, and no wiser treatment than brute force?

The boy had much reason to thank his mother, for to her intervention it was doubtless largely due that he was left to follow his bent, and haunt such picture-galleries as might be found in noblemen's houses and public sale-rooms. Then he feasted his bodily eyes on earthly beauty, as his mental gaze had been charmed with heavenly visions. From admiration to imitation was but a step, and the little hands soon began to shape such rude, but loving copies as Raffaelle, with tears in his eyes, must have smiled to see. His father, moved by motherly persuasions, as we can easily infer, bought him casts for models, that he might continue his drawing-lessons at home; his own small allowance of pocket-money went for prints; his wistful child-face presently became known to dealers, and many a cheap lot was knocked down to him with amiable haste by friendly auctioneers. Then and there began that life-long love and loyalty to the grand old masters of Germany and Italy, to Albrecht Dürer, to Michel Angelo, to Raffaelle, which knew no diminution, and which in its very commencement, revealed the eclecticism of true genius, because the giants were not the gods in those days.

But there came a time when Pegasus must be broken in to drudgery, and travel along trodden ways. By slow, it cannot be said by toilsome ascent, the young student had reached the vestibule of the temple; but

> "Every door was barred with gold, and opened but to golden keys,"

which, alas! to him were wanting. Nothing daunted, his sincere soul preferred to be a door-keeper in the house of his worship rather than a dweller in the tents of Mammon. Unable to be an artist, he was content for the time to become an artisan, and chose to learn engraving, — a craft which would keep him within sight and sound of the heaven from which he was shut out. Application was first made to Ryland, then in the zenith of his fame, engraver to the King, friend of authors and artists, himself a graceful, accomplished, and agreeable gentleman. But the marvellous eyes that pierced through mortal gloom to immortal glory saw also the darkness that brooded behind uncanny light. "I do not like the man's face," said young Blake, as he was leaving the shop with his father; "it looks as if he will live to be hanged." The negotiation failed; Blake was apprenticed to Basire; and twelve years after, the darkness that had lain so long in ambush came out and hid the day: Ryland was hanged.

His new master, Basire, was one of those workmen who magnify their office and make it honorable. The most distinguished of four generations of Basires, engravers, he is represented as a superior, liberal-minded, upright man, and a kind master. With him Blake served out his seven years of apprenticeship, as faithful, painstaking, and industrious as any blockhead. So great was the confidence which he secured, that, month after month, and year after year, he was sent out alone to Westminster Abbey and the various old churches in the neighborhood, to make drawings from the monuments, with no oversight but that of his own taste and his own conscience. And a rich reward we may well suppose his integrity brought him; in the charming solitudes of those old-time sanctuaries. Wandering up and down the consecrated aisles, — eagerly peering through the dim, religious light for the beautiful forms that had leaped from many a teeming brain now turned to dust, — reproducing, with patient hand, graceful outline and deepening shadow, — his daring, yet reverent heart held high communion with the ages that were gone. The Spirit of the Past overshadowed him. The grandeur of Gothic symbolism rose before him. Voices of dead centuries murmured low music down the fretted vault. Fair ladies and brave gentlemen came up from the solemn chambers where they had lain so long in silent state, and smiled with their olden grace. Shades of nameless poets, who had wrought their souls into a cathedral and died unknown and unhonored, passed before the dreaming boy, and claimed their immortality. Nay, once the Blessed Face shone through the cloistered twilight, and the Twelve stood round about. In this strange solitude and stranger companionship many an old problem untwined its Gordian knot, and whispered along its loosened length, —

> "I give you the end of a golden string:
> Only wind it into a ball,
> It will lead you in at Heaven's gate,
> Built in Jerusalem wall."

To an engraving of "Joseph of Arimathea among the Rocks of Albion," executed at this time, he appends, — "This is one of the Gothic artists who built the Cathedrals in what we call the Dark Ages, wandering about in sheep-skins and goat-skins; of whom the world was not worthy. Such were the Christians in all ages."

Yet, somewhere, through mediæval gloom and modern din, another spirit breathed upon him, — a spirit of green woods and blue waters, the freshness of May mornings, the prattle of tender infancy, the gambols of young lambs on the hill-side. From his childhood, Poetry, walking hand in hand with Painting, beguiled his loneliness with wild, sweet harmonies. Bred up amid the measured, melodious platitudes of the eighteenth century, that Golden Age of commonplace, he struck down through them all with simple, untaught, unconscious directness, and smote the spring of ever-living waters. Such wood-notes wild as trill in Shakespeare's verse sprang from the stricken chords beneath his hand. The little singing-birds that seem almost to have leaped unbidden into life among the gross creations of those old Afreets who

> Stood around the throne of Shakespeare,
> Sturdy, but unclean,"

carolled their clear, pure lays to him, and left a quivering echo. Fine, fleeting fantasies we have, a tender, heart-felt, heart-reaching pathos, laughter that might at any moment tremble into tears, eternal truths, draped in the garb of quaint and simple story, solemn fervors, subtile sympathies, and the winsomeness of little children at their play, — fancies glowing sometimes with the deepest color, often just tinged to the pale and changing hues of a dream, but touched with such coy grace, modulated to such free, wild rhythm, suffused with such a delicate, evanishing loveliness, that they seem scarcely to be the songs of our tangible earth, but snatches from fairy-land. Often rude in form, often defective in rhyme, and not unfrequently with even graver faults than these, their ruggedness cannot hide the gleam of the sacred fire. "The Spirit of the Age," moulding her pliant poets, was wiser than to meddle with this sterner stuff. From what hidden cave in Rare Ben Jonson's realm did the boy bring such an opal as this

SONG.

"My silks and fine array,
 My smiles and languished air,
By Love are driven away;
 And mournful, lean Despair
Brings me yew to deck my grave:
Such end true lovers have!

"His face is fair as heaven,
 Where springing buds unfold;
Oh, why to him was 't given,
 Whose heart is wintry cold?
His breast is Love's all-worshipped tomb,
Where all Love's pilgrims come.

"Bring me an axe and spade,
 Bring me a winding-sheet;
When I my grave have made,
 Let winds and tempests beat:
Then down I 'll lie, as cold as clay.
True love doth pass away."

What could the Spirit of the Age hope to do with a boy scarcely yet in his teens, who dared arraign her in such fashions as is set forth in his address

TO THE MUSES.

"Whether on Ida's shady brow,
Or in the chambers of the East,
The chambers of the Sun, that now
From ancient melody have ceased;

"Whether in heaven ye wander fair,
Or the green corners of the earth,
Or the blue regions of the air,
Where the melodious winds have birth;

"Whether on crystal rocks ye rove
Beneath the bosom of the sea,
Wandering in many a coral grove,
Fair Nine, forsaking Poetry;

"How have you left the ancient love
That bards of old enjoyed in you!
The languid strings do scarcely move,
The sound is forced, the notes are few."

Whereabouts in its Elegant Extracts would a generation that strung together sonorous couplets, and compiled them into a book to Enforce the Practice of Virtue, place such a ripple of verse as this? —

"Piping down the valleys wild,
Piping songs of pleasant glee,
On a cloud I saw a child,
And he, laughing, said to me:

"'Pipe a song about a lamb!'
So I piped with merry cheer.
'Piper, pipe that song again!'
So I piped; he wept to hear.

"'Drop thy pipe, thy happy pipe;
Sing thy songs of happy cheer!'

So I sang the same again,
  While he wept with joy to hear.

"'Piper, sit thee down and write
  In a book, that all may read!'
So he vanished from my sight,
  And I plucked a hollow reed,

"And I made a rural pen,
  And I stained the water clear,
And I wrote my happy songs,
  Every child may joy to hear."

A native of the jungle, leaping into the fine drawing-rooms of Cavendish Square, would hardly create more commotion than such a poem as "The Tiger," charging in among Epistles to the Earl of Dorset, Elegies describing the Sorrow of an Ingenuous Mind, Odes innumerable to Memory, Melancholy, Music, Independence, and all manner of odious themes.

"Tiger, tiger, burning bright
In the forests of the night,
What immortal hand or eye
Framed thy fearful symmetry?

"In what distant deeps or skies
Burned that fire within thine eyes?
On what wings dared he aspire?
What the hand dared seize the fire?

"And what shoulder, and what art,
Could twist the sinews of thy heart?
When thy heart began to beat,
What dread hand formed thy dread feet?

"What the hammer, what the chain,
Knit thy strength and forged thy brain?

What the anvil? What dread grasp
Dared thy deadly terrors clasp?

"When the stars threw down their spears,
And watered heaven with their tears,
Did he smile his work to see?
Did He who made the lamb make thee?"

Mrs. Montagu, by virtue of the "moral" in the last line, may possibly have ventured to read the "Chimney-Sweeper" at her annual festival to the swart little people; but we have not space to give the gem a setting here; nor the "Little Black Boy," with its matchless, sweet child-sadness. Indeed, scarcely one of his early poems — all written between the ages of eleven and twenty — is without its peculiar, and often its peerless charm.

Arrived at the age of twenty-one, he finished his apprenticeship to Basire, and began at once the work and worship of his life, — the latter by studying at the Royal Academy, the former by engraving for the booksellers. Introduced by a brother-artist to Flaxman, he joined him in furnishing designs for the famous Wedgwood porcelain, and so the same dinner-set gave bread and butter to genius, and nightingales' tongues to wealth. That he was not a docile, though a very devoted pupil, is indicated by his reply to Moser, the keeper, who came to him, as he was looking over prints from his beloved Raffaelle and Michael Angelo, and said, "You should not study these old, hard, stiff, and dry, unfinished works of Art: stay a little, and *I* will show you what you should study." He brought down Le Brun and Rubens. "How did I secretly rage!" says Blake. "I also spake my mind! I said to Moser, 'These things that you call finished are not even begun; how, then, can they be finished?'" The reply of the startled teacher is not recorded. In other respects, also, he swerved from Academical usage. Life, as it appeared in "a model artificially posed to enact an artificial part," became hateful to him, seemed to him a caricature of Nature, though he delighted in the noble antique figures.

Nature soon appeared to him in another shape, and altogether charming. A lively miss to whom he had paid court showed herself cold to his advances; which circumstance he was one evening bemoaning to a dark-eyed, handsome girl,—(a dangerous experiment, by the way,)—who assured him that she pitied him from her heart. "*Do* you pity me?" he eagerly asked. "Yes, I do, most sincerely." "Then I love you for that," replied the new Othello to his Desdemona; and so well did the wooing go that the dark-eyed Catharine presently became his wife, the Kate of a forty-five years' marriage. Loving, devoted, docile, she learned to be helpmeet and companion. Never, on the one side, murmuring at the narrow fortunes, nor, on the other, losing faith in the greatness to which she had bound herself, she not only ordered well her small household, but came at length to share her husband's tastes. She learned to read and write, and to work off his engravings. Nay, love endowed her with a new power, the vision and the faculty divine, and she presently learned to design with a spirit and a grace hardly to be distinguished from her husband's. No children came to make or mar their harmony; and from the summer morning in Battersea that placed her hand in his, to the summer evening in London that loosed it from his dying grasp, she was the true angel-vision, Heaven's own messenger to the dreaming poet-painter.

Being the head of a family, Blake now, as was proper, went into "society." And what a society it was to enter! And what a man was Blake to enter it! The society of President Reynolds, and Mr. Mason the poet, and Mr. Sheridan the play-actor, and pompous Dr. Burney, and abstract Dr. Delap, — all honorable men; a society that was dictated to by Dr. Johnson, and delighted by Edmund Burke, and sneered at by Horace Walpole, its untiring devotee: a society presided over by Mrs. Montagu, whom Dr. Johnson dubbed Queen of the Blues; Mrs. Carter, borrowing, by right of years, her matron's plumes; Mrs. Chapone, sensible, ugly, and benevolent; the beautiful Mrs. Sheridan; the lively, absurd, incisive Mrs. Cholmondeley; sprightly, witty Mrs. Thrale; and Hannah More, coiner of guineas, both as saint and sinner; a most piquant, trenchant, and entertaining society it was, and well might be, since the bullion of genius was so largely wrought into the circulating medium of small talk; but a society which, from sheer lack of vision, must have entertained its angels unawares. Such was the current which caught up this simple-hearted painter, this seer of unutterable things, this "eternal child,"—caught him up only to drop him, with no creditable, but with very credible haste. As a lion, he was undoubtedly thrice welcome in Rathbone Place; but when it was found that the lion would not roar them gently, nor be bound by their silken strings, but rather shook his mane somewhat contemptuously at his would-be tamers, and kept, in their grand saloons, his freedom of the wilderness, he was straightway suffered to return to his fitting solitudes. One may imagine the consternation that would be caused by this young fellow turning to Mrs. Carter, whose "talk was all instruction," or to Mrs. Chapone, bent on the "improvement of the mind," or to Miss Streatfield, with her "nose and notions *à la Grecque*," and abruptly inquiring, "Madam, did you ever see a fairy's funeral?" "Never, sir!" responds the startled Muse. "I have," pursues Blake, as calmly as if he were proposing to relate a *bon mot* which he heard at Lady Middleton's rout last night. "I was walking alone in my garden last night: there was great stillness among the branches and flowers, and more than common sweetness in the air. I heard a low and pleasant sound, and knew not whence it came. At last I saw the broad leaf of a flower move, and underneath I saw a procession of creatures of the size and color of green and gray grasshoppers, bearing a body laid out on a rose-leaf, which they buried with songs, and then disappeared. It was a fairy funeral." Or they are discussing, somewhat pompously, Herschel's late discovery of Uranus, and the immense distances of heavenly bodies, when Blake bursts out uproariously, "'T is false! I was walking down a lane the other day, and at the end of it I touched the sky with my stick." Truly, for this wild man, who obstinately refuses to let his mind be regulated, but bawls out his mad visions the louder the more they are combated, there is nothing for it but to go back to his Kitty, and the little tenement in Green Street.

But real friends Blake found, who, if they could not quite understand him, could love and honor and assist. Flaxman, the "Sculptor for Eternity," and Fuseli, the fiery-hearted Swiss painter, stood up for him manfully. His own younger brother, Robert, shared his talents, and became for a time a loved and honored member of his family, — too much honored, if we may credit an anecdote in which the brother appears to much better advantage than the husband. A dispute having one day arisen between Robert and Mrs. Blake, Mr.

Blake, after a while, deemed her to have gone too far, and bade her kneel down and beg Robert's pardon, or never see her husband's face again. Nowise convinced, she nevertheless obeyed the stern command, and acknowledged herself in the wrong. "Young woman, you lie!" retorted Robert; "*I* am in the wrong!" This beloved brother died at the age of twenty-five. During his last illness, Blake attended him with the most affectionate devotion, nor ever left the bedside till he behold the disembodied spirit leave the frail clay and soar heavenward, clapping its hands for joy!

His brother gone, though not so far away that he did not often revisit the old home, — friendly Flaxman in Italy, but more inaccessible there than Robert in the heaven which lay above this man in his perpetual infancy, — the *bas-bleus* reinclosed in the charmed circle in which Blake had so riotously disported himself, a small attempt at partnership, shop-keeping, and money-making, wellnigh "dead before it was born," — the poet began to think of publishing. The verses of which we have spoken had been seen but by few people, and the store was constantly increasing. Influence with the publishers, and money to defray expenses, were alike wanting. A copy of Lavater's "Aphorisms," translated by his fellow-countryman, Fuseli, had received upon its margins various annotations which reveal the man in his moods.

"The great art to love your enemy consists in never losing sight of *man* in him," says Lavater. "None *can* see the man in the enemy," pencils Blake. "If he is ignorantly so, he is not truly an enemy; if maliciously so, not a man. I cannot love my enemy; for my enemy is not a man, but a beast. And if I have any, I can love him as a beast, and wish to beat him." No equivocation here, surely. On superstition he comments, — "It has been long a bugbear, by reason of its having been united with hypocrisy. But let them be fairly separated, and then superstition will be honest feeling, and God, who loves all honest men, will lead the poor enthusiast in the path of holiness." Herein lies the germ of a truth. Again, Lavater says, — "A great woman not imperious, a fair woman not vain, a woman of common talents not jealous, an accomplished woman who scorns to shine, are four wonders just great enough to be divided among the four corners of the globe." Whereupon Blake adds, — "Let the men do their duty, and the women will be such wonders; the female life lives from the life of the male. See a great many female dependents, and you know the man." If this be madness, would that the madman might have bitten all mankind before he died! To the advice, "Take here the grand secret, if not of pleasing all, yet of displeasing none: court mediocrity, avoid originality, and sacrifice to fashion," he appends, with an evident reminiscence of Rathbone Place, "And go to hell."

But this private effervescence was not enough; and after he had been long thinking anxiously as to ways and means, suddenly, in the night, Robert stood before him, and revealed to him a secret by which a fac-simile of poetry and design could be produced. On rising in the morning, Mrs. Blake was sent out with a half-crown to buy the necessary materials, and with that he began an experiment which resulted in furnishing his principal means of support through life. It consisted in a species of engraving in relief both of the words and the designs of his poems, by a process peculiar and original. From his plates he printed off in any tint he chose, afterwards coloring up his designs by hand. Joseph, the sacred carpenter, had appeared in a vision, and revealed to him certain secrets of coloring. Mrs. Blake delighted to assist him in taking impressions, which she did with great skill, in tinting the designs, and in doing up the pages in boards; so that everything, except manufacturing the paper, was done by the poet and his wife. Never before, as his biographer justly remarks, was a man so literally the author of his own book. If we may credit the testimony that is given, or even judge from such proofs as Mr. Gilchrist's book can furnish, these works of his hands were exquisitely beautiful. The effect of the poems imbedded in their designs is, we are told, quite different from their effect set naked upon a blank page. It was as if he had transferred scenery and characters from that spirit-realm where his own mind wandered at will; and from wondrous lips wondrous words came fitly, and with surpassing power. Confirmation of this we find in the few plates of "Songs of Innocence" which have been recovered. Shorn of the radiant rainbow hues, the golden sheen, with which the artist, angel-taught, glorified his pictures, they still body for us the beauty of his "Happy Valley." Children revel there in unchecked play. Springing vines, in wild exuberance of life, twine around the verse, thrusting their slender coils in among the lines. Weeping willows dip their branches into translucent pools. Heavy-laden trees droop their ripe, rich clusters overhead. Under the shade of broad-spreading oaks little children climb on the tiger's yielding back and stroke the lion's tawny mane in a true Millennium.

The first series, "Songs of Innocence," was succeeded by "Songs of Experience," both subsequently bound in one volume. Then came the book of "Thel," an allegory, wherein Thel, beautiful daughter of the Seraphim, laments the shortness of her life down by the River of Adona, and is answered by the Lily of the Valley, the Little Cloud, the Lowly Worm, and the Clod of Clay; the burden of whose song is,

"But how this is, sweet maid, I know not, and I cannot know,
I ponder, and I cannot ponder: yet I live and love!"

The designs give the beautiful daughter listening to the Lily and the Cloud. The Clod is an infant wrapped in a lily-leaf. The effect of the whole poem and design together is as of an "angel's reverie."

The "Marriage of Heaven and Hell" is considered one of the most curious and original of his works. After an opening "Argument" comes a series of "Proverbs of Hell," which, however, answer very well for earth: as, "A fool sees not the same tree that a wise man sees"; "He whose face gives no light shall never become a star"; "The apple-tree never asks the beech how he shall grow, nor the lion the horse how he shall take his prey." The remainder of the book consists of "Memorable Fancies," half dream, half allegory, sublime and grotesque inextricably commingling, but all ornamented with designs most daring and imaginative in conception, and steeped in the richest color. We subjoin a description of one or two, as a curiosity. "A strip of azure sky surmounts, and of land divides, the words of the title-page, leaving on each side scant and baleful trees, little else than stem and spray. Drawn on a tiny scale lies a corpse, and one bends over it. Flames burst forth below and slant upward across the page, gorgeous with every hue. In their very core, two spirits rush together and embrace." In the seventh design is "a little island of the sea, where an infant springs to its mother's bosom.

From the birth-cleft ground a spirit has half emerged. Below, with outstretched arms and hoary beard, an awful, ancient man rushes at you, as it were, out of the page." The eleventh is "a surging of mingled fire, water, and blood, wherein roll the volumes of a huge, double-fanged serpent, his crest erect, his jaws wide open." "The ever-fluctuating color, the spectral pigmies rolling, flying, leaping among the letters, the ripe bloom of quiet corners, the living light and bursts of flame, the spires and tongues of fire vibrating with the full prism, make the page seem to move and quiver within its boundaries, and you lay the book down tenderly, as if you had been handling something sentient."

We have not space to give a description, scarcely even a catalogue, of Blake's numerous works. Wild, fragmentary, gorgeous dreams they are, tangled in with strange allegoric words and designs, that throb with their prisoned vitality. The intensity of his lines and figures it is impossible for words to convey. It is power in the fiercest action,—fire and passion, the madness and the stupor of despair, the frenzy of desire, the lurid depths of woe, that thrill and rivet you even in the comparatively lifeless rendering of this book. The mere titles of the poems give but a slight clew to their character. Ideas are upheaved in a tossing surge of words. It is a mystic, but lovely Utopia, into which "The Gates of Paradise" open. The practical name of "America" very faintly foreshadows the Ossianic Titans that glide across its pages, or the tricksy phantoms, the headlong spectres, the tongues of flame, the folds and fangs of symbolic serpents, that writhe and leap and dart and riot there. With a poem named "Europe," we should scarcely expect for a frontispiece the Ancient of Days, in unapproached grandeur, setting his "compass upon the face of the Earth,"—a vision revealed to the designer at the top of his own staircase.

Small favor and small notice these works secured from the public, which found more edification in the drunken courtship and brutal squabbles of "the First Gentleman of Europe" than in Songs of Innocence or Sculptures for Eternity. The poet's own friends constituted his public, and patronized him to the extent of their power. The volume of Songs he sold for thirty shillings and two guineas. Afterwards, with the delicate and loving design of helping the artist, who would receive help in no other way, five and even ten guineas were paid, for which sum he could hardly do enough, finishing off each picture like a miniature. One solitary patron he had, Mr. Thomas Butts, who, buying his pictures for thirty years, and turning his own house into "a perfect Blake Gallery, often supplied the painter with his sole means of subsistence." May he have his reward! Most pathetic is an anecdote related by Mr. H. C. Robinson, who found himself one morning sole visitor at an Exhibition which Blake had opened, on his own account, at his brother James's house. In view of the fact that he had bought four copies of the Descriptive Catalogue, Mr. Robinson inquired of James, the custodian, if he might not come again free. "Oh, yes! *free as long as you live!*" was the reply of the humble hosier, overjoyed at having so munificent a visitor, or a visitor at all.

We have a sense of incongruity in seeing this defiant, but sincere pencil employed by publishers to illustrate the turgid sorrow of Young's "Night Thoughts." The work was to have been issued in parts, but got no farther than the first. (It would have been no great calamity, if the poem itself had come to the same premature end!) The sonorous mourner could hardly have recognized himself in the impersonations in which he was presented, nor his progeny in the concrete objects to which they were reduced. The well-known couplet,

> "'T is greatly wise to talk with our past hours
> And ask them what report they 've borne to heaven,"

is represented by hours "drawn as aerial and shadowy beings," some of whom are bringing their scrolls to the inquirer, and others are carrying their records to heaven.

> "Oft burst my song beyond the bounds of life"

has a lovely figure, holding a lyre, and springing

into the air, but confined by a chain to the earth. Death puts off his skeleton, and appears as a solemn, draped figure; but in many cases the clerical poet is "taken at his word," with a literalness more startling than dignified.

Introduced by Flaxman to Hayley, friend and biographer of Cowper, favorably known to his contemporaries, though now wellnigh forgotten, Blake was invited to Felpham, and began there a new life. It is pleasant to look back upon this period. Hayley, the kindly, generous, vain, imprudent, impulsive country squire, not at all excepting himself in his love for mankind, pouring forth sonnets on the slightest provocation, — indeed, so given over to the vice of verse, that

> "he scarce could ope
> His mouth but out there flew a trope,"—

floating with the utmost self-complacence down the smooth current of his time; and Blake, sensitive, unique, protestant, impracticable, aggressive: it was a rare freak of Fate that brought about such companionship; yet so true courtesy was there that for four years they lived and wrought harmoniously together, — Hayley pouring out his harmless wish-wash, and Blake touching it with his fiery gleam. Their joint efforts were hardly more pecuniarily productive than Blake's single-handed struggles; but his life here had other and better fruits. In the little cottage overlooking the sea, fanned by the pure breezes, and smiled upon by sunshine of the hills, he tasted rare spiritual joy. Throwing off mortal incumbrance, — never, indeed an overweight to him, — he revelled in his clairvoyance. The lights that shimmered across the sea shone from other worlds. The purple of the gathering darkness was the curtain of God's tabernacle. Gray shadows of the gloaming assumed mortal shapes, and he talked with Moses and the prophets, and the old heroes of song. The Ladder of Heaven was firmly fixed by his garden-gate, and the angels ascended and descended. A letter written to Flaxman, soon after his arrival at Felpham, is so characteristic that we cannot refrain from transcribing it: —

"Dear Sculptor of Eternity, — We are safe arrived at our cottage, which is more beautiful than I thought it, and more convenient. It is a perfect model for cottages, and, I think, for palaces of magnificence, — only enlarging, not altering, its proportions, and adding ornaments, and not principles. Nothing can be more grand than its simplicity and usefulness. Simple, without intricacy, it seems to be the spontaneous expression of humanity, congenial to the wants of man. No other formed house can ever please me so well, nor shall I ever be persuaded, I believe, that it can be improved, either in beauty or use.

"Mr. Hayley received us with his usual brotherly affection. I have begun to work. Felpham is a sweet place for study, because it is more spiritual than London. Heaven opens here on all sides her golden gates; her windows are not obstructed by vapors; voices of celestial inhabitants are more distinctly heard, and their forms are more distinctly seen; and my cottage is also a shadow of their houses. My wife and sister are both well, courting Neptune for an embrace.

"Our journey was very pleasant; and though we had a great deal of luggage, no grumbling. All was cheerfulness and good-humor on the road, and yet we could not arrive at our cottage before half-past eleven at night, owing to the necessary shifting of our luggage from one chaise to another; for we had seven different chaises, and as many different drivers. We set out between six and seven in the morning of Thursday, with sixteen heavy boxes and portfolios full of prints.

"And now begins a new life, because another covering of earth is shaken off. I am more famed in heaven for my works than I could well conceive. In my brain are studies and chambers filled with books and pictures of old, which I wrote and painted in ages of Eternity, before my mortal life, and those works are the delight and study of archangels. Why, then, should I be anxious about the riches or fame of mortality? The Lord our Father will do for us and with us according to His Divine will, for our good.

"You, O dear Flaxman, are a sublime archangel, — my friend and companion from Eternity. In the Divine bosom is our dwelling-place. I look back into the regions of reminiscence, and behold our ancient days, before this earth appeared in its vegetated mortality to my mortal vegetated eyes. I see our houses of eternity, which can never be separated, though our mortal vehicles should stand at the remotest corners of heaven from each other.

"Farewell, my best friend! Remember me and my wife in love and friendship to our dear Mrs. Flaxman, whom we ardently desire to entertain beneath our thatched roof of rusted gold. And believe me forever to remain your grateful and affectionate

"WILLIAM BLAKE."

Other associations than spiritual ones mingle with the Felpham sojourn. A drunken soldier one day broke into his garden, and, being great of stature, despised the fewer inches of the owner. But to the conflict between spirits of earth and spirits of the skies there is but one issue, and Blake "laid hold of the intrusive blackguard, and turned him out neck and crop, in a kind of inspired frenzy." The astonished ruffian made good his retreat, but in revenge reported sundry words that exasperation had struck from his conqueror. The result was a trial for high treason at the next Quarter Sessions. Friends gathered about him, testifying to his previous character; nor was Blake himself at all dismayed. When the soldiers trumped up their false charges in court, he did not scruple to cry out, "False!" with characteristic and convincing vehemence. Had this trial occurred in our own day, it would hardly be necessary to say that he was triumphantly acquitted. But fifty years ago such a matter wore a graver aspect. In his early life he had been an advocate of the French Revolution, an associate of Price, Priestley, Godwin, and Tom Paine, a wearer of white cockade and *bonnet rouge*. He had even been instrumental in saving Tom Paine's life, by hurrying him to France, when the government was on his track; but all this was happily unknown to the Chichester lawyers, and Blake, more fortunate than some of his contemporaries, escaped the gallows.

The disturbance caused by this untoward incident, the repeated failures of literary attempts, the completion of Cowper's Life, which had been the main object of his coming, joined, doubtless, to a surfeit of Hayley, induced a return to London. He feared, too, that his imaginative faculty was failing. "The visions were angry with me at Felpham," he used afterwards to say. We regret to see, also, that he seems not always to have been in the kindest of moods towards his patron. Indeed, it was a weakness of his to fall out occasionally with his best friends; but when a man is waited upon by angels and ministers of grace, it is not surprising that he should sometimes be impatient with mere mortals. Nor is it difficult to imagine that the bland and trivial Hayley, perpetually kind, patronizing, and obvious, should, without any definite provocation, become presently insufferable to such a man as Blake.

Returning to London, he resumed the production of his "prophetic books." These he illustrated with his own peculiar and beautiful designs, "all sanded over with a sort of golden mist." Among much that is incoherent and incomprehensible may be found passages of great force, tenderness, and beauty. The concluding verses of the Preface to "Milton" we quote, as shadowing forth his great moral purpose, and as revealing also the luminous heart of the cloud that so often turns to us only its gray and obscure exterior: —

"And did those feet in ancient time
   Walk upon England's mountain green?
And was the holy Lamb of God
   On England's pleasant pastures seen?

"And did the countenance Divine
   Shine forth upon our clouded hills?
And was Jerusalem builded here
   Among these dark, Satanic hills?

"Bring me my bow of burning gold!
   Bring me my arrows of desire!
Bring me my spear! O clouds, unfold!
   Bring me my chariot of fire!

"I will not cease from mental fight,
Nor shall my sword sleep in my hand,
Till we have built Jerusalem
In England's green and pleasant land."

The same lofty aim is elsewhere expressed in the line, —

"I touch the heavens as an instrument to glorify the Lord!"

We can only glance at a few of the remaining incidents of this outwardly calm, yet inwardly eventful life. In an evil hour — though to it we owe the "Illustrations to Blair's Grave" — he fell into the hands of Cromek, the shrewd Yorkshire publisher, and was tenderly entreated, as a dove in the talons of a kite. The famous letter of Cromek to Blake is one of the finest examples on record of long-headed worldliness bearing down upon wrong-headed genius. Though Cromek clutched the palm in this case, and in some others, it is satisfactory to know that his clever turns led to no other end than poverty; and nothing worse than poverty had Blake, with all his simplicity, to encounter. But Blake, in his poverty, had meat to eat which the wily publisher knew not of.

In the wake of this failure followed another. Blake had been engaged to make twenty drawings to illustrate Ambrose Philips's "Virgil's Pastorals" for school-boys. The publishers saw them, and stood aghast, declaring he must do no more. The engravers received them with derision, and pronounced sentence, "This will never do." Encouraged, however, by the favorable opinion of a few artists who saw them, the publishers admitted, with an apology, the seventeen which had already been executed, and gave the remaining three into more docile hands. With two hundred and thirty cuts, the book now is valued only for Blake's small contribution.

Of an entirely different nature were the "Inventions from the Book of Job," which are pronounced the most remarkable series of etchings on a Scriptural theme that have been produced since the days of Rembrandt and Albrecht Dürer. Of these drawings we have copies in the second volume of the "Life," from which one can gather something of their grandeur, their bold originality, their inexhaustible and often terrible power. His representations of God the Father will hardly accord with modern taste, which generally eschews all attempt to embody the mind's conceptions of the Supreme Being; but Blake was far more closely allied to the ancient than to the modern world. His portraiture and poetry often remind us of the childlike familiarity — not rude in him, but utterly reverent — which was frequently, and sometimes offensively, displayed in the old miracle and moral plays.

These drawings, during the latter part of his life, secured him from actual want. A generous friend, Mr. Linnell, himself a struggling young artist, gave him a commission, and paid him a small weekly stipend: it was sufficient to keep the wolf from the door, and that was enough: so the wolf was kept away, his lintel was uncrossed 'gainst angels. It was little to this piper that the public had no ear for his piping, — to this painter, that there was no eye for his pictures.

> "His soul was like a star, and dwelt apart."

He had but to withdraw to his inner chamber, and all honor and recognition awaited him. The pangs of poverty or coldness he never experienced, for his life was on a higher plane: —

> "I am in God's presence night and day,
> He never turns his face away."

When a little girl of extraordinary beauty was brought to him, his kindest wish, as he stood stroking her long ringlets, was, "May God make this world to you, my child, as beautiful as it has been to me!" His own testimony declares, —

> "The angel who presided at my birth
> Said, — 'Little creature, formed of joy and mirth,
> Go, love without the help of anything on earth!'"

But much help from above came to him. The living lines that sprung beneath his pencil were but reminiscences of his spiritual home. Immortal visitants, unseen by common eyes, hung enraptured over his sketches, lent a loving ear to his songs, and left with him their legacy to Earth. There was no looking back mournfully on the past, nor forward impatiently to the future, but a rapturous, radiant, eternal now. Every morning came heavy-freighted with its own delights; every evening brought its own exceeding great reward.

So, refusing to the last to work in traces, — flying out against Reynolds, the bland and popular President of the Royal Academy, yet acknowledging with enthusiasm what he deemed to be excellence, — loving Fuseli with a steadfast love through all neglect, and hurling his indignation at a public that refused to see his worth, — flouting at Bacon, the great philosopher, and fighting for Barry, the restorer of the antique, he resolutely pursued his appointed way unmoved. But the day was fast drawing on into darkness. The firm will never quailed, but the sturdy feet faltered. Yet, as the sun went down, soft lights overspread the heavens. Young men came to him with fresh hearts, and drew out all the freshness of his own. Little children learned to watch for his footsteps over the Hampstead hills, and sat on his knee, sunning him with their caresses. Men who towered above their time, reverencing the god within, and bowing not down to the *dœmon à la mode*, gathered around him, listened to his words, and did obeisance to his genius. They never teased him with unsympathetic questioning, or enraged him with blunt contradiction. They received his visions simply, and discussed them rationally, deeming them worthy of study rather than of ridicule or vulgar incredulity. To their requests the spirits were docile. Sitting by his side at midnight, they watched while he summoned from unknown realms long-vanished shades. William Wallace arose from his "gory bed," Edward I. turned back from the lilies of France, and, forgetting their ancient hate, both stood before him with placid dignity. The man who built the Pyramids lifted his ungainly features from the ingulfing centuries; souls of blood-thirsty men, duly forced into the shape of fleas, lent their hideousness to his night; and the Evil One himself did not disdain to sit for his portrait to this undismayed magician. That these are actual portraits of concrete objects is not to be affirmed. That they are portraits of what Blake saw is as little to be denied. We are assured that his whole manner was that of a man copying, and not inventing, and the simplicity and sincerity of his life forbid any thought of intentional deceit. No criticism affected him. Nothing could shake his faith. "It must be right: I saw it so," was the beginning and end of his defence. The testimony of these friends of his is that he was of all artists the most spiritual, devoted, and single-minded. One of them says, if asked to point out among the intellectual a happy man, he should at once think of Blake. One, a young artist, finding his invention flag for a whole fortnight, had recourse to Blake.

"It is just so with us," he exclaimed, turning

to his wife, "is it not, for weeks together, when the visions forsake us? What do we do then, Kate?"

"We kneel down and pray, Mr. Blake."

To these choice spirits, these enthusiastic and confiding friends, his house was the House of the Interpreter. The little back-room, kitchen, bedroom, studio, and parlor in one, plain and neat, had for them a kind of enchantment. That royal presence lighted up the "hole" into a palace. The very walls widened with the greatness of his soul. The windows that opened on the muddy Thames seemed to overlook the river of the water of life. Among the scant furnishings, his high thoughts, set in noble words, gleamed like apples of gold in pictures of silver. Over the gulf that yawns between two worlds he flung a glorious arch, and walked tranquilly back and forth. Heaven was as much a matter-of-fact to him as earth. Of sacred things he spoke with a familiarity which, to those who did not understand him, seemed either madness or blasphemy; but his friends never misunderstood. With one exception, none who knew him personally ever thought of calling his sanity in question. To them he was a sweet, gentle, lovable man. They felt the truth of his life. They saw that

> "Only that fine madness still he did retain
> Which rightly should possess a poet's brain."

Imagination was to him the great reality. The

external, that which makes the chief consciousness of most men, was to him only staging, cumbersome and uncouth, but to be endured and made the most of. The world of the imagination was the true world. Imagination *bodied* forth the forms of things unknown in a deeper sense, perhaps, than the great dramatist meant. His poet's pen, his painter's pencil turned them to shapes, and gave to airy nothings a local habitation and a name. Nay, he denied that they were nothings. He rather asserted the actual existence of his visions, — an existence as real, though not of the same nature, as that of the bed or the table. Imagination was a kind of sixth sense, and its objects were as real as the objects of the other senses. This sense he believed to exist, though latent, in every one, and to be susceptible of development by cultivation. This is surely a very different thing from madness. Neither is it the low superstition of ghosts. He recounted no miracle, nothing supernatural. It was only that by strenuous effort and untiring devotion he had penetrated beyond the rank and file — but not beyond the possibilities of the rank and file — into the unseen world. Undoubtedly this power finally assumed undue proportions. In his isolation it led him on too unresistingly. His generation knew him not. It neglected where it should have fostered, and stared where it should have studied. He was not wily enough to conceal or gloss over his views. Often silent with congenial companions, he would thrust with boisterous assertion in the company of captious opponents. Set upon by the unfriendly and the conventional, he wilfully hurled out his wild utterances, exaggerating everything, scorning all explanation or modification, goading peculiarities into reckless extravagance, on purpose to puzzle and startle, and so avenging himself by playing off upon those who attempted to play off upon him. To the gentle, the reverent, the receptive, he too was gentle and reverent.

Nearest and dearest of all, the "beloved Kate" held him in highest honor. The ripples that disturbed the smooth flow of their early life had died away and left an unruffled current. To the childless wife, he was child, husband, and lover. No sphere so lofty, but he could come quickly down to perform the lowliest duties. The empty platter, silently placed on the dinner-table, was the signal for his descent from Parnassus to the money-earning graver. No angel-faces kept him from lighting the morning fire and setting on the breakfast-kettle before his Kitty awoke. Their life became one. Her very spirit passed into his. By day and by night her love surrounded him. In his moments of fierce inspiration, when he would arise from his bed to sketch or write the thoughts that tore his brain, she too arose and sat by his side, silent, motionless, soothing him only by the tenderness of her presence. Years and wintry fortunes made havoc of her beauty, but love renewed it day by day for the eyes of her lover, and their hands only met in firmer clasp as they neared the Dark River.

It was reached at last. No violent steep, but a gentle and gracious slope led to the cold waters that had no bitterness for him. Shining already in the glory of the Celestial City, he gazed upon the dear form that had stood by his side through all these years, and with waning strength he cried, "Stay! Keep as you are! *You* have been ever an angel to me: I will draw you." And, summoning his forces, he sketched his last portrait of the fond and faithful wife. Then, comforting her with the shortness of their separation, assuring her that he should always be about her to take care of her, he set his face steadfastly towards the Beautiful Gate. So joyful was his passage, so triumphant his march, that the very sight was to them that could behold it as if heaven itself were come down to meet him. Even the sorrowing wife could but listen enraptured to the sweet songs he chanted to his Maker's praise; but, "They are *not* mine, my beloved!" he tenderly cried; "*No!* they are *not* mine!" The strain he heard was of a higher mood; and continually sounding as he went, with melodious noise, in notes on high, he entered in through the gates into the City.

XXIX.

MY BOOK.

THE trouble about biographies is that by the time they are written the person is dead. You have heard of him remotely. You know that he sang a world's songs, won victories, founded empires, did heroes' work; but you do not know the little tender touches of his life, the things that bring him into near kinship with humanity, and set him by the household hearth without unclasping the diadem from his brow, until he is dead, and it is too late forevermore. Then with vague restlessness you visit the brook in which his troutline drooped, you pluck a leaf from the elm that shaded his regal head, you walk in the graveyard that holds in its bosom his silent dust, only to feel with unavailing regret that no sunshine of his presence can gleam upon you. The life that stirred in his voice, shone in his eye, and fortressed itself in his unconscious bearing can make to you no revelation. It is departed, none knows whither. He is as much a part of the past as if he had tended flocks for Abraham on the plains of Mamre.

This, when biographies are at their best. Generally, they are at their worst. Generally, they do not know the things you wish to learn, and when they do, they do not tell them. They give you statistics, facts, reflections, eulogies, dissertations; but what you hunger and thirst after is the man's inner life. What use is it to know what a man does, unless you know what made him do it? This you can seldom learn from memoirs. Look at the numerous brood that followed in the wake of Shelley's fame. Every one gives you, not Shelley, but himself, served up in Shelley sauce. Think of your own experience: are not the vital facts of your life hermetically sealed? Are you not a world within a world, whose history and geography may be summed up in that phrase which used to make the interior of Africa the most delightful spot in the whole atlas, — "Unexplored Region"? One person may have started an expedition here, and another there. Here one may have struck a river-course, and there one may have looked down into a valley, and all may have brought away their golden grain; but the one has not followed the river to its source, nor the other wandered bewilderingly through the valley-lands, and none have traversed the Field of the Cloth of Gold. So the geographies are all alike, boundaries, capital, chief towns, rivers. And what is true of you is doubtless true of all. Faith is not to be put in biographies.

Whether you were susceptible of calmness or were deeply turbulent, — whether you were amiable, or only amiably disposed, — whether you were inwardly blest and only superficially unrestful, safely moored even while tossing on an unquiet sea, — what you thought, what you hoped, how you felt, yes, and how you lived and loved and hated, they do not know and cannot tell. A biographer may be ever so conscientious, but he stands on the outside of the circle of his subject, and his view will lack symmetry. There is but one who, from his position in the centre, is competent to give a fair and full picture, and that is your own self. A few may possess imagination, and so partially atone for the disadvantages of position; but, a thousand to one, they will not have a chance at your life. You must die knowing that you are at the mercy of whoever can hold a pen.

Unless you take time by the forelock and write your biography yourself! Then you will be sure to do no harm, inasmuch as no one is obliged to read your narrative; and you may do much good, because, if any one does read it and become interested in you, he will have the pleasing consciousness of living in the same world with you. When he drives through your street, he can put his head out of the carriage-window and perhaps see you just going in at the front gate. Also, if you write your biography yourself, you can have your choice as to what shall go in and what shall stay out. You can make a discreet selection of your letters, giving the go-by to that especial one in which you rather — is there such a word as spooneyly? — offered yourself to your wife. Every word was as good as the bank to her, for to her you were a lover, a knight, a great brown, bearded angel, and all metaphors, however violent, fell upon good ground. But to the people who read your life you will be a trader, a lawyer, a shoemaker, who pays his butcher's bills and looks after the main chance, and the metaphors, deprived of their fire, but retaining their form, will seem incongruous, not to say ridiculous. I do not say that your wife's lover and knight and angel are not a higher and a better, yes, and a truer you, than the world's trader and lawyer; still your love-letters will probably be better off in the bosom of the love-lettered than on a bookseller's shelves. Besides these advantages, there is another in præ-humous publication. If you wait for your biography till you are dead, it is extremely probable you will lose it altogether. The world has so much to see to ahead that it can hardly spare a glance over its shoulder to take note of what is behind. Take the note yourself and make sure of it. You will then know where you are, and be master of the situation.

I purpose, therefore, to write the history of my

life, from my entrance upon it down to a period which is within the memory of men still living. In so doing, I shall not be careful to trace out that common ground which may be supposed to underlie all lives, but only indicate those features which serve to distinguish one from another. Everybody is christened, cuts his teeth, and eats bread and molasses. Silently will we, therefore, infer the bread and molasses, and swiftly stride in seven-league boots from mountain-peak to mountain-peak.

I was born of parents who, though not poor, were respectable, and I had also the additional distinction of being a precocious child. I differed from most precocious children, however, in not dying young, and that opportunity, once let slip, is now forever gone. I believe the precocious children who do not die young develop into idiots. My family have never been without well-grounded fears in that line.

Nothing of any importance happened to me after I was born till I grew up and wrote a book. Indeed, I believe I may say even that never happened, for I did not write a book. Rather a book came to pass, — somewhat like the goldsmithery of Aaron, who threw the ear-rings into the fire, and "there came out this calf!" I went out one day alone, as was my wont, in an open boat, and drifted beyond sight of land. I had heard that shipwrecked mariners sometimes throw out a bottle of papers to give their friends a clew to their fate. I threw out a bottle of papers, less out of regard to friends than to myself. They floated into a printing-press, and came forth a book, whereon I sailed safely ashore, grateful. Alas! in another confusion will there be another resource?

It is this book which is to form the first, and quite possibly the last chapter of my life and sufferings, for I don't suppose anything will ever happen to me again. To be sure, in the book I have just been reading a girl marries her groom, leaves him, rejects two lovers, kills her husband, accepts one lover, loses him, marries the second, first husband comes to light again and is shot, marries second husband over again, and goes a-journeying with second husband and first lover, first cousin and two children, in the South of France, before she is twenty-two years old. But in my country girls think themselves extremely well off for adventures with one marriage and no murder. But then the girls in my country do not have the murderous black eyes which shine so in romances.

My book being fairly set a-going, of course you wish to know what came of it. Do not pretend you don't care, for you know you do. Only look not too closely at me, or you will disconcert me. Veil now and then your intent eyes, or my story will surely droop under their steadfastness. Look sometimes into yonder sunset sky and the beautiful reticulations drawn darkly against its glowing sheets of color. You will none the less listen, and I shall all the more enjoy.

You have read much about the anxieties, the forebodings, the anticipatory tremors of new authors. So have I, but I never felt them, — not a single foreboding. I was delighted to write a book, and it never occurred to me that everybody would not be just as delighted to read it. The first time my book weighed on me was one morning when a meagre little letter came to me, which turned out to be only a card bearing the laconic inscription, —

"Twelve copies 'New Sun' sent by express, with the compliments of the Publishers."

The "New Sun" was my book. I put on my hat and walked straightway up to the hole in the rock, about a mile around the corner, where the expressman always leaves my parcels, and took up the package to bring home. It was very heavy. I balanced it first on one arm and then on the other, until, as the poet has it, —

"Both were nigh to breaking."

Then I lifted it by the cords, but they cut my fingers. Then I remembered the natural law, that internal atmospheric pressure prevents any consciousness of the enormous external pressure exerted by an atmosphere forty-five miles thick, and applied the law, saying, "These books all being inside of my head, of course I shall not feel them on the outside." So I put the package on my head, and walked on, making believe I was in a gymnasium, keeping a sharp watch fore and aft, and considering the distant rumbling of wheels a signal for dousing my colors. In my country people do not carry their burdens on their heads, nor would they be likely to account for me on the principles of Natural Philosophy. I might have been apprehended as a lunatic, but for my timely caution.

Thus the "New Suns" came home and were speedily stripped of their dun wrappings. I lingered over them, admiring their clear type, their fragrance, their crispness. I opened them wide, because they would open so frankly. I delighted myself with their fair smoothness. And then I began to read. I am ashamed to say I never read a more interesting book!

How very true it is that suffering is about equally distributed, after all! If you do not have your troubles spread out, you have them in a lump. The furies may seem to be held in abeyance, but they will only lay on their lashes all the harder when they do come. My unnatural calmness was succeeded by a storm of consternation. I pass over the few days that followed. If you ever put yourself into a pillory in the night just to see how it seemed, and then found yourself fastened there in good earnest, and day dawning, and all the marketmen and shopkeepers up and stirring, and everybody coming by in a few minutes, you will not need to ask how I felt. When you write a book, you are quite alone and your pen is entirely private; but when it comes to you so unquestionably printed, and inexorable, and out-of-doors —— Ah, me! It did not seem like a book at all, — not at all the abstraction and impersonality that were intended, but a concrete person walking out into the world with malice aforethought.

But though a writer is before critics, did it never occur to you that the critics are just as much before the writers? A critic's talk about a book is just as truly a revelation of the critic as the writer's talk in the book is a revelation of the writer. One man gives you an opinion that implies attention. He does not go into the depths of the matter, but he tells you honestly what he likes and what he does not like. This is good. This is precisely what you wish to know, and will indirectly help you. Another, from the steps of a throne, in a few sentences, it may be, or a few columns, classifies you, interprets you not only to the world, but to yourself; and for this you are immeasurably glad and grateful. It is neither praise nor censure that you value, but recognition. Let a writer but feel that a critic reaches into the *arcana* of his thought, and no assent is too hearty, nor any dissent too severe. Another glances up from his eager political strife, and with the sincerest kindness awards you a nice little bon-bon, chiefly flour and water, but flavored with sugar. Thank you. Another flounders in a wash of words, holding in solution the faintest salt of sense. Heaven help him! Another dips his spear-point in poison and lets fly. Do you not see that these people are an open book? Do you not read here the tranquillity of a self-poised life, the inner sight of clairvoyance, the bitterness of disappointed hopes and unsuccessful plans, the amiability that is not founded upon strength, the pettiness that puts pique above principle, the frankness that scorns affectation, the comprehensiveness that embraces all things in its vision, and commands not only acquiescence, but allegiance, the great-heartedness that by virtue of its own magnetism attracts all that is good?

When my poor little ewe-lamb went out into the world, I did not fear any shearing it might encounter in America. I do not mind my own countrymen. I like them, but I am not afraid of them. Two elements go to make up a book: matter and manner. The former, of course, is its author's own. He maintains it against all comers. Opposition does not terrify him, for it is a mere difference of opinion. One is just as likely to be right as another, and in a hundred years probably we shall all be found wrong together. But manner can be judged by a fixed standard. Bad English is bad English this very day, whatever you or I think about it; and bad English is a bad thing. When I know it, I avoid it, except under extreme temptation; but the trouble is, I do not know it. I am continually learning that words in certain relations are misplaced where I never suspected the smallest derangement, and, no doubt, there are many dislocations which I have not yet discovered. So far as my own people are concerned, I do not take this to heart,—because my countryman very likely perpetrates three barbarisms in correcting my one. He knows this thing that I did not, but then I know something else that he does not, and so keep the balance true. Moreover, my America, if I use bad English, whose fault is it? You have had me from the beginning. The raw material was as good as the average; why did you not work it up better? I went to the best schools you gave me. I learned everything I was set to learn. You can nowhere find a teacher who will tell you that I ever evaded a lesson. I was greedy of gain. I spared neither time nor toil. I lost no opportunity, and here I am, just as good as you made me. So, if there is any one to blame, it is you, for not giving me better facilities. The Children's Aid Society warned New York a dozen years ago that a "dangerous class of untaught" pagans was growing up in her streets; but she did not think it worth while to arouse herself and educate them, and one morning she found them burning her house over her head. You too, my country, have been repeatedly warned of your dangerous class, a class whom, with malice aforethought, you leave half educated, and, from ignorance, idle, — and now comes Nemesis! New York had a mob, and you have — me.

The real ogres were those terrible Englishmen. I was brought up on the British Quarterlies. Their high and mighty ways entered into my soul. I never did have any courage or independence, to begin with; and when they condescended to tread our shores with such lordly airs, I should have been only too glad to burn incense for a propitiation. So impressive was their loftiness, their haughty patronage, that their supercilious sneers at our provincialism were heart-rending. I came to look at everything with an eye to English judgment. It was not so much whether a book or a custom were good as whether it would be likely to meet with English approval. To be the object of their displeasure was a calamity, and at even a growl from their dreadful throats I was ready to die of terror.

But it so happened that by the time my book was set afloat, the Reviewers had lost their fangs. The war came, and they went over to the enemy, every one: "North British," "London Quarterly," "Edinburgh," and even the liberal "Westminster," had but one tone. "Blackwood" was seized with an evil spirit, and wallowed foaming.

The English people may be all right at heart. Their slow, but sure and sturdy sense may bring them at length within hailing distance of the truth. Noble men among them, Mill and Cairnes and Smith and their kind, made their voices heard in the midst of opposing din, even through the very pages which had rung with Southern cheers: but it is not the English people who make up the Quarterly Reviews. It was not the voice of Mill or Cairnes that answered first across the waters to the boom of Liberty's guns. When our blood was hot and our hearts were high, and sneers ten thousand times harder to bear than blows, we found sneers in plenty where we looked for God-speed. It may not have been the English heart, only the English head. But we could not get at the English heart, and the English head was continually thrust against ours. The fires may have burned warmly on many a hearth, but we could not see them. The only light that shot athwart the waters was from the high watch-towers, and it was lurid. This wrought a change. The English may put on airs in literature; for our little leisure leaves us short repose, and it would be strange indeed, if their civilization of centuries had not left its marks in a finer culture and a deeper thought. But when, leaving literature and coming down into the fastnesses of life, they gave us hatred for love, and scorn for reverence, — when they sneered at that which we held sacred, and reviled that which we counted honorable, — when, green-eyed and gloating, they not only saw through their glasses darkly, but all things were distorted and awry, — when devotion became to them fanaticism, and love of liberty was lust of power, — did virtue go out of them, or had it never been in? This, at least, was wrought: when one part of the temple of our reverence was undermined, the whole structure came down. They who showed themselves so morally weak cannot maintain even the intellectual or æsthetic superiority which they have assumed. Henceforth their blame or praise is not what it was. When a man rails at my country, it is little that he rails at me. If they have called the master of the house Beëlzebub, they of his household would as soon be called little flies as anything else.

(As a matter of fact, I do not suppose my little venture has ever been heard of across the ocean. You think it is very presumptuous in me ever to have thought of it; but I did not think of it. I was only afraid of it. Suppose the British Quarterly has not vision microscopic enough to discern you; you like to know how you feel in a certain contingency, even if it should never happen. Besides, so many strange things arise every day, that incongruity seems to have lost its force.)

But if we only did reverence England as once we reverenced her, this is what I would say: — "Upon my country do not visit my sins. Upon my country's fame let me fasten no blot. Wherever I am wrong, inelegant, inaccurate, provincial, visit all your reprobation upon me, —

> 'Me, me, adsum, qui feci; in me convertite ferrum,
> O Angli! mea fraus omnis,'—

upon me as a writer, not upon me as an American. Do not regard me as the exponent of American culture, or as anywhere near the high-water mark of American letters. If you will see the highest, look on the heights. If you look at me, look at me where I am: not among those whose infancy was cradled in art and luxury, whose life from the beginning has been carefully attuned to the finest issues, who for purity of language and dignity of mental bearing may throw down the gauntlet to the proudest nation in the world, — but among those wild children of the soil who take its color, who share its qualities, who give out its fragrance, who love it and lay their hearts to it and grow with it, rocky and rugged, yet cherish, it may be hoped, its little dimples of verdure here and there, — who show not what, with closest care, it might become, but what, under the broad skies and the free winds and the common dews and showers, it is. Our conservatories can boast hues as gorgeous, forms as stately, texture as fine as yours; but don't look for camellias in a cornfield."

Does this seem a little inconsistent with what I was saying just now to my home-made critics?

Very likely. But truth is many-sided, and one side you may present at home and the other abroad, according to the exigencies of the case, without being inconsistent.

O England, England! what shall recompense us for our Lost Leader? Great and Mighty One, from whose brow no hand but thine own could ever have plucked the crown! Beautiful land, sacred with the ashes of our sires, radiant with the victories of the past, brilliant with hopes for the future, —

> "O Love, I have loved you! O my soul,
> I have lost you!"

Ah, if these fatal years might be blotted out! If we could stand once again where we stood on that October day when the young Prince, whose gentle blood commanded our attention, and whose gentle ways won our hearts, bore back to his mother-land and ours the benedictions of a people! Upon that white-faced shore I shall one day look, but woe is me for the bitter memories that will spring up for the love and loyalty so ruthlessly rent away!

So I borrow your ears, my countrymen, and tell you why it is impossible to defer to you as much as one would like. Partly, it is because you talk so wide of the mark. It may not be practicable or desirable to say much; but so much the more ought what you do say to be to the point. A good carpenter needs not to vindicate his skill by hammering away hour after hour on the same shingle; but while he does strike, he hits the nail on the head. Moreover, you show by your remarks that you have such — such — well, *stupid* is what I mean, but I am afraid it would not be polite to employ that word, so I merely give you the meaning, and leave you to choose a word to your liking — notions about the nature, the facts, and the objects of writing. Look at it a moment. With your gray goose-quill you sit, O Rhadamanthus, and to your waiting audience pleasantly enough affirm that I have "taken Benlomond for my model." But when I happen to remember that the larger part of my book was written and printed not only before I had ever met Benlomond, but before he had ever been heard of in this country at least, what faith can I have in your sagacity? And when, remembering those remarkable coincidences which sometimes surprise and baffle us, which in science make Adams and Le Verrier discover the same planet at the same time without knowing anything of each other's calculations, and which in any department seem to indicate that a great tide sweeps over humanity, bearing us on its bosom whithersoever it will, so that

> "God's puppets, best and worst,
> Are we; there is no last nor first,"—

I institute an examination of Benlomond to discover those generic or specific peculiarities which are supposed to have made their mark on me, why, I find for resemblance, that the situations, look you, is both alike. There is a river in Macedon; there is also, moreover, a river in Monmouth: 't is as like as my fingers to my fingers, and there is salmons in both!

Have I taken Benlomond for my model? But why not Josephus and Ricardo and François and Michel, any and all who have poured their fancies and feelings into this mould? Why select the last disciple and ignore the first apostle? Many prophets have been in Israel whom I resemble as much, to say the least, as this Benlomond. Is it not, my friend, that, in the multitude of your words and ways, you have not found time to renew your acquaintance with these ancient worthies, and so their features have somewhat faded from your memory? But Benlomond came in but yesterday, and because he is a newspaper-topic, him you know; and because at the first blush you doubtless can read that there is a river in Monmouth and also a river in Macedon, and salmons in both,—'t is as like as my fingers to my fingers, and Monmouth was built on the model of Macedon! Ah, my eagle-eyes, Judæa, too, had its Jordan, and Damascus its Abana and Pharpar, and little Massachusetts its Merrimac, which,

"poet-tuned,
Goes singing down his meadows."

But Judæa did not type Damascus. The Merrimac bears not the sign of Abana, nor was Abana born of Jordan: all, obedient to the word of the Lord, trickle forth from their springs among the hills, and wander down, one through his vineland, one through his olive-groves, and one to meet the roaring of the mill-wheel's rage.

I lay no claim to originality. I know full well that the soil has been tilled and the seed scattered of all that is worthy in the world. Where giants have wrestled, it is not for pigmies to boast their prowess. Where the gods have trodden, let mortals walk unsandalled. The lowliest of their learners, I sit at the feet of the masters. To me, as to all the world, the great and the good of the olden times have left their legacy, and the monarchs of to-day have scattered blessings. Upon me, as upon all, have their grateful showers descended. My brow have they crowned with their goodness, and on my life have their paths dropped fatness. Dreaming under their vines and fig-trees, I have gathered in my lap and garnered in my heart their mellow fruits.

> "With them I take delight in weal
> And seek relief in woe,
> And while I understand and feel
> How much to them I owe,
> My cheeks have often been bedewed
> With tears of heartfelt gratitude."

But though with gladness I render unto Cæsar the things that are Cæsar's, he shall not have that which does not belong to him. Neither Benlomond, nor any living man, nor any one man, living or dead, has any claim to my fealty, be it worth much or little. If I cannot go in to the banquet on Olympus by the bidding of the master of the feast, I will forswear ambrosia altogether, and to the end of my days feed on millet with the peasants in the Vale of Tempe.

Then, changing ground, you smile and shake your head and say, "It is all very well, but it has not the element of immortality. Observe the difference between this writer and Charles Lamb. One is ginger-pop beer that foams and froths and is gone, while the other is the sound Madeira that will be better fifty years hence than now."

Well, what of it? Do you mean to say, that, because a man has no argosies sailing in from the isles of Eden, freighted with the juices of the tropics, he shall not brew hops in his own cellar? Because you will have none but the vintages of dead centuries, shall not the people delight their hearts with new wine? Because you are an epicure, shall there be no more cakes and ale? Go to! It is a happy fate to be a poet's Falernian, old and mellow, sealed in *amphoræ*, to be crowned with linden-garlands and the late rose. But for all earth's acres there are few Sabine farms, whither poet, sage, and statesman come to lose in the murmur of Bandusian founts the din of faction and of strife; and even there it is not always Cæcuban or Calenian, neither Formian nor Falernian, but the *vile Sabinum* in common cups and wreathed with simple myrtle, that bubbles up its welcome. So, since there must be lighter draughts, or many a poor man go thirsty, we who are but the ginger-pop of life may well rejoice, remembering that ginger-pop is nourishing and tonic, — that thousands of weary wayfarers who could never know the taste of the costly brands, and who go sadly and wearily, will be fleeter of foot and gladder of soul because of its humble and evanescent foam.

Ginger-pop beer is it that you scoff? Verily, you do an unconsidered deed. When one remembers all the liquids, medicinal, soporific, insipid, poisonous, which flood the throat of humanity, one may deem himself a favorite of Fortune to be placed so high in the catalogue. Though upon his lowliness gleam down the rosy and purple lights of rare old wines aloft, yet from his altitude he can look below upon a profane crowd in thick array of depth immeasurable, and rejoice that he is not stagnant water nor exasperated vinegar nor disappointed buttermilk. Nay, I am not only content, but exultant. It may be an ignoble satisfaction, yet I believe I would rather flash and fade in one moment of happy daylight than be corked and cobwebbed for fifty years in the gloom of an unsunned cellar, with a remote possibility, indeed, of coming up from my incarceration to moisten the lips of beauty or loosen the tongue of eloquence, but with a far surer prospect of but adding one more to the potations of the glutton and wine-bibber.

And what, after all, is this oblivion which you flaunt so threateningly? Even if I do encounter it, no misfortune will happen unto me but such as is common unto men. Of all the souls of this generation, the number that will sift through the meshes of the years is infinitesimally small. The overwhelming majority of names will turn out to be chaff, and be blown away. I shall be forgotten, but I shall be forgotten in very good company. The greater part of my kinsfolk and acquaintance, your own self, my critic, and your family and friends, will go down in the same oblivion which ingulfs me. When I am dead, I shall be no deader than the rest of you, and I shall have been a great deal more alive while I *was* alive.

I am not afraid to be forgotten. Posterity will have its own soothsayers, and somewhere among the stars, I trust, I shall be living a life so intense and complete that I shall never once think to lament that I am not mulling on a book-shelf down here. Besides, if you insist upon it, I am not going to be forgotten. You know no more about it than I do. Knowledge is not always prescience. "This will never do," ruled Jeffrey from his judgment-seat. "Order reigns in Warsaw," pronounced Sebastiani. "I have now gone through the Bible," chuckled Tom Paine, "as a man would go through a wood with an axe on his shoulder, and fell trees. Here they lie, and the priests, if they can, may replant them. They may, perhaps, stick them in the ground, but they will never make them grow." But Wordsworth to-day is reverenced by the nation that could barb no arrow sharp enough to shoot at him. The evening sky that bends above Warsaw is red with the watch-fires of her old warfare bursting anew from their smouldering ashes. And the oaks that doughty Paine fancied himself to have levelled show not so much as a scratch upon their sturdy trunks. Nay, I do not forget that even Charles Lamb was fiercely belabored by his own generation. So, when upon me you pass sentence of speedy death, I assure you that I shall live a thousand years, and there is nobody in the world who can demonstrate that I am in the wrong. Even if after a while I disappear, it proves nothing; you cannot tell whether I am really submerged, or only lying in the trough of the sea to mount the crest of the coming wave. Till the thousandth year proves me moribund, I shall stoutly maintain that I am immortal.

Concerning Charles Lamb the less you say the better. It is easy to build up a reputation for sagacity by offering incense to the gods who are already shrined. Of course there is a difference between us. A pretty rout you would make, if there were not. But, for all your adoration of Charles Lamb, I dare say he would have liked me a great deal better than he would you. Would? Why should I intrench myself in hypothesis? *Does* he not? When I knock at the door of the Inner Temple, does he not fling it wide open, and does not his face welcome me? When the red fire glows on the hearth, have I not sat far into the night, Bridget sitting beside me with heaven's own light shining in her beautiful eyes, and above her dear head the white gleam of guardian angels hovering tenderly, — herself a guardian angel now? And when Elia arches his brows, and lowers at me his storm-clouds, which I do not mind for the sunshine that will not be hidden behind them, — when in the sweet play of June lights and shadows, and the golden haze of Indian-summer, I forget even the kingly words that go ringing through the land, waking the mountain-echo, — when I look out upon this gray afternoon, and see no leaden skies, no pinched and sullen fields, but green paths, gem-bestrewn from autumn's jewelled hand, and warm light glinting through the apple-trees under which he stood that soft October day, till

> "Conscious seems the frozen sod
> And beechen slope whereon he trod," —

O Alexander, stand out of my sunshine with your bugbear of a Charles Lamb! "I have heard you for some time with patience. I have been cool,— quite cool; but don't put me in a frenzy!"

When you have satisfied yourself with the limiting, you begin on the descriptive adjectives, and pronounce me egotistical. Certainly. I should be unlike all others of my race, if I were not. It is a wise and merciful arrangement of Providence, that every one is to himself the centre of the universe. What a fatal world would this otherwise be! When one thinks what a collection of insignificances we are, how dispensable the most useful of us is to everybody, how little there is in any of us to make any one care about us, and of how small importance it is to others what becomes of us, — when one thinks that even this round earth is so small, that, if it should fall into the arms of the sun, the sun would just open his mouth and swallow it whole, and nobody ever suspect it, (*vide* Tyndall on Heat,) one must see that this self-love, self-care, and self-interest play a most important part in the Divine economy. If one did not keep himself afloat, he would surely go under. As it is, however disagreeable a person be, he likes himself, — however uninteresting, he is interested in himself. Everybody — you, my critic, as well — likes to talk about himself, if he can get other people to listen; and so long as I can get several thousand people to listen, I shall keep talking, you may be sure, and so would you. You are just as egotistical as I am, only you will not own it frankly, as I do. True, I might escape censure by using such circumlocutions as "the writer," "the author," or, still more cumbrously, by dressing out some figure, calling it Frederic or Frederika, and then, like the Delphic priestesses, uttering my sentiments through its mouth, for the space of a folio novel; but it would be my own self all the while. Besides, in order to get at the thing I wanted to say, I should have to detain you on a thousand things that I did not care about, but which would be necessary as links, because, when you have your man, you must do something with him. You cannot leave him standing, without any visible means of support. One person writes a novel of four hundred pages to convince you in a roundabout way, through thirty different characters, that a certain law, or the mode of administering it, is unjust. He does not mention himself, but makes his men and women speak his arguments. Another man writes a treatise of forty pages, and gives you his views out of his own mouth. But he does not put himself into his treatise any more than the other into his novel. For my part, I think the use of "I" is the shortest and simplest way of promulgating one's opinions. Even a *we* bulges out into twice the space that *I* requires, besides seeming to try to evade responsibility. Better say "*I*" straight out,—"*I*," responsible for my words here and elsewhere, as they used to say in Congress under the old *régime*. Besides being the most brave, "I" is also the most modest. It delivers opinions to the world through a perfectly transparent medium. "I" has no relations. It has no consciousness. It is a pure abstraction. It detains you not a moment from the subject. "The writer" does. It brings up ideas entirely detached from the theme, and is therefore impertinent. All you are after is the thing that is thought. It is not of the smallest consequence who thought it. You may be certain that it is not always the people who use "I" the most freely who think most about themselves; and if you are offended, consider whether it may not be owing to a certain modern morbidness of taste in the reader as much as to egotism in the offender.

Remember, also, that, when a writer talks of himself, he is not necessarily speaking of his own definite John Smithship, that does the marketing and pays the taxes and is a useful member of society. Not at all. It is himself as a unit of the great sum of mankind. He means himself, not as an isolated individual, but as a part of humanity. His narration is pertinent, because it relates to the human family. He brings forward a part of the common property. He does not touch that which pertains exclusively to himself. His self is self-created. His imaginative may have as large a share in the person as his descriptive powers. You do not understand me precisely? Well, what is to be done about it?

You think me arrogant. You would think so a great deal more, if you knew me better. At heart I believe I incline very much to the opinion of a friend of mine, that, "after all, nobody in the world is of much account but Susy and me," — only in my formula I leave out Susy. Think not, therefore, solely of the arrogance that is revealed, but also of the arrogance concealed, and in consideration of the greater repression pardon the great expression. It is not the persons who sin the least, but those who overcome the strongest temptations, who are the most virtuous. People endowed by nature with a sweet humility do not deserve half the credit for their lovely character that those who are naturally selfish and arrogant often deserve for being no more disagreeable than they are. Yes, it must be confessed, you are right in attributing arrogance, — though, after this meek confession and repentance, if you do not forgive me freely and fully, for past and future, your secondary will be a great deal worse than my original sin; — but you never would accuse me of "an arrogance that disdains docility," if you could see the mean-spirited way in which I sit down by the side of an editor and let him *ram-page* over my manuscript. Out fly my best thoughts, my finest figures, my sharpest epigrams, — without chloroform, — and I give no sign. I have heard that successful authors can always have everything their own way. I must be the greatest failure of the age.

"It will be much better to omit this," says the High Inquisitor, turning the thumb-screw.

"No," I writhe. "Take everything else, but leave that."

"I am glad to see that you agree with me," he responds, with Mephistophelian courtesy; and away it goes, and I say nothing, thankful that anything is left.

"Revealing somewhat of the arrogance of success," you comment, directed by your Evil Genius, upon that especial chapter which was written in a gully of the Valley of Humiliation, when I was gasping under an Ætna of rejected manuscripts, — when there was not a respectable newspaper in the country by which I had not been "declined with thanks," — when, in the desperation of my determination, I had recourse to bribery, and sent an editor a dollar with the manuscript, to pay him for the fifteen minutes it would take to read it. (*Mem.* I never heard from editor, manuscript, or dollar.) No, it may be arrogance, but it is not the arrogance of success. Whatever it was, it was in the grain. And, to look at it in another light, I cannot have been "spoiled by the indulgent praise which my early efforts received," because I have always been praised, —

"Like to the Pontic monarch of old days,
I fed on poisons, till they had no power,
But were a kind of nutriment."

The earliest event I remember is being presented with two cents by one of the "Committee" visiting the school. And if I could stand two cents in my helpless infancy, don't you suppose I can stand your penny-a-lining now I am grown up? I may have been spoiled, or I may not have been worth much to begin with; but the mischief was all done before you ever heard of me. Confine yourself to facts: dismiss conjectures. State actions: shun motives. Give results: avoid causes, if you would insure confidence in your sagacity.

Furthermore, you say that with abundant denunciation of present evils, my book contains no practical suggestions for their removal, — and this in face of the fact that, as Chaucer would say, it sneweth in that book of practical suggestions. But they are so simple that you make no account of them. So Naaman of old went to Elisha to be healed of his leprosy, expecting the prophet to come out and work a miracle with great pomp and solemnity, as was befitting the state of the Lieutenant-General of the army of Syria. And when Elisha did not so much as go to the door, but sent a servant to advise the great man to wash himself, no wonder he went away in a rage. That was a practical suggestion, indeed! However, when he suffered his wrath to subside and did as the prophet bade him, his flesh came again like unto the flesh of a little child. So if you, august complainer, will but be docile, and not insist upon being told to do some great thing that shall overturn the foundations of society, but will be content to go into your own family circle and do the seven and seventy times seven little things that I counsel you to do, you will become sweet and pure and innocent like a little child, and every one will love you, especially they which are of your own household; nor will you ever again find either lack or need of practical suggestions.

There is also a kind of stock criticism on which a large class of critics do a flourishing business. It is no new thing, for the Abbot Trublet well described it a hundred and fifty years ago. "He (the critic) has also general forms of censure and commendation, composed wholly of terms of art. He is particularly fond of such as dispense with the detail of proofs, and are most proper to make you sensible of his superiority over the author he pronounces upon. For instance, one of the most common judgments he passes upon works just published is that they have nothing new in them"; to which the modern critic has learned to add "nor do they present old things with any new force." Another general form has already been referred to, that of holding up an author of established reputation with the discriminating and scholarly command to "see the difference." "Compare with Kingsley and note the difference." "Compare one of these Essays with those of the 'Country Parson' and you will note a vast difference." "Compare the 'Religio Medici' with the 'New Sun' and the immense superiority of the former over the latter will be apparent at once,"— a form of criticism safe and therefore sagacious. Or, again we are informed that "this book might have been compressed into one half or one third or — the vulgar fraction expanding into whatever infinite decimal the critic may choose — the space it occupies. Very true. It might not have been written at all, while you are about it; as country children amuse themselves with improving on the old adage,

> "He that would thrive
> Must rise at five."

By adding

> "He who'd thrive more
> Must rise at four."

> "He who the best would be
> Must rise at three."

And so on, till they arrive at the conclusion, —

> "He who would get ahead
> Must never go to bed."

It must be confessed that these people are wise in their generation; for, to write a real criticism, to set the strength or weakness of a book in such clear lights that all may see it for themselves, to pronounce judgment with such weight that the decision shall be final, is a work of high art. It requires skill, learning, power, genius, attention. It creates risk and involves responsibility; while any noodle can make a general statement which all the other noodles shall receive as pure gold. But though such criticism may be indulged in to almost any extent, and with entire impunity, not every one can condense it into the elegant compactness of that writer who closes a protest against the verbiage of a certain author with the assertion, that "she has a *fatal* facility of expression *that will yet be the death of her*"!

But all else will I forgive and forget, if you will not tell me to stop writing. *That* I cannot and will not do. You may iterate and reiterate, that the public will tire of me. I am sorry for the public, but it is strong and will be easily rested. Sorry? No, I am not; I am glad. I should like to pay back a part of the weariness which the public has inflicted on me in the shape of lessons, lectures, sermons, speeches, customs, fashions. Why should it have the monopoly of fatiguing? Minorities have their rights as well as majorities. The spout of a tea-kettle is not to be compared, in point of bulk, to the tea-kettle, but it puts in a claim for an equal depth of water, and Nature acknowledges the claim. I cannot think of reining in yet. I have but just started. And everything is so interesting. Nothing is isolated. Nothing is insignificant. Everything you touch thrills. It seems to matter but little what you look at: only look long enough, and a life, its life, springs up. You see that it has causes and consequences, dependencies, bearings, and all manner of social interests; and before you know it, you have become involved in those interests and are one of the family. For the time, you stake all on one issue, and contend valiantly. As soon as that is decided, and you stop to take breath a moment, something else comes equally interesting and seeming equally important, and again your lance is in rest. When it comes to the *quantities* of morals, there is not much difference between one thing and another. And you ask me to fold my hands and sit still! Not I. I promise to do the best I can, but I shall do it. There are rows of blocks standing around the walls of my studio, waiting to be chiselled. They will not be Apollos, — but even Puck is a Robin Goodfellow, since,

> "In one night, ere glimpse of morn,
> His shadowy flail hath threshed the corn
> That ten day-laborers could not end."

And I shall not confine myself to my sphere. I hate my sphere. I like everything that is outside of it, — or, better still, my sphere rounds out into undefined space. I was born into the whole world. I am monarch of all I survey. Wherever I see symptoms of a pie, thither shall my fingers travel. Wherever a windmill flaps, it shall go hard but I will have a tilt at it. I shall not wait till I know what I am talking about. If I did, I never should talk at all. It is a well-known principle in educational science, that the surest way to learn anything is to teach it. How fast would Geology get on, if its professors talked only of what they knew? Planting their feet firmly on facts, they feel about in all directions for theories. By carefully noting, publishing, comparing, discussing their uncertainties, they presently arrive at a certainty. Horace might advocate nine years' delay. He was building for himself a monument that should defy the rolling years. He was setting to work in cool blood to compass immortality, and a little time, more or less, made no difference. Apollo and Bacchus could afford to wait. Beautiful daughters of beautiful mothers will exist to the world's end, and their praises will always be in order. But when, unmindful of the next generation, which will have its books and its memories, though you are unread and forgotten, mindful only of this generation which groans and travails in pain, you look on suffering that you yearn to assuage, danger of which you long to warn, sadness which you would fain dispel, burdens which you would strive, though ever so little, to lighten, delay, even for things so desirable as complete knowledge and perfect polish, becomes not only absurd, but impossible. Better shoot into the cavern, even if you do not know in what precise part of it the dragon lies coiled. The flash of your powder may reveal his whereabouts to a surer marksman. A transient immortality is of no importance; it is of importance that hearts be purified, homes made happy. Is that ignoble? Very well. But the noblest way to benefit posterity is to serve the present age,—to serve it by doing one's best, indeed, but by doing it now, not waiting for some distant day when one may do it better. A writer deserves no pardon for careless or hurried writing. As much time as he has mental ability to spend on it, so much time he should devote to it. But then speed it on its way. Shut it up for a term of years, and you will perhaps have a manuscript that says *begin* where it used to say *commence*, but in the mean time all the people whom you wished to save have died of a broken heart,—or lived with one, which is still worse. Besides, even for improvement, it is better to publish your paper than to keep it in the drawer. There, all the amendments it can receive will come from the few feeble advances in knowledge which you may be so fortunate as to make. But print it and every one immediately gives you especial attention and the benefit of his judgment. If you should happen to serve in the right wing of Orthodoxy, you will have the inestimable boon of the freest criticism from the left wing. And it is the religious newspapers for not mincing matters! Between Jew and Gentile hostility is the normal condition of things, and is carried on peaceably enough; but when Jew meets Jew, then comes the tug of war! These people obey to the letter the Apostolic injunction, and confess your faults one to another with a marvellous relish, which must furnish to the unbelieving world a lively commentary on the old text, "Behold how these Christians love one another!" When their own list of your shortcomings is exhausted, ten to one they will take up the parable of somebody else; and if little Johnny Horner sitting in the corner of his sanctum has not room in his crowded columns for the whole pie in which his brother Horner has served you up, never fear but he will put in his thumb and pick out the plums to enliven the feast withal.

One blemish which grievously annoys the bishops and other clergy is irreverence. Like their Oriental prototypes, they meet the exhortation to be of good cheer with an outcry that the exhorter blasphemeth. They are shocked with the contempt which is shown for the Divine record, with the irreverent use of Bible language. They evidently judge according to Dr. Johnson's standard: "Campbell is a good man, — a pious man. I am afraid he has not been in the inside of a church for many years; but he never passes a church without pulling off his hat; this shows he has good principles." They are of their father the Jew, who would not trample on a piece of paper lest it might contain the name of Jehovah, but who scrupled not to stone His prophets and crucify His Son. Yet though their hearts are stirred within them at liberties taken by lay writers, they are not only not shocked, but on the contrary they quite — if I may use so secular a word in so sacred a connection — chuckle over it, when such liberties emanate from clerical sources. Nobody professed himself shocked when a religious newspaper told us, with great glee, how, when a certain Dr. S. was first settled in Hartford, "Dr. Bellamy, feeling a deep interest in the success of the church in this favored spot, resolved to visit the youthful pastor, and 'see if he would do.' On arriving at the residence of his young brother, which was a new house and nicely furnished, Dr. Bellamy remarked, as Mr. S. met him at the door, 'So you have got your house all swept and garnished.' 'Yes, yes, Dr. Bellamy, all ready for evil spirits, — walk in, walk in.' We need not add, that Dr. Bellamy, after a hearty laugh, remarked, 'He 'll do, he 'll do.'"

The same paper tells of Mr. Leifchild's "journey from Bristol to Wells in company with Mr. Hall, who was a great smoker. He descended at a blacksmith's shop to relight his pipe. Making his way to the forge, he jumped aside with unwonted agility, when a huge dog growled at him. When he returned to the carriage, Mr. Leifchild observed, 'You seemed afraid of the dog, sir.' Mr. Hall instantly rejoined, 'Apostolic advice, sir, Beware of dogs.'"

The Remarker is the head and front and both wings of the Orthodox army. It is so intensely religious a newspaper that it cares little to have a long list of subscribers, but is deeply anxious to have them of sound Orthodox piety, — which is a thing to be admired (at) in this Mammon-worshipping age, and furnishes a touching illustration of the manner in which Providence tempers the wind to the shorn lamb. Now one would not wish, even if it were possible, to be any more pious than the Remarker, for fear he might die young. Yet the Remarker tells us a story of Father Hill, of Mason, N. H., who "had a parsonage full of young children": —

"The Rev. William M. Rogers of this city was once on a visit to that brother minister. The boys and girls were in full glee around him, when he quietly remarked, that he never knew before the full meaning of the Psalmist, where he says that 'the little hills rejoice on every side.'"

And it not only tells the story without any apparent horror of the Scriptural quip, but adds, that we may be sure of its truth, "We had this from the Rev. Timothy Hill, one of the juvenile group, for many years since a Western missionary."

But if it is meet and right for the clergy to wrest the words of the Divine record away from their Divine meaning, can it be a high crime for the laity to apply their Divine meanings to common things? If a clergyman may make a joke from the Bible whenever he can think of one, may not a layman use a phrase from the same source when it comes to him? If a minister may manufacture puns, may not a man borrow pungency? or are we to return to the good old times, and have the Bible once more chained to the pulpit?

But a thing truly wonderful to see is the manner in which the hostility aroused by my book swallows up all lesser hostilities. The chronic enmity between different divisions of the Church Militant disappears at its coming, and "The Remarker" and "The Furnace" lie side by side in melodious concord,—which is such a reconciliation as has rarely been seen since the day when Herod and Pilate were made friends together. The Furnace is indeed pathetic in its aversion. It is little to say that it disapproves; it cannot even tolerate me when mingled with, and, it might be hoped, modified by, other ingredients in the "Oceanic Miscellany," and insists on being warned against my approach that it may parry the blow. In pity for its woes, permit me to announce that there is a plan on foot, either to issue for its use an expurgated edition of the "Oceanic Miscellany," comprising only the most Elegant Extracts, or else to hoist a little black flag when I am coming, that the Reverend Mokanna may have time to put on his silver veil and so the gales of heaven shall not visit his face too roughly. Next, and with no unequal steps, comes "The Noticer," a paper which, apparently finding it impossible to become thoroughly regenerate, long ago gave up the attempt in despair, and now regularly divides itself off into a sort of Holy and Profane State. Unfortunately, in its eagerness to embrace a fancied opportunity to despatch a provincial victim and several metropolitan brethren at one fell swoop, it left a bar down or a gate open, and so permitted — unconsciously let us hope — a rather profane little fib or two to stray over upon the holy side. But to use its own brilliant and startling language, which, it congratulates itself those who have once heard will never forget, "Doctors differ. Editors differ. Good men differ," — a "logical division" of mankind which, so far as one may judge from "The Noticer," complies strictly with Whately's third rule for Division, viz. the Parts or Members must not be contained in one another. However, since nobody supposes difficulty of perception to be incompatible with goodness of heart, and since we permit a pious soul to puff itself out a good deal beyond its due dimensions without forfeiting its right of passage through the strait gate, we may also admit that a good man who differs so widely from other good men as to be careless of truth, is like Kinglake's Gladstone, a good man — in the worst sense of the term!

It will readily be inferred that, after all this banning with bell, book, and candle, it only remains to sigh with penitent Pet Marjorie, "My charecter is lost among the Braehead people. I hope I will be religious again, but as for regaining my charecter I despare for it." However, I shall keep on writing, — hit, if I can, miss, if I must, but shoot any way. There is a great deal of firing that kills no men and breaches no walls, but it worries the enemy. John Brown did not in the least know what he was doing. His definite attempt was a fatal failure; but the great and guilty conspiracy behind, of which he saw nothing, was smitten to the heart under his random blows; his sixteen white men and five negroes, flung blindly and recklessly against the ramparts of Slavery, were but the precursors of that great host, black and white, which has since gone down, organized and intelligent, to tread the wine-press of the wrath of God.

I fear I am committing the rhetorical error of comparing small things with great; but, if Virgil could bring in the Cyclops and their thunderbolts to illustrate his bees, and Demetrius Phalereus justify it, you will hardly count it a capital offence in me, — and I don't much care if you do, if I can only convince you that I am not going to be silent because I do not know the Alpha and Omega of things. I do not pretend to be logical, or consistent, or coherent. Nature is not. A forest of oaks burns down or is cut down, and do oaks spring again? No. Pines. Logic is baffled, but the land is bettered. A field of corn is planted, and Nature does not set herself to protect it, but sends a flock of crows to devour it; the farmers grumble, but the crows are saved alive. Freezing water contracts awhile, and then without any provocation turns about and expands; if your pitcher stands in the way, so much the worse for the pitcher, but the little fishes are grateful; and with all her whims and inconsequences, Nature gets on from year to year without once failing of seed-time and harvest, cold or heat. How is it with you and your logic, you men who have been to college and discovered what you are talking about? You who discuss politics and decide affairs, are you not continually accusing one another of sophistry, inconsistency, and shying away from the point? Take up any political or religious newspaper, and see, according to their own testimony, how deficient in logic are all these logic-mongers, — how all the learned and logical are accused by other learned and logical of false assumptions, of invalid reasoning, of foregone conclusions, of pride and prejudice and passion. One would say that the result of your profound researches was only to make you more intensely illogical than you could otherwise be.

"As skilful divers to the bottom fall
Swifter than they who cannot swim at all,

> So in the sea of sophisms, to my thinking,
> You have a strange alacrity in sinking."
>
> (*Ego et Dorset fecimus!*)

Sure I am, my humble ability in the way of unreason can never compass fallacies so stupendous as those which you attribute to one another; and I will none of your logic, but will rather rest content with the advantage, that, when I write nonsense, I know it is nonsense, while you, pardon me, write it and think it sense. But your thinking so does not make it so, and you will not rule me out of court on the strength of it. In the domain of letters is none but Squatter Sovereignty. In literature, though not in morals, might makes right. If you are cultivating the soil to its utmost capacity, I shall not meddle; but if it seems to me that you are letting it lie fallow while I can draw a furrow to some purpose, you need not warn me off with your old title-deeds; *in* my ploughshare shall go. To a better farmer I will yield right gladly, but I will not be scared away by a signboard.

When you learnedly assert that my induction is meagre, I am the farthest in the world from contradicting you. Nay, I am ready to confess not only that it is meagre, but that there is no induction at all. For, look you, induction is for hidden, not for obvious truth. If I wished to convince you, or to satisfy myself, that the earth's centre is a mass of fire, I should produce a sufficient number of caloric facts to give the statement a stable basis. But if my design were to arouse you to a true sense of earth's beautiful summer greenness, I should not go plucking grass in all directions, but should merely show you a blade or a leaf to illustrate what I meant by "green," and bid you use your own eyes for the rest. If the earth is indeed not green, but blue, my judgment pays the penalty; but there is no induction about it.

Nor need you go very far out of your way to affirm that I have not the requisite experience for writing on such and such topics. As a principle, the remark is absurd. Cannot a doctor prescribe for typhus fever, unless he has had typhus fever himself? On the contrary, is he not the better able to prescribe from always having had a sound mind in a sound body? As a fact, my experience in those things concerning which you allege its insufficiency has never been presented to you, and its discussion is therefore entirely irrelevant. If my statements are false, they are false; if my arguments are inconclusive, they are inconclusive: disprove the one and refute the other. But whether this state of things be owing to a want of experience, or inability to use experience aright, or any personal circumstance whatever, is a mätter in regard to which all the laws of courtesy forbid you to concern yourself.

You are sometimes so good as to inform me that

I am exhausting my resources, and in over-anxious kindness declare even that I have exhausted myself. Not a bit.

"It is no task for suns to shine,"

though the sputtering little tallow candle can hardly be expected to believe it.

And pray, Gentle Critic, do not tell me that I must be content simply to amuse, or *must* — anything else. Must is a hard word; be not too confident of its power. I feel a grandmotherly interest in the world and its ways; and much as I should like to amuse it, I shall never be content with that. You may not *like* to be instructed, my dear children, but instructed you shall be. You read long ago, in your story-book, that little Tommy Piper did not want his face washed, though he was very willing to be amused with soap-bubbles; but his face needed a washing, and got it. I come to you with soap-bubbles indeed, but with scrubbing-brushes also. If you take to them kindly, it will soon be over; but if you scream and struggle, I shall not only scrub the harder, but be all the longer about it.

Sometimes grave refutations are very amusing. It is astonishing to see how crank-proof sundry people are. Everything seems to them on a dead level of categorical proposition. They walk up to every statue with their measuring-line of *Barbara*, *Celarent*, *Darii*, *Ferioque Prioris*, and measure them off with equal solemnity, telling you severely that this nose is far longer than the classic rule admits, and this arm has not the swelling proportions of life, — never seeing, that, though another statue was indeed designed for an Antinoüs, this was never meant to be anything but a broomstick dressed in your grandfather's cloak, with a lantern in a pumpkin-shell for a head. O the dreariness of having to explain pleasantry! of dealing with people who do not know the difference between a blow and a "love-pat," between Quaker guns and an Armstrong battery, between a granite paving-stone and the moonshine on a mud-puddle!

But they make up for it by turning your wisdom into wish-wash; as Charles Lamb atoned for reaching his office late in the morning by leaving it early in the afternoon. Your sense must be solemn and stationary in order to be recognized. They cannot conceive that it may toss like the buoy on the tide, and yet be moored to foundations firm as the perpetual hills. On the whole

"The Robin sings in the elm;
  The cattle stand beneath
Sedate and grave, with great brown eyes,
  And fragrant meadow breath.

"They listen to the flattered bird,
  The wise-looking stupid things!
And they never understand a word
  Of all the Robin sings."

But the great consolation both for my critics and myself is, that we shall gradually get used to each other. At least, I shall furnish them abundant opportunity to get used to me. There are many books still to come, — a treatise on the Curvature of the Square, — a Dissertation on Foreign Literature, — two or three novels, — a book on Human Life, that is going to turn the world upside down, — a book on Theology, dull enough to be sensible, that is going to turn it back again, — and a bandboxful of children's stories. And when these are disposed of, I dare say I shall turn the glass and begin again.

Truly there was no need of saying all this; but when they droop their fair large ears, my gentle joy, so temptingly within hand-reach, who can restrain himself from filliping them? But I take no liberties with leviathan. Good and friendly souls, Greathearts who might crush me and do not, I should like to thank you, but perhaps you do not care. Yet bear with me a little longer in my folly; and, indeed, bear with me for the sake of the weak. Many and many there may be to whom the meat of your metaphysics is indigestible and unpalatable, but who find strength and cheer in the sincere milk of such words as I can give. To you who have already set your feet on the high places, that may be but a bruised reed which is a staff to those who are still struggling up.

Of the blessings which my book has brought me,—blessings of inward wealth that cannot be so much as named,—blessings so rich, so divine, that I sometimes think nothing ever was so beautiful as to have written a book,—I may not speak; but I trust that when all this frightful glare of day, all this rough litter, and jar, and deafening din of work shall be overpast,—when the serene Night beckons to me, and I go on into her fragrant silence and her sweet sheltering darkness,—I shall bear with me some memories that were not all of earth; some pure delights that shall glow through the charmed air, soft as night's dewy breath and lasting as her stars.

Cambridge: Stereotyped and Printed by Welch, Bigelow, & Co.

www.ingramcontent.com/pod-product-compliance
Lightning Source LLC
LaVergne TN
LVHW021121110826
845150LV00005B/913

* 9 7 8 1 4 2 5 5 5 1 1 1 7 *